SURPRISE

Encounters

WITH ARTISTS AND SCIENTISTS,
WHALES AND OTHER LIVING THINGS

BY SCOTT McVAY

Published by Wild River Books
P.O. Box 53
Stockton, New Jersey 08559
www.wildriverconsultingandpublishing.com

Distributed by Wild River Consulting & Publishing, LLC.

Design and composition:
  Cover and publication design by Tim Ogline.
  Interior design executed by Denise Petti.

Publisher's Cataloging-In-Publication Data
McVay, Scott
  Surprise Encounters with Artists and Scientists, Whales and Other Living Things

ISBN: 978-1-941948-02-6

1. Memoir. 2. Literature. 3. Poetry.
4. Scott McVay.

Printed in the United States of America

First Edition

SURPRISE

Encounters

WITH ARTISTS AND SCIENTISTS, WHALES AND OTHER LIVING THINGS

BY SCOTT McVAY

WILD RIVER BOOKS

Hella, the Alpha and the Omega
and every glowing letter in between.

Contents

An Anecdotal Biography

Wer wagt, gewinnt. — Whoever wages, wins.

Wer liebt, gewinnt. — Whoever loves, wins.

In *Leaves of Grass*, Whitman wrote, "As for me I know nothing else but miracles."

I feel the same way, as the stories that follow will affirm.

I have been a lucky guy—first and foremost, in marriage; and second in work, which I have enjoyed. My work has included serving with Army intelligence in Berlin, working with and learning from a precocious bottlenose dolphin, heading two philanthropic foundations—Robert Sterling Clark and Geraldine R. Dodge—and serving as president of the Chautauqua Institution.

When I flew across the Atlantic to Germany in 1956, I learned the numbers one to ten in German, a small start for one who was not so good at languages—at least French, Latin, and Greek. Upon arriving in Stuttgart, however, I was fortunate to be given a four-month course in German taught by a master, Werner Schwabe from Berlin. On my own I learned 500 proverbs or sayings to get into the gestalt and rhythm of the language. And the language was immediate, all about, with generous feedback.

I reveled in the proverbs since they sang of insight, rang of truth, and had a snap unlike the tired, tattered clichés of one's own language. My favorite was *"Wer wagt, gewinnt!"*—"Whoever wages, wins!"—sharper, keener than our "Nothing ventured, nothing gained," a double negative. Much later, when Hella and I got our wedding rings, we had them fashioned by a goldsmith master, Susanne Grote, sister of Hella's dear classmate, Hika, into fifteen letters, three words: *"Wer liebt, gewinnt,"* or "Whoever loves, wins."

Although I have had different jobs down the years, a common theme from May 1972 forward has been service in the field of philanthropy. Beyond the two foundations—Robert Sterling Clark Foundation and Geraldine R. Dodge Foundation, where I was founding executive director of both—I have served on the board of two others, one to the present day. I noticed that this occupation, this business of philanthropy, seems to afflict personalities. Staff arrogance, with notable exceptions, seems to bloom as the years roll by. Hat sizes grow and grow.

I relished the everyday meeting with folks I admired for their devotion to craft, be it teaching, protecting the environment, explorations of artists, or caring for animals—driven, impelled by passion and commitment, not Mammon.

In August 1969, when our girls, Catherine and Cynthia, were nine and eight years old, Hella and I took them on a journey through Mexico, coached by Mayan specialist Gillett Good Griffin. We visited nineteen archeological sites, making a Möbius path through Guanajuato, Morelia, Puebla, Oaxaca, and Jalapa. Music and laughter were everywhere.

Following a memorable evening in Taxco with a renowned innkeeper, she told us of a sacred place that she had not mentioned to any other outlander, prompted by the joy of our evening together. It happened to be far behind us. We circled back, of course, way back, hours back, to see and inhale that place. When we finally got there, it turned out to be a couple of fields bisected by a stream. What was so special? Further scrutiny revealed an amazingly pure stream where you could see every stone on the deep bottom.

We walked along the far side of the stream and saw an upwelling of pure water from the belly of the Earth about two meters in diameter, rising a couple of inches above the surface of the stream. In seconds, Catherine and Cynthia were in there, allowing the upwelling to hold first one then the other securely as if by the upstretched hand of the Lord. Hella and I went in, too, and felt connected to the miracle of life and the Earth, Mother Earth. This miracle, if you will, opened us to other miracles of place and people, some of whom are revealed in these pages. The upwelling of clear, strong, clean water became a metaphor for an enhanced view of this blessed blue-green orb as sacred, requiring our utmost stewardship.

Life seems coherent and convergent when viewed retrospectively. The connective chords here, however, are an adventurous marriage, a love of the natural world and its beauty, the allure of poetry, stick-to-it-iveness, regard for path-breaking lives, and irrepressible curiosity.

Central themes emerge. A sense of the integrity of the natural world binds many of these sketches. This perception began to open through daily study of a bottlenose dolphin named Elvar. That led to efforts to stop the killing of whales after publication of a paper in *Scientific American*, "The Last of the Great Whales." That, in turn, made possible the discovery of the six-octave song of the humpback whale, which energized conservation efforts and even astonished Japanese scientists, writers, and whalers.

Another stream of small stories grew through getting to know pioneers in education, critical issues, the arts, and the well-being of animals—the four foci for grant-making we developed at the Geraldine R. Dodge Foundation. The work of such pathfinders, assisted in part through informed philanthropy, is recorded in annual reports of the Dodge Foundation over nearly a quarter century. Viewed retrospectively, they are summarized in an essay I wrote in 2002, "The Philanthropic Tipping Point: The Intimate, Albeit Frail, Connection between Survival and the Work of the Independent Sector," which frames that set of episodes and was published in *Just Money* (2004).

It occurs to me now that what I most enjoyed was taking things on from scratch, even creating and serving as first recording secretary at Princeton University.

This is true for Hella, too, since she created the math program at Carollton School of the Sacred Heart in Coconut Grove in 1964 and the math department at Stuart Country Day School in Princeton a few years later as chair of the department. Similarly, she was not only a founder of the Whole Earth Center in Princeton, New Jersey, in 1970, but also their volunteer president for years when the culture was shaped for this organic foods store, which is flourishing today.

An exhilarating current is the theme "In Praise of Women," beginning with my resilient wife and two daughters—three priceless guides. Also, Carol Gilligan's *In a Different Voice* (1982) altered our perception of women as seeing a world of relationships rather than of people standing alone and affirmed what many of us felt about women.

While most of the folks encountered here are a source of admiration and inspiration, a small subset of stories might be seen as "foibles," to which each of us is prone. These dozen or so resonate with a note written by Francisco Goya when he undertook his singular series, *Los Caprichos*, all of which have fascinated me since undergraduate days. Goya realized his intent of exposing, with wit and discernment, follies, bias, deceit, hubris, ignorance, and self-interest, to which we all are inclined. I have included part of Goya's note in the section titled "Caprichos."

The citations scattered throughout these stories, anecdotes, and sketches are drawn from diverse authors, from Confucius to Boccaccio, who are shrewd observers of the human experiment. Their insights, like Melville's, cast a ray of light into the fables. These brief stories may touch on a single incident or be drawn over time seeking to honor lives that have contributed to the general good—and, perhaps, even reveal a lesson or two.

George Denniston, a classmate from Princeton University, wrote to me, in a letter from September 2004: "I would like you to write your autobiography. One reason for asking this is that I would like to read it! And I even have a suggestion. It does not have to be exhaustive. It can be anecdotal, just talking about those aspects of your life that you talk about readily, and that you enjoy sharing with your many friends."

Scott with George Denniston in Rick's Café in Casablanca, Morocco, in 2004 with Humphrey Bogart looking on.

When we were traveling with the Population Institute in Morocco two months later, Denniston and I continued to swap many yarns. George pushed, "Why don't you write down a few stories from your life. Write something each day." I liked George's idea of choosing select tales to share rather than just a chronological listing of events, and chose to record my stories this way.

In setting forth even these small stories, I realize that many more lurk in the mist of memory. Yet when I asked the eminent biologist, E. O. Wilson, upon the day of publication of his tome written with Bert Hölldobler, *The Ants*—with 8,000 species described—if that was all, he said no, sadly, but we had to draw a line. So, too, a line must be drawn here. We must move on and pitch out the scribbles, letters, notes, and journals to clear the way for days ahead.

Hella played an integral role in making this book. Just as with my book of poetry, *Whales Sing and Other Exuberances* (2012), where she chose the ninety-nine poems and put them in a natural sequence of nine sections (from whales to jottings in Nepal to, lastly, growing older), she encouraged this undertaking from the outset and has found a sequence and rhythm for the tales that unfold here.

Since Hella was part of much of what is recounted here, she is one with the author in trying to hold fast to the slippery truth of what happened. We created a Poetry Trail of forty-eight signs in Greenway Meadows in Princeton in 2010 as our gift to

Poetry flags created by Hella for dedication of the McVay Poetry Trail at Greenway Meadows, October 2012.

the community for the joy and privilege of raising our daughters here, living close by a university of consequence for more than half a century. The elegant design of the signs, including the bright ribbon down the left side of each like the spine of a book, and the exact placement of the signs in the landscape are thanks to Hella. The poetry along the trail seeks to reveal insights of poets planetwide over two millennia who salute the beauty, surprise, and wonder of the ineffable natural world.

Oliver Sacks, upon turning eighty—as my college classmates and I have done—wrote an op-ed for the *New York Times* on July 6, 2013, "The Joy of Old Age. (No Kidding.)," which closes:

My father, who lived to be 94, often said that the 80s had been one of the most enjoyable decades of his life. He felt, as I begin to feel, not a shrinking but an enlargement of mental life and perspective. One has had the long experience of life, not only one's own life, but others', too. One has seen triumphs and tragedies, booms and busts, revolutions and wars, great achievements and deep ambiguities, too. One has seen grand theories rise, only to be toppled by stubborn facts. One is more conscious of transience and, perhaps, of beauty. At 80, one can take a long view and have a vivid, lived sense of history not possible at an earlier age. I can imagine, feel in my bones, what a century is like, which I could not do when I was 40 or 60. I do not think of old age as an ever grimmer time that one must somehow endure and make the best of, but as a time of leisure and freedom, freed from the facetious urgencies of earlier days, free to explore whatever I wish, and to bind the thoughts and feelings of a lifetime together.

That binding for me has occurred in trying to capture quickly, yet accurately, small events along life's way that illuminated the trail, brought on the day, making bits of the journey perhaps of interest to others.

What are we, finally, but our stories.

—Scott McVay
Princeton, New Jersey, January 2015

The Decameron

I shall narrate a hundred stories or fables or
parables or histories or whatever you choose
to call them, recited in ten days by a worthy
band of seven ladies and three young men,
who assembled together during the plague
which recently took such heavy toll of life.

— Prologue to *The Decameron* (1353)
by Giovanni Boccaccio

I STILL HEAR HIS VOICE EVERY DAY

In the "Afterword" to his *Family Genealogy*, my father, Martin "Mac" Scott McVay, wrote:

> Quite probably one of our grandchildren, or certainly one of *their* children, will be living in a colony in space before 2050, as livable habitats in this new "High Frontier" will have been established some years prior.... This, of course, is predicated on the assumption that mankind will not wipe itself out in an atomic holocaust. Sad to say, man's relationship to his fellow man, unlike the great advances in science and technology, apparently has improved but little since the Stone Age.

The facts of Dad's life are not uninteresting—working as a kid at Hilltop Grocery every Saturday in Sidney, Ohio, for a silver dollar (five cents of which was spent on a hamburger at the Spot); paddling a prized canoe, the "Shawa," with Jerry Wagner, his best boyhood friend, up the canal to Port Jefferson; climbing in the Adirondacks with Al Ferguson or jousting with Bob Peare, colleagues at General Electric where he worked for thirty-three years; a three-month honeymoon in Europe footed by his bride who had invested wisely when she worked for E. F. Hutton; family trips around Colorado and the West, singing, "Who's Gonna Love You, Honey, When I'm Gone?" at the Smiths' log cabin and "There's a Gold Mine in the Sky" while strumming a banjo; working for A. L. Jones in Denver and Chet Lang in Building 2 in Schenectady; and in his sixties weighing in the wrestlers on Saturday morning in Princeton and ever giving a boost to the coaches and players, still stroking around nine holes of golf—but the enthusiasms he brought to everything he did, whether studying maps to prepare for a trip or showing a younger member of the Miller clan the wonders of Nassau Hall and environs, Mac swept you along and made you feel a part of something larger than yourself.

"Mac" McVay playing the banjo, maybe "There's a Gold Mine in the Sky," at Red Smith's cabin in foothills of the Rockies, early 1940s.

In 1980, after his eightieth birthday on June 2, my father completed *A Family Genealogy including some accounts on and comments on the times our forebears lived in.* It was a joyful undertaking, and at the suggestion of my cousin Ann Miller Nye, I wrote a "Note to the Reader about the Chronicler."

You will find scattered references to Martin Scott McVay throughout the text and a marvelous 1904 photograph at its conclusion of the author in shoulder-length golden locks sitting on his dog Rover. You will also sense the spirit of this quest, which jumps off every page. To try to catch this amazing gentleman in a few words is not possible, but I can say he is as friendly as anyone I've ever known. He loved working for the General Electric Company, but after reading this narrative, written in the last year of his eighth decade, do you not wonder for a moment that he should have been a history teacher? History was his love, and the past contains clues about tomorrow. Dad's other passion (besides Princeton and sports) is the family—both near and far—with whom he stayed in close touch down the years across five generations.

I have always thought of him as the quintessential father—somebody who is easy to be with, somebody who throws a football with a spiral, somebody you can count on, somebody who can show you how to slide your hands together for pole-vaulting like Franklin Blue, somebody who is utterly absorbed in whatever he's working on, somebody who at least a hundred persons considered among their ten best friends, somebody who married well and whose marriage remained a model of joy, health, well-being, trust, and honest talk. Hooray, too, for his spouse of fifty-three years, Margaret Lalor, without whose loving care and attention not a word would have been penned by this "preemie."

As one reads within the genealogy of the young woman "who would rather be treated than trotted," the chap who sold the defective gun, the first family member to enter Harvard (Class of 1668), the father who fell from a plank into the Delaware River and drowned, the first woman to drive a carriage through from Athens to the Ohio, the "ride and tie" trip to Princeton, the incredible organ built in a basement, the memorable stop in Somerset en route to Fort Dearborn, you hear my Father's voice and laugh with him or sometimes cry. Beyond the careful digging and faithful reporting, a bit of the human condition and our place in the stream of humanity are revealed.

The concluding sentence of this chronicle notes that man's relationship to man has changed but little since the Stone Age, and we now have lethal toys to vent our spleen, but it brings to mind a dominant aspect of the historian's personality. His gregariousness and zest for life are utterly infectious. Not only does a room light up when he enters it, or a family gathering, when he presides or spins an unforgettable yarn or two, but he has illuminated the family tree. And those who read his words will rejoice with him in the adventures and misadventures of our forebears.

At the 50th reunion of the Princeton Class of 1922 with former Princeton President Harold W. Dodds (second from left), current President Robert F. Goheen (center), and President-elect Bill Bowen (second from right). Class president of 1922 Martin McVay is seated at the far right.

One story will suggest his open-mindedness, his curiosity deep into old age about how the scenario spins out, his interest in UFOs and the High Frontier. In reply to the question of how to respond if an alien craft were to land in your backyard, some might say, "Luckily, we've got a shotgun in the house—I'll fill their hide with buckshot." My Father, on the contrary, said:

"I would invite in the alien visitor and offer him or her or it the best we've got, a dry martini."

In fact, after having one martini, he sometimes declared, "I feel like a new man. Let's give the new man a drink."

In 1946 in Schenectady, on Father's Day, I recall seeing my dad on television when there were about 1,000 sets in the area. He was "Father of the Year." It seemed fitting and just right—then and now.

From the foregoing, one could conclude that my father could have been a terrific history teacher. He comes from a family of educators, including Jacob Lindley, Class of 1800 at Princeton who founded Ohio University four years later; Dr. Herbert Russell McVay, his father, who was superintendent of schools in Sidney, Ohio; and Dr. Anna Pearl McVay, the ranking graduate of Ohio University to this day and a Latin and Greek scholar of the first rank. She was cofounder, with Dean Andrew Fleming West of Princeton University, of the American Classical League in 1917. (Dad said of Anna, "She was great fun for an hour, then I went out for a smoke.")

My Dad used to say, "All things in moderation, *even moderation.*"

I still hear his voice every day.

Celebrating the Class of 1922's 60th reunion in 1982, Martin McVay is marching in the iconic P-Rade.

GRAMPA

On May 2, 1976, our daughter Cynthia, then age fourteen, wrote a tribute to her grandfather for his seventy-sixth birthday a month later.

Grampa ages with the years. In 1900, he didn't exist until June. In 1914, he was fourteen and bought an Old Town canoe with his friend Jerry Wagner. In 1976, he now has seventy-six tree rings in his trunk. Because of this, it is easy to keep track of how old he is and to keep track of how much older Gramma is (eight months).

Grampa is bald, but where he has hair it is gray, as one might expect. However, he didn't always have dust-toned hair, for we have a picture— actually a poster—of him and his Saint Bernard, Rover, in which he has golden locks tumbling down to his shoulders. The year was 1904.

When Grampa was about twelve years old, he landed a job in a bowling alley adjacent to a bar. Gramp was very pleased with himself and with the additional income. However, his father, one of the leading citizens in town (Sidney, Ohio), was not quite as enthused as he. In fact, when he found out, he grabbed Gramp by the collar and yanked him out of the dubious place.

But what distinguishes Grampa is his nose. A large protuberance, much like a Roman's, his nose reappears on my face. He once raised a fine moustache beneath it during a trip to the British Isles in 1970, but shaved it off soon afterward, saying, "It got in the way."

Gramp was the oldest of a family of eight children. His mother died when he was young, leaving only three children, and H. R., Gramp's father, a superintendent of schools in Ohio, remarried and by his second wife had the other five children. Grampa is still very close to his two true sisters, although one lives in California (Dotty Ann) and the other in Ohio/Florida (Mary). His other five siblings are distributed across the country all the way to Anchorage, Alaska, and one is the head of the Internal Revenue Service in Oregon!

When we speak of Gramp it's usually of Grampa and his maps, or Grampa and his sports. One of his hobbies is measuring miles to and from places and calculating the time it should take between them and marking his maps up in colored markers. Winters are reserved for basketball games, spring for baseball and lacrosse, and fall for football. Otherwise, he enjoys poetry that rhymes or is written by Shakespeare.

Grampa is a dandy chauffeur. If Mom and Dad are out and Catherine or I need a ride to our piano lesson, Gramp will come by punctually in his orange and black (Tigertown colors) Dodge Dart Swinger to pick us up. He'll even entertain us with stories and exciting news and is interested in our news as well. He's a great guy when you want a story, be it his own history or his friend's. Every Sunday morning after church, he and Gramma come out to Province Line Road and he talks about the latest, and then moves back in history, reminiscing about his childhood.

Although any example may sound bland and lifeless, Gramp tells these stories with spice and vitality. Gramp can talk for three hours straight and we hang on every word. But he never tells a story that would hurt anyone or make anyone feel bad. He only aims to please the listeners.

He'll talk about making bathtub gin in college during prohibition and selling it at a large profit price, or old girlfriends, or how he "married Gramma for her money," or his job at the Spot Restaurant in Sidney.

On Grampa's and Gramma's fortieth wedding anniversary, all of the family—including first, second, and third cousins and great-aunts and uncles—came together and gave the oldy-weds a surprise party. But Gram and Gramp surprised and touched us all by singing one of their favorite numbers, "Who's Gonna to Love You, Honey, When I'm Gone," and not even tough cousin Mark could keep from letting a tear slide down his cheek.

THE EUREKA STOCKADE

By and by there was a result, and I think it
may be called the finest thing in Australian
history. It was a revolution—small in size;
but great politically; it was a strike for
liberty, a struggle for principle, a stand
against injustice and oppression ... It is
another instance of a victory won by a lost
battle. It adds an honorable page to history;
the people know it and are proud of it.
They keep green the memory of the men
who fell at the Eureka stockade, and Peter
Lalor has his monument.

> — Samuel Clemens, aka Mark Twain,
> after visiting the Victorian Goldfields
> in 1895

After my Dad completed the McVay family history in 1980, he
remarked, "I think your mother's family, the Lalors, may be more
interesting."

My parents visited Ireland in the late 1970s to explore the Lalor
family history. No one stood taller than Peter Lalor, not a direct ancestor
but a relative, who had immigrated to Australia as a young man drawn
there, like others, by the gold in the ground near Ballarat, Victoria, north
of Melbourne.

Hella and I visited New Zealand and Australia in early 1996, a five-
week trip that included a swing through the gold-mining region and

nearby Ballarat. As we were rolling down a street in Ballarat on January 26, having bought a Eureka flag, Hella spotted a monument on the median with Peter Lalor atop it and said, "Stop the bus." On all four sides were descriptions of Peter Lalor's role in the Eureka Rebellion of December 3, 1854, his election to Parliament in 1856, and his election as Speaker of the Legislative Assembly in 1880.

What happened? In the early 1850s, the Victorian gold miners suffered under a number of injustices. They were without political rights. They were not entitled to vote in elections, and they were not represented in the Legislative Council. The miners' main grievance was the exorbitant cost of the gold mining license. It was hard to pay when their finds were often insufficient to provide for basic necessities.

While the events that sparked the Eureka Rebellion were specific to the Ballarat gold fields, the underlying grievances had been the subject of public meetings, civil disobedience, and protests for almost three years.

On October 17, 1854, at the Eureka Hotel where Scottish miner James Scobie had been murdered ten days prior, between 5,000 and 10,000 miners gathered to protest that James Bentley, the hotel proprietor and prime murder suspect, had not been charged. Bentley and his wife, Catherine, fled for their lives as the hotel was burnt down.

On October 23, the arrests of miners McIntyre and Fletcher for the Eureka Hotel fire prompted a mass meeting that attracted 4,000 miners. The meeting determined to establish "a Digger's Right Society," to maintain their rights.

On November 11, a crowd of more than 10,000 miners gathered at Bakery Hill, directly opposite the government encampment, and the Ballarat Reform League was created. A resolution was passed, *that it is the inalienable right of every citizen to have a voice in making the laws he is called on to obey, that taxation without representation is tyranny.* The Eureka Flag, a blue flag designed by a Canadian miner, "Captain" Henry

Ross, and bearing nothing but the Southern Cross, was flown for the first time. An oath of allegiance was sworn: "We swear by the Southern Cross to stand truly by each other and fight to defend our rights and liberties."

The stockade itself was a ramshackle affair hastily constructed over the following days from timber and overturned carts. The structure was never meant to be a military stockade or fortress. In Lalor's words, "it was nothing more than an enclosure to keep our own men together, and was never erected with an eye to military defense." Lalor had already outlined a plan whereby "if the government forces came to attack us, we should meet them on the Gravel Pits, and if compelled, we should retreat by the heights of the old Canadian Gully, and there make our final stand."

At 3 a.m. on Sunday, December 3, 1854, a party of 276 police and military personnel under the command of Captain J. W. Thomas approached the Eureka Stockade, and a battle ensued. There is no agreement as to which side fired first, but the battle was fierce, brief, and terribly one-sided. The ramshackle army of miners was hopelessly outclassed by a military regiment and was routed in about ten minutes. During the height of the battle, Lalor was shot in his left arm, took refuge under some timber, and was smuggled out of the stockade and hidden. His arm was later amputated.

According to Lalor's report, fourteen miners (mostly Irish) died inside the stockade and an additional eight died later from injuries they sustained. A further dozen were wounded but recovered. Three months after the Eureka Stockade, Peter Lalor wrote: "As the inhuman brutalities practiced by the troops are so well known, it is unnecessary for me to repeat them. There were 34 digger casualties of which 22 died. The unusual proportion of the killed to wounded, is owing to the butchery of the military and troopers after the surrender."

Of the soldiers and police, six were killed, including Captain Wise.

Martial law was imposed and all armed resistance collapsed. News of the battle spread quickly to Melbourne and other gold field regions, turning a perceived government military victory in repressing a minor insurrection into a public relations disaster. Thousands of people in Melbourne turned out to condemn the authorities, in defiance of their mayor and some legislative councilors, who tried to rally support for the government. In Ballarat, only one man responded to the call for special constables, although in Melbourne 1,500 were sworn in and armed with batons. Many people voiced their support for the diggers' requested reforms.

My Dad was right. On the McVay side of the family, no one is as luminous as Peter Lalor, who sparked the writing of the Constitution of Australia and led the country. He was from the clan in Ireland that led to my mother, Margaret Lalor.

Since 2006, we proudly fly the blue and white Eureka flag with the white Southern Cross on a blue field at our home.

Eureka flag catching a light breeze before our home.

TUESDAY

Mother and Dad singing their song, "Who's Gonna Love You, Honey, When I'm Gone?" at a surprise 40th wedding anniversary party at 40 McCosh Circle, Princeton, New Jersey, May 3, 1970.

On Sunday
she did not recognize Poppadoppa,
her life's center for 55 years,
the decline is swift, remorseless,
plummet of a falcon, then a seeming hold,
　　just above the ground.

At first the friskiest of 43 in the main house
taking stairs up and down and up for three
years
then at year's turn
so helpless
she was moved to the Home in Back,
a sharp slide in strength and mobility,
the knee's problem
was now the body's complaint
'though she didn't complain.

A hip operation
not to walk again
but to pedal (oo-hoo)
into the meadow beyond,

then Sunday, not to find
that wonderful picture
of Pop, taken by Hella at the P-Rade
in 1982, when he marched
with his Class at their 60th,
the Class of 1922,
almost as firm an entity
as Nassau Hall,
that revered picture was
nowhere to find
'til spotted in the dust
behind the stuttering set,

But Mother said she
didn't appear to know
that chap, if she said that
for she talks little now,
she's in another zone
and I thought she, stout
soul, was crossing the Great Divide,
more real more definite
than Pike's Peak before
the Continental Divide
where you could toss
a snowball in summer.

The only flicker of the
old Mom was a flash
of wit as I roused her,
and she looked at me
through shorter eyelashes,
I asked what she was
dreaming of and she said
holding me in her gaze,
my name.

Yet today was something else
as I thought to pop in
and say hello en route to the next-
to-last train to Washington,
she still asleep
in the half-lit room
I roused her a little
by taking her left shoulder in my hand,
touching her face with a cold hand
from outside,
she looked, smiled
touched my face
with her right hand
looking at first then not looking
eyes shut but blinking
a little faster
her fingertip gently probing
along the face to the ear
then touching the ear
the central organ
of which the body is an appendage
as deftly
as completely
as Helen Keller might,
not letting go.

I've long since missed
the next-to-last train at 7:35
my legs are shaking
uncontrollably

I straighten up a little
for she is lying down
and her soft dry fingertips
refocus on the chin
I can barely stand

How can she hold her skinny arm so long
aloft
does it not ache, too?
she touches she squeezes a little
in a practiced way
I'm in her thrall,
wobbling a little,
realizing there is life
beyond words and meaning,
that we reach out to the last
to touch the faces of our children,
that old woman with a still
pretty face,
holding my face and me
there for the longest time
I've known since Dad was dying
in Athens, making sure I'm still there
and not off again.

Why don't my knees
stop rattling,
this visit unlike any other,
going on like trains
to the Capitol,
who said it's hard
to make a graceful exit,
I might be there yet
and not on the last train,
were it not for the
black woman who
enters the room and says
Good Morning to which
I reply, then my
Mother says Good Morning
to me and smiles.
"Peg, do you want breakfast?"
the nurse asks.

November 4, 1987

EARLY MEMORIES

My earliest memory occurred before my fourth birthday. I fell into a rain barrel in our backyard on Lindholm Road in Shaker Heights, Ohio. My arms were pinned at my side. No one was around. The water rose to the rim. I could not breathe.

I began to rock a bit. And then some more. The barrel tipped over, and I fell out.

Shortly thereafter, my father, who worked for General Electric, was transferred to Denver. Every weekend we traveled into the beaconing Rocky Mountains to explore our new territory. One Sunday, after a picnic lunch, my sister Sally, age two, and I, four, had gathered bottle caps of every color: red, orange, yellow, green from cherry, orange, lemon, lime sodas. But there was only one purple bottle cap from a grape soda. We were squabbling over it in the backseat, and my father said, "Knock it off, or I will spank you, Scott." Things quieted down for a bit, and then heated up again. Dad pulled over beside a wall of rock with a drop-off on the other side of the road. A car came up behind us, and a woman, seeing our blue Ohio plates, shouted, "Yoo-hoo, we're from Mansfield!" My typically ever-courteous father said, "So what," and paddled me as forewarned. That was one of three spankings I ever got, each one deserved.

Another memory recurs from my first day in first grade. Mother asked what had happened. "I met Marilyn. Yes, and she has green eyes!"

"Oh?"

"And when you look into those green eyes, you can tell she is past six," I said.

I listened to the radio, as most kids did then, to Jack Armstrong, *The All American Boy*, *The Shadow Knows*, *The Lone Ranger*, and *Captain Midnight*, between five and six o'clock every weekday. For *Captain Midnight*, one could get their magic decoder if three Ovaltine tops were sent in. We did just that, tossing away the tasteless Ovaltine. I waited and waited for that decoder, pressing my mother for the packet in the mail. Finally, it arrived, and I wrote down the letters and numbers given. To my dismay—I was hoping for an answer to the riddle of the universe— the "answer" was: "Buy More Ovaltine."

Somewhat later, just after I had learned to ride a bicycle—my Dad ever cautioned, "Watch out for wobbly kids on wobbly bikes"—I announced one afternoon that I was running away. My ever-obliging Mother asked, "Will you be having a last supper?" Well, yes, that's a good idea. "How about packing a small suitcase?" Yes, toothbrush and pajamas. After that "last" supper, as the light was failing, I set forth on my wobbly bike, bag atop the handlebars. I got as far as the corner before I turned around and came home, much relieved.

The amusement park in Denver is Elitch Gardens. With another family we went there one evening, perhaps on my tenth birthday. No one was interested in going on the roller coaster, so I went alone. Partway through the ride, the power quit. I was suspended almost upside down with only a thin leather strap across a fat wide seat, dangling. When the conveyance finally began to move again, I relaxed. Haven't been on a roller coaster since.

We learned of the attack on Pearl Harbor, December 7, 1941, in the voice of President Franklin Delano Roosevelt on the car radio when motoring through the Rockies. Later, we were encouraged to plant Victory gardens. I put down seeds for green peas and eagerly awaited the outcome. Sadly, so few peas showed up that my mother put them together with Birds Eye peas to make adequate portions.

At the little dry goods store in Park Hill run by three sisters, where I often swept the sidewalk, I bought a corncob pipe for a nickel. Nine years old, I stuffed the bowl with fresh coffee grounds, lit up, and inhaled. I coughed and coughed. I felt ill, and I never smoked again after this experience. And I did not have a cup of coffee until I was forty with a piece of New York cheesecake.

In elementary school, I served as an altar boy at the Sacred Heart Church. Vivid memories include swinging the on-fire incense out and back, inhaling on the back swing, and being warned by the priest when we held the paten under the chins of the believers with outstretched tongues that if the host, being the body of Christ, fell to the floor, it was cause for damnation. Finally, I completed my Nine First Fridays—a series of devotional practices—in the third grade, since, I was told, I would then have a chance for forgiveness before I kicked the bucket. What a bargain. But as a third grader, I did not mention it; for added insurance I did it again as a sixth grader when I noised it about. I completed the Nine First Fridays on my twelfth birthday on June 1, 1945, the day we departed for Schenectady and my Dad's new assignment back East at headquarters.

FOR WHOM DO YOU WANT TO CADDY?

With the turf 'neath our tread
and the blue overhead,
And the song of the lark in the whin [wind]
There's the flag and the green, with
the bunkers between—
Now will you be over or in?

— Arthur Conan Doyle,
"A Lay of the Links" (1898)

When school was out in 1946, I had just turned thirteen and became a caddy at the Mohawk Golf Club in Schenectady, New York. I was assigned badge number 77 by the pro, a scratch golfer from Beaumont, Texas, with a certain ease and an east Texas drawl.

I carried two bags every morning and two bags every afternoon all summer long, keeping exact records on the tips. One was paid $1.50 for carrying a single bag or $2.50 for carrying two bags. The tips for two brought the total, typically, to $3.00 in the morning and $3.00 in the afternoon. Real money!

On the side I had a ball business and swept the bottom of the mucky pond below the tee on the fourth hole every Sunday evening. I had a five-foot bamboo pole, a net bag over my shoulder, and crouched as I sashayed, back and forth, covering the entire soggy pond.

At the end of the first season, the pro made me caddy number one.

The same routine of caddying every day, two bags in the morning and two in the afternoon, continued for a second year in 1947 when I was fourteen, from the day school let out until it reopened at summer's end.

The record-keeping even included keeping track of those who cheated. On the very first round my first year, on the fifth hole, the man I was working for was asked, "Sam, what did you get?"

He said, "Six."

I whispered to him, "It was seven, sir," trying to explain.

"Shut up, kid."

Improved lies, moving the ball to a better spot, were routine. I figured about 37 percent of the golfers cheated, but after my first round experience, I said nothing.

It was August in the summer of 1948. The cover of *Life* magazine that week featured Alice and Marlene Bauer, twenty-one and sixteen years old, professional golfers. They were coming to play against our golf pro at the club in Schenectady and the lead male member.

With the glamorous Bauer sisters coming to town, the pro asked me, "For whom do you want to caddy?"

Since Marlene was close to my age, I said Marlene. Marlene, a child prodigy who first gripped a club at age three, was among the dozen women who began the Ladies Professional Golf Association. She had won twenty-six LPGA Tour victories by 1972. Decades later, she was named to the World Golf Hall of Fame.

Well, Alice turned out to be the charmer that day, talkative, laughing, and full of fun. Marlene was somewhat dour, quiet, and subdued. But the joyful crowds surpassed any other day at the Club.

We lived right along the eleventh hole and often balls would be knocked over a row of tall trees into our yard. I used to run out and give the ball to the player, but sometimes I would wait it out and see if he found it. An ethical dilemma!

After three summers of caddying and even playing in caddy

tournaments, I quit the game and took up tennis, which I expected to play all my life. Playing tennis took far less time, and one played the game pretty much the way one recalled it. With golf, however, one remembers the best score one ever had on a given hole. Old man par is remorseless. And golf took too much time!

THE TEENS?

After caddying, a continuing fact of my life was working every summer. At sixteen, I worked in a factory at the General Electric company as a material handler for Herman, who taught me the essence of my job and a poem, "The Wheel of Fortune," which he made me memorize and did not let me write down. That poem was forgotten, but not those lines my father quoted from Shakespeare, Browning, and Thomas Moore. Herman wanted me to come to Glen Falls, his home, some Friday or Saturday night, to learn the facts of life. I passed up his invitation.

The next summer I worked in another huge building as a crane follower for a deft crane operator, who trained me how to safely hook up loads of sheet metal or pallets freighted with goods. The safety angle was critical since these hooked-up items had to pass over the heads of scores of workers without mishap. When he was guiding the package from point A to point B, he moved in only two dimensions, forward or backward and up or down, never diagonally, he explained, since he had only two hands. Every summer I worked until I earned nearly $600, when I would cease to be a deduction on my father's taxes.

I loved the out-of-doors, not just caddying dawn to dusk but in winter ice-skating for two to three hours after school on the frozen fairway of the tenth hole at Mohawk Golf Club. When I got too cold from playing hockey with racing-blade skates (I managed to deeply puncture my upper thigh three times), I ducked inside a hut warmed by a wood-burning stove that fogged up my glasses if I forgot to go in backwards. My favorite spot for reading a book in summer was in the very top of the tall tree that was part of the edge of the eleventh hole before our home at 1912 East

Country Club Drive. The trunk of the tree opened into five branches, forming a perfect seat for swaying in the breeze as golf balls whizzed past.

In the spring of sophomore year in high school, 1949, I met with an advisor at Nott Terrace High School in Schenectady. My question for her was, "What are the career options if I want to work outside?"

She said there were two possibilities: a long linesman for the telephone company or a forester who stood atop a tower and looked for fires. Hmm. No mention of, say, field biologist.

In April of that year, Dad, an expert, courteous driver, was teaching me how to drive. He asked me to pull over.

"You are not going anywhere."

"Whaddaya mean? I'm in the fraternity with the cross-country guys, and on the ski and tennis teams."

"Unless we move to Alaska, you're not going anyplace."

He had gone to the New York Public Library and saw that Phillips Exeter Academy was one of the better schools, and we were going there the next day, Saturday, for an interview. The admissions window was about to close.

I burst into tears. "How could you spring this on me? We always talk things over."

That was when he mentioned a recent bonus and felt he could swing it.

We drove to Exeter, New Hampshire. I met with Mr. Rounds and squeaked in. Did okay academically, but did not get renowned English teacher D'arcy Curwen nor Mr. Finch, the top math teacher in New England. I was on the edge of campus in Dutch House. Didn't make a team.

But Dad was right: I wasn't going anywhere in my hometown.

It turned out that many in our graduating class at Exeter went to Harvard (seventy), Yale (forty), or Princeton (thirty-five).

The last summer before entering college, I worked again for GE, but this time in an office. The work was boring and tedious, unlike the two prior summers in the factory. On my last day, I put a note in the suggestion box that our office could be eliminated with the office to the left and to the right being joined. How unfeeling for my colleagues!

After earning $600, I was invited to be a counselor for twenty-five kids on a lake in the Adirondacks where families had summer homes. The lake was four miles long with one entrance at the southern tip where cars parked, and each family had a boat. At the northern end was a clubhouse, where our activities were centered. One day I remember planning a paddle to an island in the lake in the dark early morning where all of the kids climbed to the high point for viewing the sunrise and cooking breakfast over an open fire. A month-long project was creating a big swing for going out over the water with a carefully built seat with everyone's initials on it. On the last day, we tried it out. It worked only when someone gave a big push and the rider sailed into the lake. The ropes were too long to get anything going by oneself.

The month was a lot of fun just before going to college. I was enthused at the prospect, not apprehensive, just as I was at ten years old in going to Camp Holy Cross in Cañon City, Colorado, where I learned to swim, was a member of the Ute Tribe and renamed Peaceful Badger, or when I entered the armed services and was assigned to Europe. The future beckoned.

AMONG THE OCCASIONALLY UNZIPPED

In September 1951, Sam Sloan and I were assigned to a dormitory room at Princeton on the second floor of Pyne Hall. That was a fortuitous arrangement since we continued to room together for four years, sometimes as part of a larger group.

Hard to believe, but the first year we had men who made the beds. Sam noticed that the level of his bottle of whiskey was dropping faster than he remembered. Our man was Tony, who was short, squat, and affable. So Sam lightly marked the level of whiskey in the bottle. Sam, ever tidy, kept his class schedule on his desk. One day, he headed off to class only to find the class canceled. He came back to the room and found Tony sleeping and snoring in his bed. I don't believe Sam reported him, but the next year, "the maids" were eliminated.

Sam grew up in New York City where his father had been a publisher and his mother became a prolific writer of both novels and poetry, living to an advanced age. Sam loved Dixieland jazz so we went occasionally to Jimmy Ryan's and Eddie Condon's on 53rd Street to hear the very best in smoked-filled rooms.

In November, I called my Irish Catholic Mother to say I was quietly leaving the church. It wasn't working for me.

Mother shot back, "It's that Sam Sloan from New York City!" not blaming me but rather my circumstances. With my parents' confidence in me and their unwavering support, I had nothing to push against. Also, somehow, I couldn't let them down.

In the summer of 1952, between freshman and sophomore years in college, Sam Sloan, eighteen and I, nineteen, motored across the country in Sam's new blue Chevrolet convertible, often sleeping out-of-doors under an open sky. Our journey was more leisurely than our grandson Philip's trip in 2014, since we had forty days and visited classmates along the way.

The worst night was when we tried to sleep in the sand beside the Great Salt Lake, after a bobbing-like-a-cork swim, near Salt Lake City. We dug hip holes and pulled mosquito netting over our heads. Still, the mosquitoes and gnats and fleas had a feast. Not asleep by two in the morning, we packed up and drove up a nearby mountain where we threw down sleeping bags at a turn in the road. At four o'clock, a steady stream of cars ground up the mountain in the dark to the mines, each dumping a cloud of dust on us.

At the North Rim of the Grand Canyon, we approach the chasm for a good look. It does not drop off cleanly like the South Rim but is rather round and full of pebbles. Sam wore leather street shoes, and I worried that he was too far out and could slip and slide down. I urged him to please back up. He said he was okay.

"Then give me the keys."

Another unpredictable night, under a full moon, found us in the Southwest sleeping in a farmer's field. Partway through the night, Sam let out a whoop and started rolling in his sleeping bag under the barbed-wire fence. I felt the large tongue of a cow lapping my cheek and quickly followed Sam.

We relished Mesa Verde, Canyon de Chelly, Bryce and Zion, the Mojave Desert, Sante Fe, and Taos.

Another memorable summer occurred in 1954, between junior and senior years in college when I took a job as a bellhop at Terrace Gables Hotel in Falmouth Heights on Cape Cod. The hours were excellent—from, say, three in the afternoon until eleven, and the next day from seven to three, then twenty-four hours off. I was paired with René, a Frenchman even taller than I at six foot five. I learned as much about humanity, special demands, and needs that summer as I did as a caddy, and, as ever, about how one's attentiveness affected the scale of tips.

Sometimes, I would hitchhike up to Kennebunkport, Maine, to visit my sister Sally, who had a summer job as a waitress. One day I put my thumb up, and an old white-haired gentleman in a broken straw hat with a grass spear sticking out of his mouth stopped.

"Where are you going?"

"To Boston."

"I'll get you started."

It was Harold W. Dodds—the president of Princeton University. I introduced myself, and he said, "You look familiar."

What is he going to say? Anyway, that fall I was invited to a tea at Prospect House, his residence.

Over the summer I designed and built a chair for myself. The notion was to find driftwood but none was suitable. I found some stark hard trees in the woods that had apparently been hit by lightning. The limbs were perfect. I created a large ample X for the back, and a small x for the front. The seat and back were heavy twine. A typical chair is seventeen inches off the ground, but this one was twenty-one inches, just right for my frame. I also made and sold sand dollar necklaces. I cooked the sand dollars until they were hard. I used silver chains and silver wire for attachment. They sold briskly, especially to the three dozen waitresses in the hotel from a nearby Catholic school. Sadly, the sand dollars fell apart after a couple of weeks. Luckily for the intrepid salesman, summer was quickly over.

I brought the chair back to college, and it was excellent for reading. One day in the late fall when returning from a football game, I saw the chair ablaze in our fireplace. What had happened? Sam said someone sat in it, and the chair collapsed. Knowing how much I cared about that chair, Sam said he thought it beyond repair and pitched it into the roaring fire. I expect he did the right thing, but it didn't feel that way at the moment.

On the Saturday before graduation in 1955, I was best man to Sam when he married Toddy, and they spent the first night at the Black Bass Hotel in Bucks County, Pennsylvania. That marriage produced four attractive children. Today Sam lives south of Santa Fe, and he is an elegant photographer, so much so that his annual black-and-white Christmas cards have been treasured and saved as something spare in a cluttered world.

In 2012, I sent Sam a copy of my poetry book, *Whales Sing and Other Exuberances*. The ninety-eighth of ninety-nine poems is "old men":

> they are first & foremost
> slow
> skin is thin and red, hair is spare and white
> you repeat for them everything
> twice thrice
> then say, "forget it."
> they don't walk, they shuffle
> they don't saunter, they wander & squint
> new knees, new hips, triple bypass
> a paunch, a well-tended paunch
> a distended paunch
> bent forward, hanging onto the balustrade
> pills, pills, pills and …
>
> UNZIPPED!

Sam replied, thanking me for the book. Playing off this poem Sam, fit as ever, closed with: "Among the occasionally Unzipped."

WHO WOULD LIKE TO WRITE FOR THE POST WEEKLY NEWSPAPER?

In the fall of 1955, when I was about three weeks into basic training with the 8th Infantry "Golden Arrow" Division, Company E, at Fort Carson, Colorado, over the squawk box a voice said, "Whoever would like to write a piece for the post weekly newspaper, please submit blah, blah, blah ..."

We had this sergeant who was trying to shape up 200 raw recruits through a variety of standard army training tactics. Four of us kind of bonded: Bob Denning, a nice guy from Grand Junction, Colorado, from a Mormon family who had a lumber business; Bill Chasteen, a lawyer from Yale who smoked and had a somewhat cynical take on life; and a fellow named Tony Chavez, who was the most proficient chap in the platoon and could readily go up a rope hand over hand and quickly. In the course of basic training I encouraged Chavez, who was also smarter than anybody else, in my opinion, to go after his high school diploma by mail, which he did successfully.

Whenever the sergeant would say, "Take five!" we would drop to the ground for a break. I would pull a paperback out of my back pocket, and the sergeant said, "You can do anything you like, smoke, talk, but McVay, you can't read!"

When we were crawling under barbed wire with rifle shots being fired above our heads, this sergeant would bark such things as, "All I want to see is asses and elbows!"

This may have been common parlance, but he had dozens of other ways of speaking that seemed singularly, quite charmingly, all his own. I began to jot them down.

So with the invitation from the editor of the post weekly ringing in my ears, I wrote a little piece completely in the argot of this fellow's colorful speech. And I dropped it off.

Publication date arrived, and I was leaning in the doorjamb of a room where the mail was placed in slots for the post's personnel. Our sergeant approached his and pulled out the paper. My piece formed a narrow column down the middle of the first page and continued inside.

It occurred to me then—and only then—that I had handed this fellow my head on a silver platter, and we had many weeks still to go.

He held the paper close to his face, moving his head back and forth on each line of the column, his face tightening.

He turned the page rapidly, jaw set. I shivered from stem to stern at my utter stupidity.

Then he looked up, slapped his knee, and said, "This is the first goddamn good piece I have ever seen in this paper!"

This suggests that we all like to hear what sounds familiar, maybe even in our own voice.

The orders for the next assignment were cut. I was told to report to the company commander. He said he saw that after a Christmas break, I was assigned to report to Fort Holabird in Baltimore for training in intelligence. He said, "McVay, if we had only known. You know that is *not* the regular army."

What did he mean? Perhaps in the regular army there may be a tat of hostility toward an assignment that may lead to wearing civilian clothes. I would have worn the uniform gladly.

WHO WAS IN THE RIGHT?

We've all experienced a key moment in life
that we can call a "turning point." A certain
event unleashes another and then another
and another.

— Marcela Serrano, *Ten Women*

Basic training at Fort Carson, Colorado, was behind me. I had
enjoyed it. In January 1956, I reported in at Fort Holabird in Baltimore
for what I thought would be a sixteen-week course to become a special
agent in the Counter Intelligence Corps.

At that time every able-bodied male was required to join the armed
services. One could be drafted and serve for two years. Or, by committing
to three years, one could be an officer, a language specialist, or work in
intelligence. I chose intelligence, and, in effect—luckily, it turned out—
gained all three.

My top-secret clearance was approved before I enlisted in the Army
for three years. A perfunctory interview process—standing and walking
through—took place upon arrival. A lieutenant, as I recall, asked if I had
any questions. I said no.

Then, on the bulletin board the assignments were posted. My name,
Martin S. McVay, black on white, was assigned to the nine-week analyst
course, which I viewed as glorified clerk typist training, not interrogation
or running cases. I was crushed.

Jack Riddle from Denver noted my dismay and anguish. I had dated
his sister Mary Ellen the prior summer. Jack was an officer who had been

at Fort Holabird for four years, knew the ropes, and he suggested I apply for a transfer to the commander of the post—an application made in seven copies.

I said I would apply for an interview related to possible reassignment.

When the sergeant in charge of the Casual Company (the interim spot before assignment) saw my application, he challenged it. He was tall, ramrod straight in posture, had piercing brown eyes, and a deep voice: "McVay, who the hell do you think you are?"

"Er, nobody special, sir."

"Sergeant!"

"Yes, sergeant."

He said he had been at that Casual Company for four years. Forty men had applied for a transfer, as had I, and all were denied. Not one was approved. "The US Army," he said, "is not inclined to think it made a mistake."

He asked again, "WHO THE HELL DO YOU THINK YOU ARE?!"

"Nobody special, sergeant."

Three days passed. Then I was instructed to report to a small building for an interview. Two men, officers—a major and a captain—invited me to sit down.

They asked me a lot of questions. The interview was not going especially well. Then, at the twenty-minute mark, one said, "The year was 1845. The place: what is now Texas. We were at war with forces to the South. Who was in the right?"

I replied, "It depended upon where you were standing, sir." I felt that the US perhaps was not "in the right," but it seemed as though my loyalty was being tested, not just a familiarity with history. Ulysses S. Grant called this war the most "wicked war" ever waged. Historians on both sides of the border describe it as little more than a land grab.*

The rest of the forty-minute interview went a little better (maybe a B-plus), and the officers bid me goodbye.

As I walked out the door, a large American flag snapped in the breeze backlit by the sun. That was a moment of intense gratitude for the fact that in America, sometimes, a matter may be appealed for review. I felt I had blown it, but I had had my chance.

Two days passed, and I was called before a colonel, a major, and a captain—all new faces—and stood before them.

The colonel asked me a few routine questions for less than ten minutes. Then he said, "If we transfer you, McVay, please don't mention it. These reviews are a pain in the ass."

In my mind I clicked my heels. I saluted and said, "Thank you, colonel."

That was the first of five critical moments that led to Hella. Second was getting assigned to Germany. Third, getting German language training for four months in Stuttgart from a splendid elderly gentleman from Berlin, Werner Schwabe. Fourth, being fourth in the course among eight CIC special agents when the top four were sent to Berlin, the hot spot of the Cold War. Fifth, thanks to a Yale linguist Peter Merrill, I met Hella—on September 19, 1956.

*The *New York Times*, October 31, 2013

THE WALK-IN

Brandenburg Gate as seen from West Berlin
with Soviet War Memorial off camera on left.

In the three years I was in Berlin, my principal job was participating in the interrogation or interviewing of three or four refugees every day who were referred to us from the Marienfelde Refugee Center.

At that time (1956–1958), one thousand refugees from East Germany (the Deutsche Demokratische Republik, the DDR) came streaming into Berlin every day, for years, until the wall was built in 1961. That flow led to a drain of some three million enterprising souls from the east, largely East Germany but also a few from Poland and Czechoslovakia. Most of them came seeking greater opportunity and freedom of expression, and we figured about 20 percent were "sent" by the Stasi or Soviet Intelligence with a mission to penetrate West German businesses and the government.

A lead example is Günter Guillaume, the trusted aide to Willy Brandt, former mayor of West Berlin and architect of the Ostpolitik, when he was chancellor of West Germany (1969–74). Guillaume, a refugee in 1969 who was working for the East, it turned out, with equal diligence and devotion, undid Willy Brandt and his regime in 1974. This betrayal was retold in the play *Democracy* by Michael Frayn (2003), which was a hit in London and later in New York.

Very few of the refugees were much interested in working for the East even though they might have nominally said so. In any event this was part of our mission as special agents of the Counter Intelligence Corps in Berlin, to talk with those who were among the "more interesting" in that daily flood of one thousand seeking a place in the West where they could live and develop their lives and their families. We did good work as part of a small group that included George Mitchell, later senator from Maine.

Another minor task was dealing with the "walk-ins" at the gate on Clay-Allee Boulevard. When we did not know someone's name, or when we thought they may be using an alias, duly noted, for the purposes of a brief report, we noted simply "FNU LNU," or "first name unknown, last name unknown." Rarely did a walk-in offer much of interest for us, but one day a chap appeared and I spoke with him. He claimed to be working for the Soviets. I said, "Prove it."

He said, "What do you want me to do?"

"Tomorrow at the Soviet War Memorial inside West Berlin on this side of the Brandenburg Gate, when the changing of the guard occurs, have the relief soldier carry a green book in his left hand."

I reported this to my superior. The next day I was sitting across the street in a car when the changing of the guard occurred. A green book was in the left hand of the new soldier who carried his weapon in his right hand. I reported this back in Dahlem, and the CIA took charge of the matter. This was no longer counterintelligence.

In 2004, we took our daughters to the play *Democracy* in New York after its London opening. Why? I was hoping thereby to suggest the nature of our counterintelligence work in Berlin.

WHEN SHOULD ONE BE ONESELF?

Daydreams are the stuff of life.
— Anna Quindlen, author, on *Radio Times*,
WHYY, May 11, 2012

When I returned home in November 1958 after nearly three years' service in Berlin, I read *The Organization Man* (1956) by William H. Whyte (1917–1999). I was looking for work and needed a little guidance. The book was a best seller then and has become a classic in the meantime since Whyte defined corporate conformity and warned against its growth.

The book contained tips in applying for a job and handling the interview situation. For example, when asked on the application form, "Do you daydream?" Whyte advised that one should not be so naïve as to say yes. And therefore, he suggested in effect that you lie. And so on.

I wrote Whyte a letter commending him on the book, but inquiring when should one be oneself? If hired, one would certainly want to get along, picking up on the signals in the environment—fitting in. At what point, sir, should one trust oneself and say what one thinks? When does the adaptive behavior stop, if ever? There was no reply.

Years went by. In 1974, when I was in New York at the Robert Sterling Clark Foundation, I signed up for an excursion with other grant-makers to a distant point in Brooklyn. Upon arriving at the point of departure, I saw a list of participants and noted that "Holly" Whyte was among them. When he boarded the bus, I sat beside him.

I should note that Whyte led an exemplary life and had a strong influence then and now on shaping the configuration of urban spaces, for he believed in their sanctity and importance. He was a mentor to Jane Jacobs, the great critic and champion of cities. So too he inspired Fred Kent to found and lead as president the Project for Public Spaces, and Fred counted on his guidance down the years.

Even though sixteen years had passed since I wrote Whyte that letter, I was still puzzled by the questions I posed to the author and by the fact that he did not acknowledge it, as busy as he was.

When I identified myself and mentioned the letter, Whyte said he remembered it and, indeed, carried it around with him for months, since the question continued to confound him, too, and he found no right way to reply to it.

Yet we have to keep asking the tough questions.

The Golden Thread

Storytelling is a method of teaching, a way
to gain trust, to communicate effectively,
to inspire imaginative thinking, and to
provide a foundation for the thinking that
is basic to literacy. … It can place us among
the vast chain of teachers since ancient
times who have compelled their students to
learn through the sheer power of the story
to captivate, inspire, and transform the
imagination.

— from *The Golden Thread: Storytelling
in Teaching and Learning*, 2006,
by Susan Danoff

HELLA: A SLIVER OF THE STORY

It does not seem difficult to write a little something about someone you do not know. The challenge is to write about one with whom you have been living for fifty-seven years.

Where to begin? Perhaps at the beginning. One fortuitous evening, September 19, 1956, Peter Merrill, a colleague in Berlin who took me under his wing, asked me, "Do you like Dixieland jazz?" Love it. And we were off to the Die Eierschale (The Eggshell), a place with music and draft beer favored by students.

That very day I had seen Nefertiti (ca.1370–1330 BC) for the first time at East Berlin's Neues Museum and marveled at the ancient Egyptian queen, whose beauty was caught by the hand of a master sculptor, Thutmose. I gasped in amazement at the incomparable work that had, miraculously, survived down thirty-three centuries.

My first glimpse of Hella was of her laughing, hair swept up like the sweep of Nefertiti's headgear. When I introduced myself to ask her to dance, I said I was Till Eulenspiegel, the troubadour-prankster who traveled from town to town entertaining with songs and stories in the Middle Ages. We danced to Dixieland jazz, and I invited her to a ballet in Charlottenburg for which I had two tickets.

I was excited. On the designated day, I took a nap to be fresh, and I overslept. When I got to the theater the program was half over. During intermission, I walked up and down the aisles and about looking for her. When the performance was over, I stationed myself outside where I could see everyone as they left. I spotted her scooting away and raced after her. She told me later she had bought a ticket in the loge, saw me, and ducked down in her seat. I apologized and invited her to Kottlers, a Schwäbisch restaurant where a man played a zither. "No thanks," she demurred, but eventually agreed.

On Hella's twenty-first birthday, October 27, 1956, I sent her twenty red roses and one yellow one to suggest we go from the formal *Sie* (you) to the more familiar *du* in our relationship. On Thanksgiving, I turned up with a turkey from the PX (post exchange) and cooked a dinner for her family with all the trimmings à la USA.

We saw each other regularly for two years. Among our favorite haunts was Die Stachelschweine (The Porcupines), a political cabaret with six actors, including Wolfgang Neus and Wolfgang Müller, where skits captured moments in the lives of Berliners who lived in a red sea of 400,000 Soviet soldiers in the DDR (East Germany) who could sweep into West Berlin (overseen by the Americans, British, and French) at any time. This dazzlingly incisive cabaret made us hunger for something analogous when we came to America. It took a while before Second City in Chicago emerged and its derivative *Saturday Night Live* burst onto the scene.

We were given six weeks of R&R (rest and relaxation) every year for supposedly hazardous duty. Once, with a colleague, I traveled to Vienna and environs for a couple of weeks, enjoyed the renowned Helmut Qualtiger—the 300-pound satirist—and the Viennese Opera. But I returned to Berlin after one week, I so missed Hella.

In April 1957, Hella and I drove in my beige Volkswagen Bug to Spain when the Free University had a break and thoroughly relished the élan of the country south of the Pyrenees. Under fascist dictator Franco, a lad with a weapon stood by the entrance to every town. We enjoyed the fishing villages south of Barcelona and often ate fresh-caught seafood at tabernas along the coast. It was in the sailors' quarter of Barcelona that we decided to marry eighteen months hence when Hella had completed her degree in mathematics and psychology at the Free University of Berlin. We traveled to Granada, Seville, and on to Madrid, where we blinked in amazement at Goya's *Caprichos* and *The Disasters of War* and the paintings of Velázquez. Along the way we would often picnic on local provisions of meat, cheese, fruit, and bread that Hella, then as now, could fashion into something delectable.

In the spring of 1958, we went to Denmark and Sweden, where we bought a lot of Danish furniture designed mainly by the legendary Hans Wegner: a teak and oak dining table, two bear chairs, a sideboard, a sewing table, a nest of tables, and more. We had dinner at the home of my parents' friends, Torbin and Weebika Klitgaard, who had a sailboat named "MCVAY."

A thrilling exercise, also that spring, was choosing our dishes, our glasses, and our flatware. We chose Arzberg for elegance and simplicity, going to the warehouse to pick from among the seconds plates that all looked perfect to us. We chose a complete line of Gralglas and are amazed to still have a few to this day. We chose utensils designed by Wilhelm Wagenfeld and produced by Württembergische Metallwarenfabrik (WMF). To our surprise, at the next international design show in Milano, our china, stemware, and flatware were featured on the cover of the catalog. Beautiful and functional design has ever fascinated us.

Following a civil ceremony, we married on August 9, 1958, at a small Catholic chapel in Berlin-Haselhorst, near Hella's home. My sister Sally came over from the States. In attendance, too, were colleagues from my unit, Bob and Linda Kausen, two Jim Griffins. Hella's family and friends included her grandfather, age seventy-eight, who rowed every day, took cold showers, and looked like Bismarck with a substantial well-formed mustache.

Let me be clear: I cannot even begin to tell the story of Hella's experiences as a girl during the war, where she moved between her home in Berlin before it was bombed out and Pirna-Neuendorf (near Dresden) to avoid Nazi schooling and Allied bombing, and East Prussia. It was thanks to two kind French prisoners on the family farm in East Prussia that her family was tipped off that the Russians would overrun them soon. How did they know? From meetings with the Red Cross. Hella, with her mother and younger brother, caught the last train back to Berlin early in 1945. Realizing that Berlin would also soon be overrun by the Russian army, they joined the trek of 15 million people towards the west. The Brits were still strafing the roads where women and children moved, killing many. The hardship continued after moving back to Berlin in the fall of 1945, living with her grandmother in then–East Berlin until 1948, when her family had the good luck of getting an apartment in West Berlin and finally starting a good education. Only she can tell of that, and the incredibly important role of her grandmother, Mina Knox, in her early years.

*Hella as a girl with baby carriage
containing three dolls and a bear.*

When we arrived in the States in November 1958, my father planned the first day for Hella in America with two events. The first was the Dartmouth–Princeton football game, the last of the season, which we shivered through during a blizzard with snow and sleet moving sideways. Her view was not unlike the Lacandon Indians from San Cristóbal de la Casas, whom anthropologist Robert Laughlin brought to America and who, some years later, saw a similar game that made little sense to them. The second was dinner in New York at the top German restaurant, Lüchow's on 14th Street, which had a huge Christmas tree and all the joy of the coming holidays in the décor.

All of our furniture had been shipped to New Orleans, awaiting word of an address in San Francisco where we expected to live. But in short order Hella was hired as number two in the Fine Hall math library at Princeton University, the epicenter of mathematics in tandem with the Institute for Advanced Study. She could not believe that her math gods came and went every day. For example, early on, Kurt Gödel, Einstein's best buddy, wanted to get into some classified material, and Hella had the key. She was not allowed to leave him alone in there, even though she was not a citizen yet. They found themselves on their knees sorting out stuff he was interested in.

Eventually, I got a job, too, as the first recording secretary at the University, and the Danish furniture was routed from New Orleans to Princeton.

After Cynthia's birth in September 1961, Hella returned to work, since a Scandinavian woman came in to help out with our two little ones. She worked for Alonzo Church, a prominent professor of mathematics at Princeton and the editor of the *Journal of Symbolic Logic*. Professor Church was something of a night owl, and he often left her notes regarding what he wanted. Alan Turing, who cracked the German Enigma machine in World War II and devised the Turing machine—a model for a general-purpose computer—completed his mathematics dissertation at Princeton in 1938 under Church. As Eric Schmidt, chairman of Google, put it, "Every time you use a phone or a computer, you use the ideas that Alan Turing invented. Alan discovered intelligence in computers, and today he surrounds us, a true hero of mankind." In 2008, a panel of professors named Alan Turing "Princeton's second most influential alumnus after only James Madison."

After I took a job to study the behavior and communication of the bottlenose dolphin in Coconut Grove, Florida, Hella was invited to teach mathematics at Carrollton School of the Sacred Heart where many young upper-class Cuban girls were taught. She said she couldn't do it since she had two small girls, Catherine, three, and Cynthia, one. The nuns said they could take care of the girls and so Hella taught math with her usual élan, and the girls thanked her after every class with a curtsy. She had taught earlier the New Math in a Princeton public school, after the Soviets launched Sputnik.

When we returned to Princeton for my tenth reunion in 1965, President Robert F. Goheen asked me to be his special assistant in One Nassau Hall. The Sacred Heart network alerted Mother Joan Kirby, and Hella was hired as the first chair of the math department at Stuart Country Day School, a position she held for eighteen years with grace and competence. I knew from former colleagues on the faculty that Hella was often an unofficial ombudsman for the lay faculty to the administration. If she felt a suggestion was just, she would present it, and typically it carried. For years she also did the scheduling of all classes in the Upper School, a tricky proposition, which she handled deftly.

Many amusing and happy incidents occurred. Wishing them happy Easter egg hunting, Hella presented the students at the Sacred Heart school with a conundrum about Easter. Why is the rabbit, a mammal, carrying Easter eggs in a basket? Where do you find this in the Bible?

How did these pagan symbols of fertility get into this day of Christian jubilation?

Or, once on April first, she invited her students to clasp the back of their heads. Did they feel any knobs? Yes, what do they mean, Mrs. McVay? Phrenology was a serious topic a while back. Hella suggested that one knob might be for "algebraicus" another for "calculi," indicating mathematical talents. Will this be on the test? No, and April Fools'! Hella felt bad about this since students are vulnerable and trust their teacher. On another April first, all the girls wore purple, Hella's favorite color, and pinned their hair up. Stuart celebrated its fiftieth anniversary in September 2013, and dozens of her former students thanked her for the difference she and math have made in their lives.

One summer, in 1966, the Aga Khan's brothers sought out Hella to tutor his daughter by Rita Hayworth, Yasmin, age sixteen, whose weight at birth was matched with rubies on a scale. A wonderfully warm young woman, she had been isolated in Swiss boarding schools and did not have a chance to develop everyday skills. Hella helped her with math, some science, and self-sufficiency. Yasmin sent her postcards and little notes for years in thanks. Today Princess Yasmin Aga Khan is a philanthropist known for raising awareness of Alzheimer's disease, which afflicted her mother.

As with any great teacher, it is give, give, give. Hella worked for years as a volunteer with Planned Parenthood of the Mercer Area, first with a caring, smart Nigerian gynecologist, Dr. E., and later with another capable physician, Dr. T. Hella wore a white coat and greeted and spoke with each woman who sought health services. This gave every woman confidence that her issues would be attentively and confidentially treated. Hella's generous caring service was honored in 1996 when she received the Volunteer of the Year award and two years later the Sanger Circle Award. She was instrumental in recruiting Senator Tim Wirth to speak in 1994 after the Cairo conference; and Janet Benshoof, president of the Center for Reproductive Law and Policy, and Congresswoman Pat Schroeder to speak at the spirited annual luncheon.

On Earth Day 1970, Hella was one of the founders of the Whole Earth Center, an organic foods store, located now at the corner of Nassau and Harrison Streets in Princeton. The founding is less relevant than the fact that she served on the board for many years, most of them as president, when the essential character and ethos of the store were shaped and honed through issue after issue, from battling bovine growth hormone to encouraging lawns free of pesticides. I remember some of the board meetings, often in our home, lasting up to five hours as crucial decisions were thrashed out. Today, the store has a thriving luncheon center, where townspeople and academics gather.

In 1988, I arranged for a trip of the board of the W. Alton Jones Foundation to Indonesia, a place of immense biological diversity. We had some crackerjack biologists with us—Adrian Forsythe, Tom Lovejoy, and Russ Mittermeier, among others. On the island of Borneo (Kalimantan), eighteen of us were walking across a meadow when two orangutans appeared in the distance, coming down a tree in a long hedgerow. The lead orang came at us on all fours, rocking forward on the sides of the hands (in contrast to the gorilla on the knuckles). He headed right for Hella, just as every cat or dog or child on other occasions, and leapt into

Hella is embraced by a mature male orangutan in Kalimantan in 1988.

her arms. I was slack-jawed, yet shot off a roll of film to capture the moment. When the mature male orang wandered off, we asked how did it feel? She smiled and said she had never had such a wrap-around hug and that he smelled good—not like a zoo animal.

All of this does not note that Hella is such good company. I get goosebumps, for example, when I hear her voice, see her handwriting or drawings, experience her imaginative and ever-varied cuisine, or see the flowering things that occur as the seasons turn in our garden between the streams, and wonder at the beauty and arrangement of art and seating in our home. Among the subtle creations on our land by her hand are such works as *Empty Nesters*, consisting of three nests cradled in an open cone with abundant feathers; *Homage to the Dogwoods*, a spirit house inspired by those we saw in Laos; and the Poetry Flags created for the dedication of our Poetry Trail.

The poem, "The Woman Who Loved Only Beauty," written on Hella's birthday, October 27, 2004, is my effort to try to catch the ineffable in her love of beauty and pursuit of mathematics.

Hella being greeted by President Bill Clinton, after he was re-elected in 1997.

THE WOMAN WHO LOVED ONLY BEAUTY

The wonder of mathematics is that it
captures precisely in a few symbols
what can only be described clumsily with
many words.

— Kenneth Chang, the *New York Times*,
October 24, 2004, "Week in Review"

My "air dish," my dish of air, my ephemeral being,
my lighter than air, not mine at all
but a creature divine
whom I accompany
in the garden in the kitchen
to Ireland, China, Alaska, Morocco…

"Beauty is the first test:
there is no permanent place
in the world for ugly mathematics,"
according to G. H. Hardy (25).

"Mathematics is there.
It's this jewel we uncover,"
according to a chap who wrote or
coauthored 1,475 academic papers,
many monumental, all substantial

"You know, Riemann had
a very short list of papers,
Gödel had a short list.
Gauss was very prolific
as was Euler of course."

This guy did math in more than
twenty-five countries ...
your curiosity and search for beauty
and truth has taken you to
a hundred countries and
more than 40 states and provinces.

This man who loved only numbers
said, "A mathematician is a machine
for turning coffee into theorems."
For 25 years you turned fresh perked
into light, life, and truth in the classroom.

Your theorem for life
is give, give, give
give to the girls
give to the grandkids
give to whomever falls within your aura.

especially (unworthy) me ...
what you and this mathematician
have in common
is that your reality overtakes mine.

He had 485 coauthors and no kids
you have one coauthor, me,
who scribbles to hint at his love of
the life you lead poetically.

We have (yikes) 48 years together
and we do not know how many to go
but we live each day in a pretty place
where every object carries meaning.

You, seeker of beauty, truth, and justice,
I, your Sancho Panza, your Tonto,
on this birthday of Oppenheimer
and you, I salute the balm of your heart,
the light of your mind,
endlessly enchanting.

October 27, 2004

THE RITUALS OF LIFE AND DEATH

Thanks to the anthropological studies of Franz Boas, Ruth Benedict, Margaret Mead, and others, we as a society began to look at other cultures—the Inuit, Samoan, New Guinean—through the lenses of their major rituals of birth, marriage, and death. In fact, in the early 1960s, we began to wonder about our own rituals, which had morphed into the realm and control of doctors for the first event and of morticians (who had renamed themselves funeral directors) for the last event.

The routine procedure for births in our community in 1960 gave the obstetrician/gynecologist almost unquestioned authority to knock out the expectant mother with a spinal block. She was unconscious of the delivery of her infant—one of life's surpassing events. That was the case with our firstborn on the first day of spring, 1960.

When number two was expected eighteen months later, we had learned of a Dr. Costan Bernard, a farmer and the father of five, who delivered children by natural childbirth and was celebrated for his spirit and humanity. Though he worked out of the Hunterdon Medical Center, just north of Flemington an hour's drive north of our home, Hella signed up with him and prepared for the second blessed event.

On September 1, 1961, we were invited to the home of Kline and Lois Fulmer, who had honeymooned in the Soviet Union and stayed on, to celebrate the birthday of their second son, Tom Fulmer, an architect like his dad.

It was a lovely evening. We had lined up the sitter to stay all night if necessary. Hella would give me a nod for every contraction, and I was closely timing the intervals. During the circulation of the appetizers, I felt that we had better get going. Hella said, have you seen what they are having for dinner? Well, we did enjoy the dinner, even as I became more anxious and apprehensive. (Another couple had announced quite noisily that they were expecting a baby and might have to leave any minute.)

The contractions occurred more frequently, and we eventually left quietly, arriving at the hospital about 11:45 p.m. Dr. Bernard was most welcoming, even leaving on the radio when Jean Shepherd was wrapping up a story. The baby arrived not long after midnight. Hella was wide awake and happy. We were elated.

The book that influenced us was *Thank You, Dr. Lamaze* by Marjorie Karmel. Hella was similarly persuaded by the La Leche League to breast-feed rather than bottle-feed.

Two years later, Peter Putnam (Class of 1942), and his wife, Durinda, invited me to join the board of the Princeton Memorial Association. We had all read Jessica Mitford's *The American Way of Death* (1963) and were moved by her sprightly exposé of abuses in the funeral home industry. She documented the ways in which funeral directors take advantage of the shock and grief of family and loved ones to convince them to pay far more than necessary for funeral costs. As a society we had let slip any thought of how we treat a member of the family when it comes to dealing with "shuffling off that mortal coil."

I interviewed a number of local funeral directors to uncover all the costs of death, saying I was putting my affairs in order, writing a will, taking out life insurance, et cetera, and I wanted to factor in the cost of death. The typical response was to say, come back in fifty years. I said, let's say it happens tomorrow. The reply was that it might happen in California. I said, let's suppose it happens on Nassau Street.

I was shown a number of caskets. I explained I wanted to be cremated. The fellow said that the body would at a minimum have to be transported in a sheet, but no one did that—they had a pine box for

$300 for transport to the crematorium (the very one where Einstein was cremated).

He asked, "How tall are you?"

"Six foot four."

"Oh, the box is only six feet."

Beginning to take things seriously, he announced, "We could chop off the feet." (Nooooooo.) "Or perhaps, flex the knees."

Years passed. My father died in 1983 after a trip to Greece. I opened a large envelope, and his clear hand said, "Dear Scott, Go down to the Princeton cemetery ..." It is not that far from Palmer Square where my folks lived for a quarter century. He had a plot in the old part to my surprise, when only a few plots remained on the far margins.

I asked the caretaker, Mr. Sutphen, "How was it that my father got this plot?"

"He came down here a lot, and I liked him," he replied.

My father wrote further, "Pace off seventy-five steps to the northeast and mark well the stone of my classmate, Edmund DeLong ..." He was the first reporter on the scene the night of the Lindbergh kidnapping. Dad and Mother's stone was to be identical, modest, with only the years noted.

In accordance with his wishes, he was cremated, and I made a box for the cremains, burning in along the sides of the top, "FROM ATHENS, TO PRINCETON, FROM ATHENS, TO PRINCETON." My sister Sally tossed in a pair of orange and black Argyle socks she knitted for him, and we nailed the box shut. We planted a couple of bonsai trees beside my parents' headstone.

For a half century, my wife and I have specified, too, that we wish to be cremated. We have purchased a niche in a new columbarium close by, top tier, which looks due east to my parents' grave.

When my time comes, we may not know (nor care) whether the

knees are flexed or not, the feet chopped off, nor whether per chance the wooden coffins are now a bit larger to accommodate a taller populace.

CATHERINE

Catherine speaking in 2010 at rally for first responders, recovery workers, and survivors at press conference before the US Capitol to urge the passage of the James Zadroga 9/11 Health and Compensation Act.

When Catherine was born on March 21, the first day of spring, 1960, our birth announcement had a drawing from Wilhelm Busch with a new baby bursting with life and joy in the middle of a feather bed with the parents almost falling out on the sides.

One year later a photographer took an extraordinary series of images of Catherine in our home on Alexander Road that capture the essence of her curiosity and exploratory spirit, from climbing the stairs to taking a bath to a wistful look standing in her crib after we had said good night.

She was happy to have a little sister, Cynthia, eighteen months younger, and sought to make her feel welcome and loved.

She learned to swim at age four during our two years in Coconut Grove, Florida, and swam happily with dolphins at a place in the Keys where a woman, Betty Brothers, kept two dolphins in a tidal pool. Betty had a way with dolphins and even wrote a children's book about them.

In 1966, our family hiked along the Appalachian Trail in the Presidential range with Jutta Cords, a family friend and Catherine's elementary school teacher, her daughter, Claudia, and Hella's brother Frank. As a teen, Catherine helped organize and lead our group to six huts: Greenleaf, Galehead, Zealand Falls, Mizpah Spring, Lake of the Clouds, and Madison Spring. Each hut is staffed by young people who pack in the food, prepare it, and put on a skit after supper. At the first hut, Catherine asked if any of the crew played chess. They said yes, after they had finished their chores. She won. That happened again at the next hut. At the third hut, a ringer was sent in who beat her.

Walking together across "the rooftop of New England" was thrilling. A high point was hearing a string quartet play across the Lake in the Clouds near sunset as we approached the hut.

When I took a gig in December 1977 as assistant naturalist on a boat from San Diego, California, to Baja to observe the southern migration of California gray whales with Ted Walker over Christmas, Catherine played chess with Thomas Pigford, a professor of nuclear engineering at Berkeley and graduate of MIT who was on the President's Commission to investigate the Three Mile Island near-meltdown. He encouraged her to apply to MIT, and when she got in, three women professors called to urge her to accept admission.

She decided to go to Princeton to study civil engineering with a focus on hydrology. Her grandfather was overjoyed since he had been opposed to coeducation but did a 180-degree turn upon her admission and took her to lunch once a week. She wrote nine profiles on members of the faculty, including Frank von Hippel, former hut boy and Rhodes

Scholar, who has been in the forefront of efforts to reduce the nuclear threat and stockpiles. She was also active in Outdoor Action. One time in leading a bunch of freshmen on the Upper Delaware River in Pennsylvania, notable for hawks and eagles, a hurricane drenched them all. They hauled out, went to a laundry to dry their clothes, and then paddled on.

After graduation, Catherine took a job with ICOS, an Italian firm that had built the foundation of the World Trade towers. Her first job was at a large waste dump in New Jersey. Her second was at Colstrip, Montana, working on an ICOS $25 million contract with Bechtel to put in slurry walls to hold unwanted chemicals due to burning coal. Her third assignment took her to Ashkelon, Israel, just north of the Gaza Strip, where at age twenty-four she was in charge of building the foundation of the second-biggest power plant in Israel. At first she worked two shifts from seven in the morning until eleven at night six days a week. At the five-month mark, she had sufficiently tamed the job to go to single shifts six days a week. It was tough because in Israel at that time women were not holding positions of consequence nor serving in the Knesset (the national legislature of Israel). With 125 men working for her, we were told that she was among the ranking women in the country. With Golda Meir the fourth Prime Minister from 1969–74, it is hard to think of women

Catherine on construction site of foundation for the second-biggest power plant in Israel, Ashkelon, 1984.

in a subordinate role, but then only eight to ten women were in the Knesset.

At Hella's suggestion, Catherine hired a young woman, Erella Ronel, born on a kibbutz, who had been a student of Hella's at Stuart. Erella had just finished her studies in Jerusalem and knew her way around the country. She in turn introduced Catherine to a young man named Gofer Gershon, who on the first date presented her with sixty red roses. Whoa. It turned out that his family was part of a moshav and they cultivated two acres of red roses, some of which were shipped daily to Europe. When we visited, we drove all over Israel, and Gofer pointed out hills that had, say, nine planes and missiles under them.

The Israeli experience probably prepared Catherine for all that followed since it was a challenging crucible. One night she got a call from one of her four foremen who were in a fight at a local bar and who asked her to come over and settle the dispute. She called Gofer, a big guy, who stayed outside. Catherine listened for a few minutes and said, "You all go home right now and get some sleep. I will see you at seven in the morning." They all showed up rubbing the sand out of their eyes.

When she returned to the States, her boss, Mr. Ressi, said that her next assignment would be to work in South Korea. Catherine needed a change of pace and chose, rather, to go to Wharton and earn an MBA, which she did. But, to this day, when she points out a crane and its capacity, she is not referring to a bird.

She then worked in financial services in New York and met a classmate from Princeton, Thomas Hughes. The first thing she said about him was, "He was an English major!"

"There are a lot of unemployed English majors," I remarked.

"But you and Grandpa were English majors!"

We saw a lot of Tom the next year. One evening at our place, Catherine went to bed early, and we chatted with Tom at some length.

At midnight, we said we were going to bed. Tom said he wanted a word with me. Tom wanted to ask Catherine to marry him, but first, he wondered if we had any questions about him and his family, all New Yorkers. The very fact that he asked put him in a special category.

Catherine and Tom were married on September 24, 1988, in the Princeton University Chapel by Dean Ernest Gordon, the Scottish chaplain who was incarcerated in World War II for three years in a Japanese prison camp. He wrote a book about it, *Through the Valley of the Kwai*, which was later made into a film called *To End All Wars*. Gordon also was the only person who brought Martin Luther King, Jr., to Princeton—twice. The reception was held at Stuart Country Day School, the images from which stream on our computer screen along with hundreds of others.

In April 1995, Catherine published a book, *Get the Lead Out: NYPIRG's Handbook for Lead Poisoning Prevention*, with Chris Meyer. It was the first book designed to empower all New Yorkers to be vigilant

Tom and Catherine after their marriage in September 1988,
in the Princeton University Chapel.

and knowledgeable about the
lead poisoning crisis and to
help reduce the toxic effects
of lead. It ran through three
editions   totaling   15,000
books.

Besides the raising of two
sons, Philip and Matthew, an
impressive work in progress,
Catherine has earned acclaim
as a leading citizen of Lower
Manhattan since the tragedy
of two planes being steered
into the Twin Towers on
September 11, 2001, barely
a block from their home
on the fourteenth floor at
176 Broadway. A television

Get the Lead Out: NYPIRG's Handbook
for Lead Poisoning Prevention, *showing
Philip with age mates on cover, 1995.
Ralph Nader said,* "Get the Lead Out *gives
you the know-how for a fast effective start
against this toxic plague in your community.*"

camera in their apartment recorded the still-roiling fires for the five
months when the family had to vacate the premises. Superstorm Sandy
flooded downtown Manhattan and swamped much of the subway
system. In anticipating storms to come, Governor Andrew Cuomo has
created the NY Rising Community Reconstruction program and named
Catherine cochair of Lower Manhattan.

In no way can I attempt to summarize the nature and extent of her
determined leadership. But Pulitzer Prize–winning journalist Anthony
DePalma turned his reporting for the *New York Times* into the definitive
book, *City of Dust: Illness, Arrogance, and 9/11* (2010) and devotes chapter
eight, "Life and Dust," to Catherine's ordeal and leadership (pages 145–
167). For seven years she was vice chair of Manhattan's Community

Board Number 1 and is now in the second term of chair for two more years, representing the now 65,000 citizens who live below Canal Street.

She received Stuart Country Day School's highest alumni accolade, the Barbara Boggs Sigmund Award, in 2006. When Barbara was mayor of Princeton, Catherine had worked with her to create a fitness trail and bicycle paths. In her remarks Catherine tried to sum up what she had learned in fighting for the health of the first responders, testifying in Washington, working with those in the city and in Albany to steer a course that took folks who lived in Lower Manhattan into account. She acknowledges that without Tom's unflagging unfailing support it would not have been possible.

Catherine, chair of Community Board #1, Lower Manhattan, 2014.

CYNTHIA

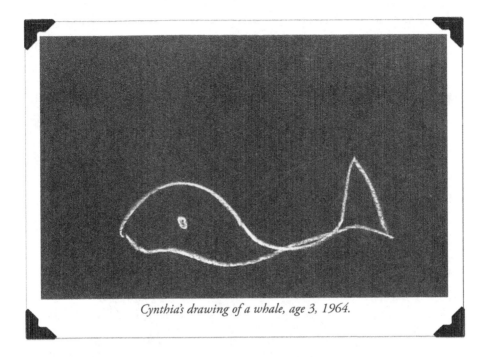

Cynthia's drawing of a whale, age 3, 1964.

When she was three years old, Cynthia drew a whale that is as definitive as Herman Melville's description of a whale as "a spouting fish with a horizontal tail." Melville knew the whale was a mammal, and he explained that his contracted definition is "the result of expanded meditation."

In September 2013, Cynthia's kindergarten teacher, residing now for many years in Maine, brought back small stories written by her pupils in 1967. Cynthia's were observant and fresh. One related to an event when her father camped out west with a friend in an open field by a full moon, and a cow licked his face. He and his friend Sam Sloan rolled rapidly away in their sleeping bags under the fence.

That same weekend, when Stuart Country Day School was celebrating the fiftieth anniversary of its founding, Cynthia and her teammates were inducted into Stuart's Athletic Hall of Fame for their unbeaten basketball team in 1979. The final game, with Cynthia the lead scorer, is noted on the plaque. Art by alumnae was hung about, and one from her collage series was hung on the column in the main hall of the beautiful school designed by Jean Labatut.

Group shot of preschool class at Stuart Country Day School with Cynthia front and center and Catherine a little to the right. Montessori teachers are Irene MacDonald and Millie Harford.

Athletics and the making of captivating art are ribbons through her exploratory life. Her major at Harvard in biology (her minor was in visual and environmental design) led to a senior thesis on the vocalizations of two species of capuchin monkeys, *Cebus abifrons* and *Cebus apella*, based on recording calls in Amazonian Peru over eleven weeks and analyzing them. E. O. Wilson said she could publish this research in three parts as a doctoral dissertation.

After Harvard, she and three other graduating seniors undertook the writing of the first edition of *Let's Go: Mexico* as part of a travel series published by Harvard Student Agencies. She covered one-fourth of the country, the northwest, living frugally. One time on the phone she said she was paying $2 a night for lodging.

"Can't you find a better place?" we asked. She said this was the hub for daily forays into the surroundings.

She went to work for the World Wildlife Fund in Washington, was assigned to Guatemala and Mexico, and had a hand in the creation in 1985 of the Monarch Butterfly Biosphere Reserve located four hours north by car and a little west of Mexico City. We did not get there for years, but were overwhelmed by the tens of millions of monarchs draped on trees and flitting about everywhere. Excited local caretakers asked Hella: "Are you Cintia's mother?" in a lilting Mexican way.

At Wharton, Catherine alerted Cynthia about the Lauder Institute, a brand-new program that also awards a master's along with an MBA that Cynthia entered with a focus on Brazil. She studied in São Paulo one summer and worked in Rio the next.

In her second year at Wharton, Cynthia was director of choreography for the Wharton Follies production, *Between the Balance Sheets*. She applied for a job at McKinsey, the lead consulting firm to corporations and countries around the world. She got the job.

Cynthia's marriage to Kenny, a fellow Wharton alumnus, did not last, but they have a spectacular daughter, Tess, now a junior at Washington University studying environmental biology. She is equally talented as an athlete and an artist. Just before Christmas 2013, she made a sprightly video, about a friend and herself, jumping on and off hay bales and emerging from and retreating to a shed, performing Hindu dance moves in unison, to the delight of all.

After five years at McKinsey, Cynthia was asked to organize a retreat in Scottsdale, Arizona, for 400 professionals (and their spouses) from the Northeast offices. What was her plan? She organized the meeting into teams by undergraduate major and life experience. The directors were anything but business majors—they had studied and practiced astrophysics, music, composing and performance, you name it. Apparently, the meeting was one of the best.

Carter Bales, a director of McKinsey from 1978 to 1998, said* the two tests for anyone at McKinsey are: Will you become a great problem-solver, and will you become a great leader? In 2014, Bales says, "She is highly gifted in both. Interesting investing opportunities would flow to her because she is so powerfully magnetic as a human being." Cynthia considers him a key mentor.

After McKinsey, Cynthia became an independent consultant and had dozens of clients. She had to list them in her application to join the Obama administration as director of innovation for the Peace Corps, a position she took going into the Peace Corps's fiftieth year.

Cynthia McVay shakes President Obama's hand when she was Director of Innovation at the Peace Corps in 2012.

In 1999, when she was living in New York on East 81st, a half block from the Metropolitan Museum of Art, she bought eighty-three acres in Esopus, south of Kingston, near the Hudson River. She renovated an old farmhouse at Field Farm. Then, after meeting Elric Endersby, a barn wizard, she looked at forty or fifty barns and bought a big old one in Gouverneur on the northern

Interior of Cynthia's barn at Field Farm.

edge of New York State, near Canada, and brought it down, each post and beam neatly marked, in three forty-foot trailers for reassemblage. She wanted to keep the integrity of the barn and the land, which got top marks later for its healthy biodiversity from a New York State wildlife specialist. She put in eight-by-eight-foot windows. Three beds were built by hand. The place will doubtless be featured in *Architectural Digest* since it is not only distinctive and inviting, but it is also brimming with works of art of her own design, including one sundial work that reaches for the sky.

Cynthia is featured in an illustrated article in the Spring 2014 issue of *Wharton Magazine* with images from and of the barn, including her beloved Labrador, Charlotte.

What she loves most is the quality of light on the property and the joy of views in all directions. Early on, she put in a pool and entertains friends regularly from many phases of her life—college, grad school, and her several jobs.

*From a feature profile on Cynthia, "The Monkey-Calling, Intuitively Strategic Artist," *Wharton Magazine,* Spring 2014.

Cynthia McVay in an article in Wharton Magazine, *Spring, 2014, titled "The Monkey-Calling, Intuitively Strategic Artist."*

IN PRAISE OF WOMEN

In my twenties I read the book *The Natural Superiority of Women* (1953, Macmillan) by Ashley Montagu and found its well-articulated thesis persuasive.

Montagu was a British American anthropologist (1905–1999) who chaired his department at Rutgers and lived nearby. He wrote sixty books, spoke often locally, and, not surprisingly, had many capable young women as colleagues.

"Women love the human race; men behave as if they were, on the whole, hostile to it … it is precisely in the capacity to love, in their cooperativeness rather than aggressiveness, that the superiority of women to men is demonstrated; for … as far as the human species is concerned, its evolutionary destiny, its very survival, are more closely tied to the capacity for love and cooperation than to anything else."

From the standpoint of survival, the female is vastly more important biologically, he pointed out, than is the male. She is the more valuable part of the species' capital because she is the principal maintainer and protector of the species during children's most tender periods of development.

Vendettas and internecine conflicts are essentially masculine activities, he underscored, and the most pathological form that such activities take—namely war—is exclusively a masculine invention.

Above all, women are more interested in human relationships, in which they can creatively love and be loved. As long as this remains the true genius of women, the world will be safe for humanity.

These thoughts prepared me—along with my experience with women colleagues and recipients of our foundation grant-making—for

Carol Gilligan's path-finding book, *In a Different Voice* (1982, Harvard University Press). Harvard Press called it "the little book that started a revolution, making women's voices heard."

The culture was changing. It was in the air and in the music. I had worked for Princeton at a time when my boss, President Robert F. Goheen, was trying to bring about coeducation with an aging board of trustees. A university survey in 1966 of alumni revealed something startling. While alumni out five years, typically twenty-seven years old, were 90 percent in favor of coeducation, those out fifty years at seventy-two years old were 90 percent against it. The feminist movement was underway, pointing at inequities of opportunity and reward.

The thesis of women working within a web of relationships prepared me to view *In a Different Voice* as an evolutionary perception of the nature of women based on impressive scholarship with ramifications for education. My wife was teaching mathematics in an all-girls' school, and our daughters were on an awakened track.

Gilligan, a psychology professor at Harvard, espoused the idea that women see "the world comprised of relationships rather than of people standing alone, a world coheres through human connection rather than through systems of rules." Two other thoughts affirm her compelling thesis:

"Illuminating life as a web rather than a succession of relationships, women portray autonomy rather than attachment as the illusory and dangerous quest. In this way, women's development points toward a different history of human attachment, stressing continuity and change in configuration, rather a replacement and separation."

"[T]he moral judgments of women differ from those of men in the greater extent to which women's judgments are tied to feelings of empathy and compassion and are concerned with the resolution of real as opposed to hypothetical dilemmas."

Gilligan had earned her doctorate at Harvard and began teaching there with renowned psychologist Erik Erikson. In 1970, she became a research assistant to Lawrence Kohlberg, who adapted Jean Piaget's psychological theory about moral reasoning as the basis for ethical behavior. Kohlberg argued that girls, on average, reached a lower level of moral development than boys. Gilligan countered, based upon her studies and interviews, that women's morality was not less developed but simply different from that of men.

At the Dodge Foundation, we backed an empirical study of Gilligan's thesis by funding a project at Emma Willard School, the oldest girls' preparatory school in America.

My nomination of Gilligan for a John Heinz Award in 1998 led to her to receive an unrestricted award of $250,000.

Since 1995, the John Heinz Awards have been given annually in five categories of Senator Heinz's life: arts and humanities, environment, human condition, public policy, and technology, the economy, and employment. Dr. Gilligan received the award in the human condition category.

In summer 2003, I made remarks in praise of women to the ever-resourceful Chautauqua Women's Club, offering dozens of examples of women's natural superiority and different ways of looking at events. For example, have you ever noticed that when a man receives an award, he may approach the microphone with an "aw shucks" attitude, perhaps a false humility, in effect saying, "you noticed?" Women, on the other hand, invariably start by saying, "This gives me a chance to acknowledge the whole team," as Gilligan noted that women see life as a web of relationships. Men often take the credit for themselves. Women say they are a seamless part of the team.

Throughout my life I have endeavored to offer the name of a qualified woman whenever invited to suggest a candidate for an interesting job.

My own personal heroes beyond my wife and daughters—who amaze me continuously—are Shirley Tilghman, the nineteenth president of Princeton University and a biologist with a passion for the arts, and Theo Colborn, a pharmacologist-biologist who has tackled the plague of health woes caused by endocrine disruption.

In the intensive Grant Study of 268 students begun at Harvard University in 1938, intended to track them through their entire lives, the early researchers did not pay much attention to their relationships. According to George Vaillant, the study director in recent decades, having a warm childhood was powerful and predictive. In his most recent summary of the work, *Triumphs of Experience*, he wrote, "It was the capacity for intimate relationships that predicted flourishing in all aspects of these men's lives."*

As our daughter Cynthia put it the other day, "Women seem to have the empathy gene built in. Men may be able to acquire it if they start early."

As Gabriel García Márquez wrote, "The only new idea that could save humanity in the twenty-first century is for women to take over the management of the world."

*From David Brooks's piece in the *New York Times*, "The Heart Grows Smarter," November 5, 2012

Postscript

This book is replete with women of staggering accomplishments. The poets Adrienne Rich, Gwendolyn Brooks, Rita Dove, Naomi Shihab Nye, Jane Hirshfield, and Pattiann Rogers offer fresh takes on what it feels like to be alive. Philanthropists Brooke Astor and Theresa Heinz have stretched thinking about giving in New York City and nationally. Scientists who have improved our perceptions include Margaret Mead,

Cynthia Moss, Dian Fossey, Margaret Geller, Sylvia Earle, and Aimee Morgana, in anthropology, understanding elephants, probing the psyche and society of mountain gorillas, mapping a swatch of the cosmos, life in the oceans, and interspecies communication, respectively.

Others who have altered our world for the better big time include Isak Dinesen, my favorite storyteller; Barbara Boggs Sigmund, a mayor of grace and accomplishment; Toshiko Takaezu, a beloved potter who made vessels never before imagined; Elizabeth Diefendorf, a librarian who found a new way to cherish books of consequence; Gloria Steinem, the voice of the women's movement; and Wendy Kopp, whose Teach for America has sent bright motivated college graduates to teach in poor urban and rural schools.

AN EMBODIMENT OF THE MAN

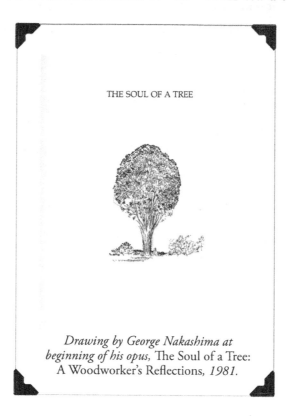

THE SOUL OF A TREE

Drawing by George Nakashima at beginning of his opus, The Soul of a Tree: A Woodworker's Reflections, *1981.*

A tree provides perhaps our most intimate contact with nature. A tree sits like an avatar, an embodiment of the immutable, far beyond the pains of man.

— George Nakashima, the opening sentence of his book, *The Soul of a Tree: A Woodworker's Reflections*

Not long after coming back to the States and moving to Princeton, Hella and I got to know George Nakashima (1905–1990), a woodworker perhaps without peer whose furniture and architecture have won acclaim worldwide. In Pondicherry, India, where he worked with and became a disciple of Sri Aurobindo, he designed and supervised the construction of Golconda, the primary disciples' residence at the ashram (1937–39), which we visited in January 2008. He was given the Sanskrit name "Sundarananda" ("one who delights in beauty") by Sri Aurobindo himself.

After our house fire in 1982, we bought eight of his chairs, four of the Conoid first designed in 1969, for our Hans Wegner dining table. He created a frame for Benton Murdoch Spruance's artist's proof of *The Last Thrust*, from his series on *Moby-Dick*. We were invited to the Nakashima's annual celebration of the dogwood blossoms and to hear any disciple of Aurobindo who came through.

George wrote his opus, *The Soul of a Tree: A Woodworker's Reflections* (1981), illustrated by his matchless drawings and by photographs of his tables and chairs and lamps, and kindly inscribed it for us.

On our twenty-fifth wedding anniversary, August 9, 1983, Hella and I took a balloon ride at dawn from just north of Lambertville, New Jersey. It was thrilling as we were carried by the wind east by southeast, with deer bounding across hill and meadow, mist lifting, and birds flying about. The hour seemed like a full day rich with infinite sensations. We landed in a farmer's field, and, as is the old French custom, uncorked a bottle of champagne for the farmer and for us.

We then drove across the Delaware River for breakfast at Mother's, George's favorite local restaurant.

Then we drove to the shore, Island Beach State Park, for a day of swimming, sunning, and beach walks, crowned by one of Hella's delicious picnic lunches.

Upon returning home, our mailbox contained a single letter, not the usual stack of bills and promotions. It was a four-page handwritten letter from George, wherein he said a piece of English walnut wood had come into his possession that he felt was singular in the last hundred years—maybe in the life of the planet.

A sketch showed how he thought a peace altar or table might be made from it. He showed further a sketch of a catwalk over water to a geodesic dome that might house the peace altar and that looked like a sphere with its reflection.

The next day I called George to see if we might raise a little money to make this happen. George said, "No, I just wanted to know what you thought."

Later, the first great Peace Altar was finished, delivered to the Cathedral of Saint John the Divine in New York and dedicated by the dean, Reverend James Parks Morton.

After George Nakashima's death, his daughter Mira Nakashima-Yarnall completed Peace Altar number two, which went to the Russian Academy of Art in Moscow. Then Peace Altar number three went to Poindicherry, where George had lived and worked after attending MIT and living in Paris. Mira also made a table for our grandson Philip when he was born in 1991, which is the centerpiece of his parents' home in Lower Manhattan.

Peace Altar number four, from the same extraordinary burl of English walnut, is destined to go to the Reverend Bishop Desmond Tutu's Institute for Justice and Reconciliation in Cape Town.

In reflecting on the immense contributions of George Nakashima twenty-five years after his death, I pause to note his own words: "My life has been a long search across the tumbling screes on mountain slopes around the world to find small points of glowing truth."

Yes, and he created glowing truth in his work. His paean to the tree and its cherished wood is found in what he created. He was a rare American who received Japan's National Treasure recognition. A two-hour-long documentary called *Elegant Craftsman*, released in 1985 by National Geographic, sought to catch his spirit in action. The Metropolitan Museum of Art has a room at the entrance to its Japan section in his honor, and his home, studio, and workshop have become a National Historic Landmark.

For us to have his furniture in our home is a daily reminder of his presence, his search for beauty and function in wood, and a spirit divining our place on Earth.

OKAY, SPORTS FANS, DON'T TOUCH THAT DIAL

Jean Shepherd (1921–1999), who grew up on the south side of Chicago, was a colorful personality on WOR Radio, 50,000 watts out of New York, and an amazing storyteller.

He had a huge following in the Greater New York area and held forth with yarn after yarn every weeknight and Saturday mornings.

Through a staff sergeant in Berlin, I learned of and learned to love the dazzling Danish writer and supreme storyteller, Karen von Blixen (1885–1962), pen name Isak Dinesen. Her book *Seven Gothic Tales* (1934) was a spellbinder for me. *Out of Africa* is her better-known work, mainly through the movie starring Meryl Streep and Robert Redford, and is about the years Dinesen ran a large coffee plantation in Kenya.

So, as a way of saying thanks to Shep for stories of his Chicago boyhood and many others—his book *In God We Trust, All Others Pay Cash* and his publication of *The America of George Ade*—and for reading of the poetry of Robert W. Service, in the early 1960s I mailed him a copy of *Seven Gothic Tales*, suggesting he start in the middle with the fourth story, "The Dreamers."

The following Saturday, Hella and I were driving with our young daughters in Bucks County, and I turn on Shepherd at 10:15 a.m. He opened with, "Okay, sports fans, don't touch that dial."

And then he proceeded to read aloud the first part of "The Dreamers," a compelling story of a man pursuing a woman across Europe, following one whiff of a clue after another, told by a man in a dhow in the Indian Ocean one hundred years later, thereby removed in both space and time, contributing to the surreal aspect of the story. Without commercial interruption, Shepherd read until 10:43, leaving us breathless and spellbound.

He said that *Seven Gothic Tales* had just come into his possession. He regularly warned his radio audience that he did not acknowledge communications from them. He said further that he gave the book to the best writer he knew, who promptly walked down the hall and dropped his typewriter down the elevator shaft.

Postscript

I regret that even though I took three courses in English literature from professor and Rhodes Scholar Edward Dudley Humes Johnson, not once did he mention nor recommend Isak Dinesen, even though he knew and admired her.

The Art of Listening

So if I am right that we are storytelling
creatures, and as long as we permit ourselves
to be quiet for a while now and then, the
eternal narrative will continue.

Many words will be written on the wind
and the sand, or end up in some obscure
digital vault. But the storytelling will go on
until the last human being stops listening.
Then we can send the great chronicle of
humanity out into the endless universe.

— *The Art of Listening*
by Henning Mankell,
translated from the Swedish
by Tiina Nunnally

THE MONKEY-ROPE

Moby-Dick: or, The Whale (1851) by Herman Melville is the book that changed my life, a grail of what was possible in literature and in the life of the seas. The work was read closely in a course taught by Lawrence Thompson, who cautioned us not to neglect chapters on "the whale stuff." Professor Thompson was the lead scholar on the book, having written *Melville's Quarrel with God* (1952), which contended that the work was essentially heretical—anti-Christian—as would be seen as the epic tale unfolded. Young Melville had dedicated his opus, "In token of my admiration for his genius, this book is inscribed to Nathaniel Hawthorne." Thompson pointed out that when Melville sent the book to Hawthorne, a note was affixed, "I have written a wicked book and feel spotless as a lamb."

Thompson was Robert Frost's biographer, but after seeing the way Thompson took apart the quest for the white whale by careful dissection and analysis, the poet began to distance himself. Thompson told me later that he thought maybe the only way to convey the nature and life of the four-time Pulitzer Prize–winning Frost was to begin with the letters (volume one) of what became a three-volume acclaimed biography.

Moby-Dick is a tremendous yarn, brilliantly told, and it was a tragedy that it bombed in Melville's own lifetime. This is a little like van Gogh, who sold only a a few paintings out of 2,000 works of art, or Emily Dickinson, publishing fewer than a dozen poems in her lifetime from more than 1,800 found and published by her sister after her death.

Also, seen in the light of subsequent whale science (or cetology), Melville's account of what we knew of whales then was accurate. Consider only the dazzling definition of the "Hump Back" whale in chapter thirty-two, "Cetology": "He is the most gamesome and light-hearted of all the whales, making more gay foam and white water generally than any other of them."

That thought prepares one, if you will, for our discovery of the six-octave songs of humpback whales (*Science*, 1971). If by some miracle, we could bring Melville back for an hour, we would play those tapes that have inspired so many musicians, scientists, and conservationists.

If I go to only one chapter, chapter seventy-two, "The Monkey-Rope," might well be a point of relevance for this book. Picture the situation. Queequeg, the lead harpooner, is on the back of a slippery mostly submerged whale stripping off the blubber. In Ishmael's voice we learn, "It was a humorously perilous business for both of us ... the monkey-rope was fast at both ends; fast to Queequeg's broad canvas belt, and fast to my narrow leather one. So that for better or for worse, we two, for the time were wedded; and should poor Queequeg sink to rise no more, then both usage and honor demanded, that instead of cutting the cord, it should drag me down in his wake. So, then, an elongated Siamese ligature united us. Queequeg was my own inseparable twin brother; nor could I any way get rid of the dangerous liabilities which the hempen bond entailed."

Ishmael continues, as any of us might, "I saw this situation of mine was the precise situation of every mortal that breathes; only in most cases, he, one way or other, has this Siamese connexion [sic] with a plurality of other mortals."

The depth of this insight carries through this volume, and whale stuff keeps coming up for air throughout the larger narrative.

The interstitching of whale science and writing about the whales is reflected, for example, in an invitation received years ago to speak at Kent State University when a distinguished scholar of *Moby-Dick* (two books!) was retiring and a three-day conference was convened in his honor. My challenge, as the last speaker, was to describe the accuracy of Melville in depicting the whale against current knowledge of what we know of this still-unknowable tribe. The preparation was fun and the response of Melville scholars encouraging. I learned that Melville, like Aristotle on the dolphin, was surprisingly accurate about the whale in the absence of very little science.

In 2011, on the 150th anniversary of the publication of *Moby-Dick*, British cetologist Philip Hoare kindly invited me to be a reader of the chapter "The Fountain" from the book. It was an honor since it was an imaginative salute, and each reading was released on a different day and accompanied by a particular original artwork.

As recently as May 30, 2013, as part of the World Science Forum, under the model of the great whale—designed and built by Richard Ellis—at the American Museum of Natural History, I gave a talk on Arctic whales after three midcareer women scientists spoke of narwhal behavior, bowhead whale songs, and the challenges of underwater filming in the Arctic.

None of this, and more, would have happened without Herman Melville's masterpiece *Moby-Dick* being woven into my spirit and impelling me first to seek to understand the phonations of the bottlenose dolphin, then writing a piece for *Scientific American* that became the underlying rationale for whale protection. This led to me serving on the US delegation to the International Whaling Commission, discovering the humpback whale's song, and leading two expeditions to the Alaskan Arctic to film, observe, and record the majestic bowhead whale, the second documented by the National Film Board of Canada.

Each undertaking propelled the next with the words of Melville in his twenties ringing in my ears, such as: "Can leviathan long endure so wide a chase and so remorseless a havoc?"

Also, I thought, perhaps naïvely, that greater knowledge of whales and other nonhuman forms of life would lead to more restraint in our exploitation of the living systems that comprise this Earth.

A PIVOTAL DATE

People ask me, how is it that I, an English major, became so intimately involved in working with whales and their preservation? They may ask, too, was this an extension of my fascination with cetaceans sparked by Melville's *Moby-Dick*? Probably. These are fair questions since many of these sketches or tales or anecdotes are about whales.

On December 7, 1961, John C. Lilly, MD, came to Princeton to speak in Eno Hall at the invitation of Jack Vernon, a professor of psychology. Lilly had written the first of ten books, *Man and Dolphin*, in which he postulated a big idea—namely, that the bottlenose dolphin may possess a level of cognition and awareness not dissimilar to us, a notion that was immediately challenged the way most new ideas are. Indeed, Lilly went even further by suggesting that this ubiquitous aquatic mammal may exceed us in range and level of awareness, despite lacking an opposing thumb and forefinger. (See my poem "Maps.")

After Lilly's talk, I waited until everyone had left. Then I asked him, "Where are you going now?"

"New York."

"How?"

"By train."

"May I ride in with you? I have a number of questions."

"Sure."

I had typed out eighty-three questions about the book, impelled by my fascination with the dolphin's quick wit and resilience in dealing with the manifold challenges of captivity, and we got through fifty-one or fifty-two of them. Lilly later invited me to come to work with him at his Coconut Grove laboratory, Communication Research Institute. I demurred, saying that I was a literature major who had read *Moby-Dick* closely, and that many young scientists were pounding on his door for the chance to work with him. He replied that I was the "most curious."

Lilly kept pushing me. In the summer of 1963, Hella and I with the girls traveled to New Orleans and the Southeast for the express purpose of exploring the possibility. Some weeks later I took the job and stayed nearly two years.

It is quite a coincidence to note that in 1968 in the basement in Eno Hall—directly below where Lilly spoke—in Mark Konishi's laboratory, I did the spectrographic analysis of the humpback whale tapes that led to my discovery, description, and analysis of their songs.

Postscript

The last time I was with Dr. Lilly was on January 26, 1996, at the Fourth Annual Whales Alive Conference at the Four Seasons Resort on Maui.

I had just given the keynote address, "When Will We Crack the Whale Code?", when I was asked to have a conversation with Lilly. The organizers had asked that the interview occur standing up. Why? They were afraid that Lilly might veer into talking about sleep tanks or LSD. He was wearing a white Navy cap with "CETACEAN NATION" handwritten on it, and he appeared in fine fettle, answering all questions posed.

Shortly thereafter, Lilly sold his papers to Stanford University. He died in 2001 at the age of eighty-six.

MAPS

What are maps
after all
but metaphors
for what we don't know?
At each juncture
of the human record of
perception of where we are
we see a little of
the near at hand
but want to know
what's over the rise
in the hill or
the far horizon at sea.

Copernicus & Kepler
gave us the first big
reorientation
Darwin & Wallace
a new map
for thinking about origins
and how we came to be.
Freud & Jung
poked up awareness
of the unmapped unconscious
Margaret Geller,

saints be praised,
gave us the first map
of the universe
that others have been
fleshing out ever since.
Yes, maps are metaphors
of the little we know
and a hint of where we
have to go.

May 5, 2010

A THIRD EYE

The year was 1963. The place was a Marriott hotel in Washington. The occasion was the first-ever meeting of whale biologists, at a time when very few had any experience of studying the living, breathing, spouting whale alive in its element.

The speaker was a British anthropologist, Gregory Bateson (1904–1980), the third husband of Margaret Mead (from 1936 to 1950) and the only one whom she loved according to her autobiography, *Blackberry Winter* (1972).

Gregory, author of *Steps to an Ecology of Mind* (1972), had been hired by John C. Lilly, MD, to run the St. Thomas Lab of the Communication Research Institute based in Coconut Grove, Florida. His topic was "The Possible Intelligence of the Bottlenose Dolphin."

Gregory came to the podium, looked out at the audience, and said, "I detect certain hostility in the room."

Many had their arms crossed skeptically.

"I do not know if it is directed at me personally or the topic I wish to discuss with you this morning. But as a consequence, I am going to take my prepared remarks and drop them in the wastebasket."

Kerplunk!

As Gregory stood before the old codgers, he created the impression of a rumpled, unmade bed. Particularly noteworthy was the way his shirt opened near the waist to frame his belly button in a triangle.

Gregory took an oblique approach to his subject, by describing the behavior of wolves and then, like a land crab, crept sideways toward his theme.

When it was over, I hurried to the front of the room to say, "Gregory, that was a good talk. And to think you took your prepared remarks and dropped them in the wastebasket!"

Gregory put his arm around me and said, "Scott, I have been working on that talk for years."

Gregory was famous for the concept of the double bind (1956)—that is, you are damned if you do or damned if you don't. The victim of a double bind receives contradictory signals (for example, a child is encouraged to speak freely, but is criticized or silenced whenever he or she actually does so).

In an elegant article, "Observations of a Cetacean Community," in *Mind in the Waters* (1974), Bateson wrote about seven dolphins of diverse species at Whaler's Cove at Sea Life Park in Hawaii. The seven had a particular "sleep formation," and number four in the pecking order was Haole, who was removed one day for experimental purposes. Oddly and interestingly, the other six could not get their swimming formation in the absence of Haole.

Fast forward. Margaret Mead died in 1978, and the American Museum of Natural History had an invitational memorial service to honor her life and work. Hella and I had lunch beforehand with Gregory, who was dying of a half-dozen ailments.

The service was organized in such a way that nine speakers, in a semicircle from right to left in alphabetical order, spoke for five minutes. Gregory was the first, then Buckminster Fuller; number five was Mary Catherine Bateson, gifted daughter of Margaret and Gregory, and last, Barbara Walters.

Hella said quietly to me that our beloved Bateson could not hem and haw, clear his throat, shuffle and scratch. He had to speak directly to the topic of Margaret Mead, perhaps the pioneering cultural anthropologist. Well, he did not. He hemmed and hawed, cleared his throat, shuffled and scratched. All the while his shirt was parted near the waist, and his navel looked out at the audience like a third eye.

Bucky Fuller, the inventor and designer of the tetrahedron, spoke next. We had heard him years earlier speak at McCosh 10 Hall at Princeton University to a packed audience, beginning at eight o'clock and ending, I understand, at four in the morning. Bucky stood at the service like a compact fireplug, after Gregory's large ungainliness. He said, "On many occasions, Margaret urged me to be brief, to wrap it up. Well, we know she is looking down on these proceedings. Let me come right to the point." He looked up, and put his hands together, saying, "Margaret, I love you," and sat down in a minute and a half.

Postscript

In 1994, we traveled throughout Papua New Guinea with Meg Taylor, the daughter of an Australian, Jim Taylor—who was among the first to visit Stone Age people, numbering roughly 50,000, in the Tari Gap who thought they were all of humanity. After the war, Taylor married and settled at Goroka in the Eastern Highlands. Meg Taylor was well educated, became Papua New Guinea's ambassador to the United States (1989–94), and served on the board of the World Wildlife Fund. On the board's visit in 1994 to a village on the Sepik River, where our faces were painted in a lively and graphic manner (interesting Christmas cards that year!), a little marker indicated that Margaret Mead and Gregory Bateson had worked there sixty years earlier.

Among the books selected by the *New York Times Book Review*'s Ten Best Books of 2014 is *Euphoria* by Lily King. This novel, drawing on the known details of a 1933 field trip to the Sepik River in New Guinea, when Margaret Mead and her second husband, Reo Fortune, briefly collaborated with Gregory Bateson, who would become her third husband, is a "taut, witty, fiercely intelligent tale of competing egos and desires in a landscape of exotic menace …" as noted in Emily Eakin's review of June 6, 2014. Eakin notes further that for Bankson (a lightly veiled Bateson), "it's Nell's (Margaret's) brain that excites him, her drive and discipline, her easy way with the natives, her scandalously impressionistic field notes, her poetry-laden talk, her naked curiosity, her freedom."

My favorite sentence in this exquisite book is uttered by Nell: "We're always, in everything we do in this world, limited by subjectivity." That is a cautionary thought for anyone trying to put together "an anecdotal biography."

BEING IN RIGHT RELATION—
KINSHIP WITH ALL LIFE

In the fall of 1963, I left a secure position as the first recording secretary at Princeton University to take the job at Communication Research Institute in Coconut Grove, Florida, offered by John Cunningham Lilly, MD. The risk of the move became intensified in our minds by the fact that President Kennedy was shot in November when we were still in a motel with two little girls, and the palm trees rattled like a stage set as if they were part of the unreality.

The first week, four persons independently urged me to get *Kinship With All Life* (1954, Harper and Row) by J. Allen Boone. I got it and was spellbound as I read it. The first half describes Boone's initially unhappy assignment of being a companion to a celebrity dog, Strongheart, of movie renown, but as the days went by Boone became enchanted by the dog's attentiveness and found that he was attuned to and "in right relation" to his surroundings in ways new to Boone. The thesis of the book is that in right relation to their animal companions and countless aspects of the living world, humans become more in tune with their fellows.

I wrote Allen Boone, then eighty-one years old in California, about my new work with dolphins. Seven bottlenose dolphins were in tanks in an old bank building, including Elvar, allegedly the most precocious in captivity. I said that I was profoundly inspired by his observations in *Kinship With All Life*. Mr. Boone wrote back a long longhand letter cheering us on.

Years later, in 1976, I saw that two copies of the book were in

Geraldine Rockefeller Dodge's estate, one with many penciled notations in the margins, reflecting her love of animals.

It turned out that among the seven dolphins in captivity and under study, their levels of awareness and cognition seemed unevenly distributed. The most curious, by a country mile, was Elvar, who was already renowned through Dr. Lilly's writings—in particular, his *Man and Dolphin* book published in 1961. I worked directly with Elvar on a variety of experiments six days a week, morning and afternoon, for months on end.

Lilly's aim was to teach Elvar and another dolphin English. His strategy was to present Elvar with a series of from one to ten consonant-vowels, in random order, for repetition. Some 198 of these consonant-vowels or vowel-consonants are found in the English language. I would say, "eez-ooze-or," and Elvar would snap right back through his blowhole something pretty close to the original, but higher pitched. Typically, he would give back the exact number of items up to ten, but in the case of a single syllable like "tee," he usually gave back two syllables since his fine-grained

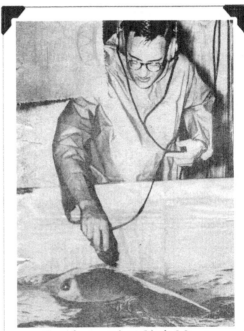

On February 14, 1964, the Miami Herald *Sunday magazine published an article describing some of our work at the Communication Research Institute. Here Scott is shown recording Elvar's sonic emissions.*

acoustical analysis revealed two sounds, "t" and "ee". (See paper in *Science* 147, 1965, "Vocal Mimicry in Tursiops: Ability to Match Numbers and Durations of Human Vocal Bursts," by John C. Lilly.)

Lilly did not conduct these experiments directly since his relationship with Elvar had soured after he planted a sleeve guide in Elvar's brain to map his neurological structure. In fairness, Lilly said he did the same thing to himself since he did not want to subject the dolphin to anything he couldn't handle. But ever afterwards, Elvar would hose down Lilly whenever he came near the tank.

The speed of dolphin interchanges among themselves is about four times as swift as those among humans. So, our speech must sound super slow to them and way down at the bottom of a well. Lilly concluded that we must either speed up our speech by four times or employ a vocoder to transfer our sonic emissions in real time at four times the pitch. He engaged a lovely gentleman, Dr. Will Munson of Bell Labs, who helped develop the vocoder, to come down periodically and work with us.

I would usually signal the end of a session by saying the name of the Institute in falsetto, "Com-mun-i-ca-tion Re-search In-sti-tute." Elvar's rapid reply hit the rhythm and number of syllables with particular feeling for the last word, "in-sti-tute."

After Hella, I believe no other entity has had a larger influence on my subsequent life than Elvar, for he taught me how to pay close attention to the most subtle and oblique signals, and he always gave his best to experiments often not worthy of his capacity. I was happy to be among those to perform the experiments, but my interest actually lay in trying to figure out what is going on sonically among the dolphins— trying to eavesdrop on their very different aquatic world where they navigate entirely by sound, whether in the depths or at night or during a storm or in everyday feeding and traveling.

Tragically, Elvar died of pneumonia in May 1965, and my mourning in part took the form of a five- or six-page poem that I sealed in an envelope not to be opened until twenty-five years later. Tragically, our house was burned to the ground in February 1981, and we lost that poem—at the twenty-three-year mark in our marriage.

When I came back to my tenth college reunion in June 1965, President Robert F. Goheen asked me to return to Princeton as his special assistant, which I accepted readily. One of the first calls he asked me to make was to Carl Kaysen, president of the Institute for Advanced Study. The woman who picked up the phone said in staccato falsetto, "IN-STI-TUTE," in much the same cadence Elvar had.

After the fire, Hella and I were left homeless and bereft of the life we had built over nearly a quarter century. We felt less self-sufficient and needed all kinds of help, from an architect to a builder to a lawyer and so on. Someone said he knew a good hypnotist and that maybe he could help me dredge up the poem from the unconscious.

One Saturday, I sat on a couch with a pad and pen in hand. As the gentleman was putting me under (something I had resisted all my life since I wanted to maintain a semblance of control—what an illusion!), I began to feel guilty about taking up his time since it was a long dirge I was trying to dredge up. But I did seem to get snatches of the poem, maybe 30 to 40 percent, and when I surfaced, I explained my guilt and frustration to him. He said, please come back next week, and we will finish this. I did not go back, but will remember Elvar for the kind, resourceful guide he was to sharpen pick-up and response.

Many memories of him linger yet. At the very end of a session where Elvar was rewarded for sonic responses with a butterfish, he made his mouth and throat move as if he were swallowing the fish. Sometimes, he would keep the fish in his mouth. When I had left the plastic-bedecked area, I looked back unobtrusively and saw that he stuffed the fish down the outflow of the tank, thereby raising the water level four inches. Even a little more water provided more wiggle room and reduced slightly the stress of captivity for an ocean-going mammal.

A violinist kept pestering Lilly to allow him to come to the laboratory and play for Elvar. Lilly was most reluctant since he thought that music might be far more interesting to Elvar than our slow deadly speech patterns and that the experience might have a negative effect on our work.

Nonetheless, Lilly eventually relented, and on a Sunday, the violinist came to the lab and sawed away on his instrument. Elvar was lolling in the tank, taking this all in. After a little bit, Elvar defecated four times, spewing the green remainders of fish he had eaten earlier.

The man, personally insulted, stalked out of the laboratory. Lilly, however, said he thought Elvar liked the music, but the man—through the odd filter of our culture—had misread the signs.

ULTIMATE FIDELITY

My studies to map the sonic domain of the bottlenose dolphin took place on Monday through Saturday. On Sundays, our family would sometimes travel to the Keys or to the west coast of Florida or up the east coast. I located nine individuals (seven women and two men essentially unknown to each other) who "kept" dolphins under an array of circumstances. In the case of the women, each had "bonded" with an individual dolphin. The men had two or three dolphins. I urged each one to keep a diary of observations, no detail being too trivial. One woman near Naples swam every day with a dolphin to whom she fed fresh pieces of fish. Even though live fish swim through a tidal pool, a dolphin rarely reverts to eating them once it has been hand-fed.

After nearly a year of daily swims and feeding the dolphin from her hand, this woman had to travel to New York for four days. In her absence, the dolphin refused to take fish from anyone else and was in danger of becoming dehydrated, since all water is absorbed from the fish consumed. When the woman returned, the dolphin was jubilant. He caught a live, wriggling fish in his teeth and offered it as a gift. The dolphin also kept her in the tidal pool for hours, not wanting her to leave again. It was just how a devoted pet—or child—will eye you sadly when you pull out luggage for a trip.

This is interesting, but you do not have science until you have at least two examples of a phenomenon.

Independently, a couple of months later another woman on the East Coast (unknown to the first) had a nearly identical experience. She, too, happened to go to New York. For how long? Four days. Hmm. Her dolphin became despondent. It looked as though she would die of dehydration—so faithful was she to the bonding that had occurred. But upon the woman's return, a squirming, live fish was presented clasped in the teeth of the now-animate dolphin. All was forgiven.

In the case of these two dolphins, it appeared that they would not eat again but rather would endure death by dehydration than continue to live "unconnected." One hears of instances among us where the death of a spouse seems to trigger the death of the other in a long-married couple. We know from the work of Susan Cohen at the Animal Medical Center in New York that the grief experience felt by a person in the loss of a beloved pet can be as acute and lengthy as that felt after the death of a dear friend or mate. So, too, each of us knows how a dog or cat, upon the death or departure of the human to whom it is linked, can grieve to death.

In all of Shakepeare, among many deaths, only one person died of a broken heart—Enobarbus, the faithful manservant of Antony, who had spoken immortal words of Cleopatra:

> Age cannot wither her, nor custom stale
> Her infinite variety: other women cloy
> The appetites they feed: but she makes hungry
> Where most she satisfies, for vilest things
> Become themselves in her: that the holy priests
> Bless her when she is riggish.

However, Antony, whom Enobarbus had known through times of glory and pain, had become so changed by this legendary woman, Enobarbus could not go on.

Dolphins and dogs might empathize with Enobarbus, since their empathy suggests the depth of the relationship. Sometimes, it seems, they would rather die than continue to live if the relationship is broken.

HOW CAN A DOLPHIN SAVE A HUMAN?

Another rare event, observed, filmed, and recorded on April 1, 1964 (no joke), at CRI's other laboratory on the island of Saint Thomas, occurred outside the protocol of our regular work.

A bright, educated woman lived a few miles away. A connoisseur of art, she was an accomplished athlete who would sometimes spend hours swimming in the waters below her home. She was confounded by the enigma of how a dolphin could purportedly save a struggling nonswimmer at sea (even though three cases were known from the literature, and we had two further accounts in letters to the laboratory, one from a Navy Seal in Thailand).

First, one assumes that the drowning person would be thrashing and disoriented. Second, if he saw a fin, he might think it a shark. Third, even if this panicked person had the self-possession to grab the dorsal fin, exhaustion would soon slacken his grip. The woman persistently queried the director of the Institute, "How could a drowning person be rescued by a dolphin?"

One Sunday, she accepted the standing invitation to visit the lab with its tidal pool and a female dolphin three or four years old. What follows was recorded in air and underwater, and it was filmed. That data is now in the Lilly archives at Stanford University.

The woman entered the water with this conundrum crowding out any other thought. She happened to lie face down in the water assuming "the dead man's float," something she never did, she told me later when I took down verbatim her first-person account. From behind, the dolphin swam onto the woman's back and clasped its flippers firmly under her arms and began to propel her around the pool with its powerful tail flukes.

At first she resisted. She was unused to letting go or losing control. She noticed, however, at the first quarter turn that she could see and breathe. The weight and vertical stroking of the flukes lifted her head clear of the water as the two—joined by a belly-to-back Siamese connection—made a circuit of the pool to the gasps of onlookers. She "let go." She told me she relaxed as deeply and as fully as she ever had. The dolphin made two complete circuits of the pool and then shot straight up in the air, releasing the woman gently and precisely on her knees on the cement lip of the pool. She said softly, "I understand."

Postscript

This account and the prior one were rewritten from the first chapter of *The Biophilia Hypothesis*, "A Siamese Connexion with a Plurality of Other Mortals," by the author, edited by Stephen R. Kellert and Edward O. Wilson, Island Press, 1993.

A PALE BLUE DOT

In my two years of working in John C. Lilly's lab, the most inquiring visitor was the astrophysicist Carl Sagan in 1964. His questions probed the soul of our work of trying to peel back the map of what we did not know about the bottlenose dolphin.

His own fertile imagination about the cetacean mind was reflected in his conjectures about the meaning of the six-octave song of the humpback whale (Payne & McVay, *Science*, 1971) that were cited in *Mind in the Waters* (Scribner's, 1974) and other ruminations:

"The cetaceans hold an important lesson for us. This is not about whales and dolphins, but about ourselves. There is at least moderately convincing evidence that there is another class of intelligent beings on Earth besides ourselves. They have behaved benignly and in many cases affectionately towards us. We have systematically slaughtered them.

"It is at this point that the ultimate significance of dolphins in the search for extraterrestrial intelligence emerges. It is not a question of whether we are essentially prepared in the long run to confront a message from the stars. It is whether we can develop a sense that beings with quite different evolutionary histories, beings who may look far different from us, even 'monstrous,' may, nevertheless, be worthy of friendship and reverence, brotherhood and trust ..." (p.74)

In fact, Sagan put our original recordings of our humpback whale songs (Frank Watlington, 1960s, SOFAR station in Bermuda) on both Voyager II and Voyager I, launched in 1977 on August 20 and September 5, respectively, from Cape Canaveral, as part of those small packages that sailed across our solar system photographing the planets and their moons, and using their gravitational pull as a slingshot to accelerate their velocity to the next planet. The images sent back are still among our most stunning and revelatory. Indeed, dollar for dollar, those unmanned but beautifully conceived and executed spacecraft may have been our finest investment in the entire NASA space program.

It was a time of rare geometric arrangement of the four outer planets, Jupiter, Saturn, Uranus, and Neptune, which occurs only every 175 years. The five-year lifetime of the two devices was stretched to twelve years and more. Of the thousands of images sent back to Earth of the planets and their moons, perhaps the most arresting was taken after Voyager I had traversed the solar system and looked back at the string of planets, one of which was "a pale blue dot." The image suggests our unending responsibility and stewardship for this orb we call home.

Carl was a rare and articulate genius, the furthest reach of which was revealed in his writings (600 papers, twenty books written or coedited), his television series (*Cosmos*) and films based upon his writing and lectures (*Contact*).

Carl was also an ardent advocate for reducing and eliminating nuclear weapons. With Richard Turco, Owen Toon, Thomas Ackerman, and James Pollack, Sagan published a paper in *Science* in 1983 that contained first estimates of the total smoke and dust emissions from a major nuclear exchange, which showed that temperatures on Earth would be lowered and the sun's rays would not penetrate the dust layers for months. It was Turco, the leader of the team known as TTAPS after their surname initials, who had also studied the effects of massive volcanic eruptions that contributed to the model, who coined the term "nuclear winter." In 1990, all of the team's estimates were updated and refined.

The W. Alton Jones Foundation of Charlottesville, Virginia, was in these years the lead philanthropy working on the reduction of the nuclear threat, devoting 40 percent of its resources to that purpose under the leadership of George Perkovich. I served on that board for twenty years.

The Jones Foundation committed $100,000 to a conference, chaired by George Woodwell, involving American and Soviet scientists in touch by satellite. I recall the turning point of the conference occurred when Ralph Nader asked, "If we see that volcanic eruptions, or nuclear debris, would cause us to be unable to raise crops anywhere on Earth, then even a so-called first strike would be, inevitably, suicidal, is that not right?" Carl Sagan acknowledged that was precisely the point.

When Neil deGrasse Tyson, director of the Hayden Planetarium, was asked, "What are the greatest books ever written about astronomy?" he replied, "Because the field of study changes so rapidly, any book that's great in one decade becomes hopelessly obsolete by the next. But if I am forced to pick one, it would be Carl Sagan's *Cosmos* (1980). Not for the science it taught, but for how effectively the book shared why science matters—or should matter—to every citizen of the world."

A RARE AND ORIGINAL SPECULATION

The year was 1964. The place was the Communication Research Institute in Coconut Grove, Florida. The occasion was a site visit to evaluate an application for support from the National Science Foundation, the Office of Naval Research, or some other funding agency.

John Lilly was waxing eloquently about the extraordinary acoustical capacity of the bottlenose dolphin. Through echolocation, images are reflected back from sonic beams they project through the melon in the front of their heads. They can find their prey; "see" other forms of life; detect rocks, docks, and other barriers; even detect the mental state of fellow dolphins by scanning their lungs.

Lilly went on to suggest a rare and original idea that the mighty sperm whale—which with a brain of eighteen to twenty pounds in contrast to our three pounder, routinely dives down a mile, and hangs out for an hour pursuing squid—might have the ability "to speak" in three-dimensional images. He elaborated on this theory by noting that sperm whales have been masters of the seas for some 25 million years, navigating by echolocation, with the reflections of their sonic click sequences showing the configurations of what lay before them.

Why shouldn't they be able to mimic precisely those return images and thereby "converse" in them?

Lilly had to leave the session briefly. At that point, Kenneth S. Norris (1924–1998), part of the review panel and an esteemed professor of Natural History at the University of California at Santa Cruz, said, "You see what sort of cockamamie stuff is going on here?"

As I recall, the Institute did not get the grant.

Norris is credited with the idea that dolphins can pop out a flat flounder in the sand by a targeted blast of clicks before snaring it.

About ten years later, there was a television program in which Norris, in a loud colorful shirt, was standing on a bluff in Hawaii with a crescent of spinner dolphins resting below him in the water after a night's diving and foraging. Norris repeated word for word Lilly's idea about how sperm whales might communicate sonically with three-dimensional images, as if the thought had just occurred to him.

TWO SCIENTISTS FROM WOODS HOLE

In the December 2011 issue of the *Smithsonian*, Eric Wagner's "Call of the Leviathan" focuses on three scientists and their specialties: Hal Whitehead (sperm whales), Bill Gilly (squid), and Kelly Benoit-Bird (a marine scientist studying the acoustic decipherment of how whales interact with the layer of phytoplankton that rise and fall with the light). Wagner mentions "two scientists from the Woods Hole Oceanographic Institution" who confirmed for the first time in 1957 that sperm whales make a series of loud clicks, as had been reported by sailors for a long time.

In the article, those pioneering scientists are unnamed. They were William E. Schevill (1906–1994), biologist, and William A. Watkins (1926–2004), bio-acoustician, who were the meticulous founders of contemporary cetology. Over a forty-year span they recorded and analyzed more than seventy species of marine mammals and created a collection of more than 6,000 recordings with field observations organized by database. On a phonograph record, they put recordings of eighteen species of whales and porpoises (1962), including the aforementioned sperm whale recording.

Of four patterns of clicks Whitehead identified, "codas are the distinct patterns of clicks when whales are socializing." It might be noted here that a jewel of a paper by Watkins and Schevill (1977) documented an imaginative experiment using an array of hydrophones 100 miles off the New Jersey coast in the Baltimore canyon. Watkins detected two pods of sperm whales converging briefly (for less than a minute!). The click coda of one member of one pod interlocks with the coda of a member of the other pod: 9-7-9-7-9, et cetera, in an elegant, precise way. The accompanying disc is a robust confirmation of what occurred.

Over many years, Schevill and Watkins were mentors, guides, and encouragers to me. In 1964, they visited us in Coconut Grove, for they were curious about the work of John Lilly.

In 1965, Schevill wrote and asked me to find out about a purported collection of 5,000 whaling artifacts possessed by Barbara (later Kristina) Johnson on Cleveland Lane in Princeton. I tapped on her door, and, yep, there were that many, including priceless whaling logs and a pair of whale jawbones marking the entrance to the property. Johnson eventually sold most of them and gave some items to the American Folk Art Museum in New York.

When I was invited by Dennis Flanagan to write an article on the plight of the great whales for *Scientific American* in 1965, which became the baseline document for whale conservation, Schevill kindly read a draft. Later, thanks to him, I was invited to contribute a chapter to a book, *The Whale Problem* (1974, Harvard University Press), titled "Reflections on the Management of Whaling."

When I was organizing my first expedition to study, record, and film the bowhead whale in the Alaskan Arctic, Schevill asked me to check out Herbert Aldrich's vivid description of the sounds of the bowhead from 1889:

"With bowhead whales the cry is something like the hoo-hoo-hoo of the hoot-owl, although longer drawn out, and more of a humming sound than a hoot. Beginning on F, the tone may rise to G, A, B, and sometimes C, before slanting back to F again."

Before the computer Bill Schevill kept his whale notes, coded by topics, on punch cards in shoeboxes and used knitting needles to retrieve the wanted information.

Once in the early 1980s, I organized a day on whales at Boston's Museum of Science. Naturally, I invited Mr. Schevill, who was a Harvard undergraduate who did not pursue an advanced degree—he just created and set the bar for observing and recording whales. In spite of his stature and standing in the field, he was a modest, unassuming man—however quick-witted and curious—and he said I could interview him.

It may have been then he said, "When you put a dolphin in captivity, it's like putting a person in a telephone booth who is getting all wrong numbers."

I called Bill Watkins from time to time to learn of latest developments. In my last conversation with him, he said that the relationship between the mighty sperm whale and the squid is an ancient one. Note the lashes on the crown of the whale. Watkins thought that when the sperm whale dives—often to a depth of a mile, staying down for a good hour—that they sometimes shut down their click streams for echolocation. They seem to know where the squid are, which comprise the heart and soul of their diet, and would surge to grasp squid with their toothed lower jaw out of long experience and ritual. As with the moth that folds its wings and drops suddenly upon the approach of the clicking bat, sometimes the squid is snared, sometimes not.

It seems inattentive that the recent *Smithsonian* article, "Call of the Leviathan" leaves unnamed "the two scientists from Woods Hole," since on the shoulders of William Schevill and William Watkins the entire scaffolding of what we know today of living whales has been built. For me, they were priceless standard setters, kind guides, and true friends.

LOOKING FORWARD

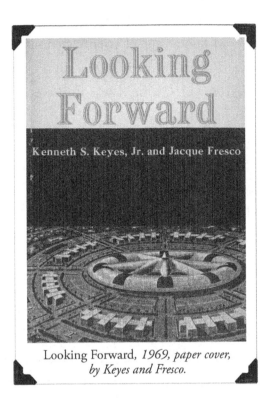

Looking Forward, *1969, paper cover,*
by Keyes and Fresco.

On a Saturday early in 1964, Ken Keyes, Jr. (1921–1995), a brilliant man in a wheelchair, visited the Communication Research Institute laboratory.

Keyes was a searching intelligence, a writer of fifteen books on personal growth and social consciousness, and the son of a man who operated a large real estate operation in South Florida.

After the tour, Keyes said there was someone he wanted me to meet, a man by the name of Jacque Fresco who was designing an environment for humanity fifty years hence. Keyes said Fresco lived in a small house in a string of similar houses, but when you entered his place you felt as though you were stepping ahead in time. He said further that Fresco gave talks in his home every Friday, Saturday, and Sunday evening and asked visitors to contribute a dollar to his work.

Hella and I went with Keyes to Fresco's place the next Friday evening. Perhaps another thirty persons showed up as well.

As a kid, I had read quite a bit of science fiction, such as *Stranger in a Strange Land* by Robert Heinlein, *Dune* by Frank Herbert, and *Childhood's End* by Arthur C. Clarke. I was future-oriented before the future began to overwhelm us.

The fast-talking Jacques Fresco delivered a mesmerizing message by first critiquing our society and then offering his ideas for what could be, a field he later came to call sociocyberneering [sic].

I was impressed by the presentation but kept wondering, throughout, what are his sources? What are his references? Whom does he admire?

When the talk and the Q&A were finished, Fresco scooted over to us and said, "Dr. McVay, thank you for coming this evening. You must have a million questions, but let me give you a reading list noting the origin of some of my thinking and points of departure."

The one-page list of readings noted the titles, authors, dates, and place of publication of scores of books and journal articles, each of which was labeled with one, two, or three asterisks indicating "beginner," "intermediate," and "advanced." The references included B. F. Skinner, Alfred Korzybski, Buckminster Fuller, Thorstein Veblen, Edward Bellamy, H. G. Wells, Norbert Weiner, and others.

We found a certain resonance in Fresco's talks at his place because of ideas not unrelated to my early readings and my then-daily preoccupation with mapping the dolphins' level of awareness. This was a time of optimism and exploration. We went back a few more times.

Jacque Fresco, ninety-eight years old (born March 13, 1916), is alive and well and working still with his colleague Roxanne Meadows on The

Venus Project, located in Venus, Florida. The Venus Project represents his vision of a future without poverty, crime, war, corruption, or waste.

In 1969, we were surprised when Jacque Fresco sent us a book called *Looking Forward* (with Ken Keyes, Jr.). In the first third he went after the foibles and shortcomings of contemporary human society acerbically.

The last two-thirds of the book laid out his grand design for the human experiment through the experience of a couple he named Scott and Hella. We read a chapter together every night. We couldn't handle more in a single gulp. We did not know whether to be flattered or to sue him. But in the end it was a bit poignant to see Jacques's view of the future through a couple carrying our names, Scott and Hella.

Illustration of Scott and Hella's Room, page 97, Looking Forward.

YOU CALL ME ON YOUR LAST DAY?

In the summer of 1966, Hella and I, along with our two daughters, Catherine (age six) and Cynthia (nearly age five), spent a week in Rome, another week in Berlin, and a final week in London.

On the Friday of our week in Rome, we called Bruno Vailati (1914–1990), the Italian analog to Jacques Cousteau of France, who was the leading underwater filmmaker in Italy.

Vailati had visited our laboratory in Coconut Grove the prior year and had urged us to be sure to call him when in Rome.

He said, "How can you call me on your last day?" Yet he invited us to come to his studio to look at underwater footage, including Arctic polar bears paddling underwater.

After that, we were walking the streets of Rome with Bruno, who was, he said, among the six top intelligence officers in World War II. He said he was involved in the release of British generals and admirals before war's end.

He had recently recruited casts of thousands who populated Hollywood blockbuster films in the Coliseum and elsewhere. That work gave him the resources to pursue his love of underwater filmmaking.

Hella noticed his form-fitting shirt with darts, trim figure, and white patent leather shoes without socks. Women waved, even from across the street, and cried, "Bruno!" He gestured in a subdued way in reply.

Bruno took us to the oldest rowing club in Europe for luncheon. A groaning board of most appealing fresh food stretched along a long wall from one end of the room to another. We filled our plates with fresh seafood, meat, fruit, cheeses, and salads.

What about you, Bruno? "I'm ordering à la carte."

The waitress asked him, "What would you like, sir?"

"Watercress salad."

When we returned to the States, my Dad took the girls to Buxton's, a local family restaurant, for a hamburger. Partway through, he asked them, "How are your burgers?"

"Fine," piped up Cynthia, "but nothing like Rome."

Connections That Illuminate

I believe that life is chaotic, a jumble of
accidents, ambitions, misconceptions,
bold intentions, lazy happenstances,
and unintended consequences, yet I also
believe that there are connections that
illuminate our world, revealing its endless
mystery and wonder.

— *Barack Obama: The Story*
by David Maraniss

HOW WAS THE WHALE SONG DISCOVERED?

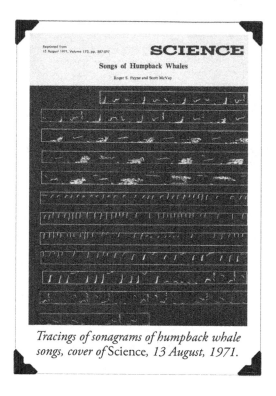

Tracings of sonagrams of humpback whale songs, cover of Science, *13 August, 1971.*

Before the 1960s, no one suspected the existence of whale song. Its discovery forced us to confront the possibility of alien intelligence — not in outer space but right here on earth.

— David Rothenberg, *Thousand Mile Song*, 2008, Basic Books

For a very long time we have underestimated the nature of communication in the animal kingdom.

In a pioneering study at Harvard in 1939, Donald Griffin, as a graduate student, discovered and documented a bat's capacity to detect insects by echolocation, a sense wholly lacking in us or so latent as to be trivial. It was ten years later that echolocation was detected in the bottlenose dolphin in a lab near St. Augustine, Florida.

Karl von Frisch was among the first to observe and describe the "waggle dance" in the honeybee, whereby a working bee indicates the direction and distance of nectar to other bees. For this research von Frisch received the Nobel Prize in 1973.

In a long path-breaking career at Cornell, Thomas Eisner managed to crack the chemical codes of bugs in thousands of experiments.

Bonnie Bassler, a Princeton neurobiologist and recipient of a MacArthur Fellowship, is a pioneer in describing how bacteria "talk" to one another, which leads to "tiny conspiracies."

During my two years with Lilly in the early 1960s, I devoured books on linguistics, since I felt they would provide clues to how we could crack the cetacean code. Among the linguists I read most closely then were Edward Sapir, Robert Hall, Benjamin Lee Whorf, and John Chadwick, who described the English architect Michael Ventris's deciphering of Linear B, a syllabic script used for writing Mycenaean Greek (a journey described in Chadwick's book *The Decipherment of Linear B*). In 2013, Margalit Fox published *The Riddle of the Labyrinth: The Quest to Crack an Ancient Code* that completes the Linear B story with the work of Alice Kober, a devoted scholar, whose insights were indispensable to Ventris.

The point is that whenever we look closely at any facet of the animal kingdom, we are astonished by what we learn of its workings, which are both more complex than we imagined and more simple and elegant.

In thinking about the discovery of the song of the humpback whale, it is useful to be aware of this long-unfolding trajectory.

In 1968, biologist Roger Payne brought me audiotapes by Frank Watlington of the Palisade Sofar Station in Bermuda. Roger had read my article in *Scientific American*, "The Last of the Great Whales," in 1966 and knew from my work with John Lilly that I could use a sound spectrograph. That technology was primitive in contrast to today when one can get a sonic printout in real time in seconds. Yet that arduous process then allowed me to study the new sonogram closely as the next one was being etched.

In the basement of Eno Hall, directly below the place where I had met Lilly in 1961, was a Kay 6061B Sound Spectrograph in the lab of Mark Konishi, a biologist then studying the degree of precision barn owls use in detecting sound on the ground in the dark. It was the only sound spectrograph on the Princeton campus.

In my spare time, nights and weekends, I made sonogram after sonogram. Each one took 2.65 minutes. I studied the last one as the next one was being made. I made hundreds, thousands of them. After some weeks, it became clear that out of the seeming cacophony of sound, clear patterns emerged. Individual whales seemed to be singing long, complex songs, of seven to thirty minutes in duration. This was analogous to birds who sing brief repetitive songs. The whales then sing them again, hour after hour.

In Rothenberg's book, on page sixteen, he quotes me as saying, "What is science if not bean-counting and patient observation? I literally spread out these printouts on the living room floor at home and kept looking and looking at them. Hella came over and studied with me. We finally looked at each other in astonishment and said, 'My God, it repeats.' There was a regular pattern with form and shape. With the alien song all graphed out, frequency against time, the McVays could see its intelligible structure."

The surprise was that all the whales were singing the same song, but not in synchrony with one another. And it was a six-octave song in six distinct themes. It was also, to our ears, utterly beautiful. We did not then know it was only the males who sing.

When Roger Payne and I published a cover article in *Science* in 1971, we wrote, "It is from studies of the herd sojourning in these waters (south of Bermuda) that we have become aware of what we believe to be the humpbacks' most extraordinary feature—they emit a series of surprisingly beautiful sounds." To our delight, the editor did not redline out this subjective observation of "surprisingly beautiful sounds" from an otherwise objective paper.

Our discovery and description added to Melville's succinct definition of the humpback, "He is the most gamesome and light-hearted of all the whales, making more gay foam and white water generally than any other of them."

More amazing than the discovery, description, and analysis of humpback whale song, in my view, was Katy Payne's subsequent discovery that the song evolves over time. Elements are dropped and elements are added. After four, five, or six years, another song emerges. In observing the evolution of the song of the Atlantic humpback whale over half a century, we have not found repeated what we described from the 1960s.

Also, that is as true of the well-known population of humpbacks recorded off Maui and the Big Island in Hawaii, where the evolving song cycle has not repeated itself.

Fourteen discreet song cycles are now being studied in the Indian Ocean and elsewhere, and they are also evolving in their separate ways.

For what purpose do the males sing? We do not know. Is the song for courtship of females as are the feathers of the peacock, the colorful bowers of bowerbirds, the blue feet of the blue-footed booby? That hypothesis appears wrong. We do not have a single example of a female responding to a male whale song from a half century of observations, especially in Hawaii where the studies have been continuous.

Today some 400 papers on the songs of humpback whales have been published, refining and extending aspects of the essential analysis.

So what's going on? It appears to be a male thing—perhaps to establish a hierarchy among males. All males sing the same song at a given time, but even the "Caruso" of the group does not seem to fare any better with the ladies.

In 1995, when Roger Payne, recipient of a MacArthur award in 1984 and director and narrator of the IMAX film *Whales* (1995), published his long-awaited book on whales, *Among Whales* (Scribner), he inscribed a copy to me: "For Scott, who started me out in conservation and who started us both with songs."

In a new book, *The Cultural Lives of Whales and Dolphins* by Hal Whitehead and Luke Rendell (University of Chicago Press, 2014), the authors note "three of the most compelling features of humpback songs, their complexity, evolution, and beauty." According to E. O. Wilson, perhaps the world's most prominent zoologist, "the song of the humpback whale may be the most elaborate single display known in any animal species."

The public picked up on the beauty, power, and grace of the song thanks to Roger Payne's issue of a record of the songs, which topped the recording charts and set the stage for public demand that the slaughter of whales be reduced if not stopped altogether.

In 2007, David Rothenberg came to our home and tape-recorded an interview of nearly four hours with me, parts of which turn up in his book *Thousand Mile Song* (Basic Books, 2008). He lays out, with verve and panache, much of our journey of musical discovery.

Rothenberg concludes: "In space we had reached the moon, and in the ocean depths we had heard the whales sing."

HUCK FINN, MOBY-DICK, AND THE VIETNAM WAR

Ōe Kenzaburō and Scott in front of tempura restaurant in Tokyo on August 11, 1970.

Thanks to the kind support of Edwin Reischauer (1910–1990), former ambassador to Japan (1961–66) and professor of Japanese History and Culture at Harvard, the writer Ōe (pronounced "oi") Kenzaburō received an opportunity to come to Harvard in 1966 for a few weeks.

During that time he came to Princeton to meet with Richard Falk, a lead spokesman against the Vietnam War. In Princeton, Ōe gave a talk intriguingly titled, "Huck Finn, Moby-Dick, and the Vietnam War."

Regarding the United States' escalating involvement in Vietnam, Ōe suggested that it was rooted in our culture. Huck Finn felt compelled "to light out for the territory." Ahab's obsession with the pursuit of the white whale, after that whale had taken one of his legs, was anchored in a way by the thought, "As for me, I am tormented by the everlasting itch for things remote."

Ōe came to our home, and we spoke of our quest to understand the whale and reduce—if not stop altogether—the killing of whales. In those years it was an unchecked slaughter, and we hoped at least to reduce the catch to one that was sustainable. Year after year, as many whales were taken as possible, and they were simply counted up in what the International Whaling Commission called "blue whale units," further clouding the exact tally.

In August 1970, at the behest of the New York Zoological Society (now the Wildlife Conservation Society), Hella and I traveled to Japan to initiate a whale conservation effort there, working with leading scientists as counseled by Ambassador Reischauer in a three-hour meeting in his Boston home. That undertaking is chronicled in a forty-three-page report to the Society

We met with Ōe a couple of times in Tokyo. On the first occasion, he gave us a little book of his adventures in America in 1966 and said one chapter was devoted to his translation and interpretation of my poem "The Marguerite Flower" (1962), based on a note in the *Norwegian Whaling Gazette* provided by a Japanese whaler/scientist, Nishiwaki.

Ōe said to ask a student to translate that chapter. Back at the International House that evening, a scholar kindly gave us a rough translation, which appeared excellent. (That book with the chapter of Ōe's translation of my poem and his interpretation was sadly lost in our fire in 1981, as was the scholar's translation.)

We explained to Ōe that we were working with six scientists who were led by Dr. Seiji Kaya, former rector of the University of Tokyo and a leading physicist. They called themselves Kujira oh Mamora Kai (the Committee for the Preservation of Whales). Ōe said he wrote three books while still a student at Tokyo University, and that if Seiji Kaya did not really lead the effort to manage whale killing, then Ōe would call a rally since he could pull in 5,000 attendees on short notice. We felt that Dr. Kaya and his colleagues across the disciplines were committed, and they actually delivered on three goals that we thought would take them three years within eighteen months.

Our mission in Japan was blessed by making available the record of the *Songs of Humpback Whales* for the first time in person and on a one-hour NHK television program that reached 33 million Japanese homes, as well as through major articles in Japan's largest circulation dailies, the *Asahi Shimbun* and the *Mainichi Shimbun*.

Ōe Kenzaburō wrote later in "The Day When Whales will be Extinct":*

I have met a cetologist from America,
and he described in detail the current
situations of whales that we suspect
may be extinguished. He was speaking
as if he were the representative of whales
that are to be extinguished. However, while
listening to him, I was thinking about *Homo sapiens*.
After a while I had an ominous dream.

One desolate twilight evening
on a high tower overlooking a valley
deep in the woods where I grew up,
together with several adults
I stood looking toward the West.
The dream was unlike other dreams,
because I was no longer a child

but was now one of those adults,
and yet in the sense that
I had been included in the group
as the one who least understood what was going on,
this dream was after all like all the others,
it became like one of those daily nightmares,
as the western sky took on a dark red hue
without a sign of light,
and we all sunk into the darkness and
were buffeted by profuse winds which blew up.
One old man, bursting the silent atmosphere of
expectation, said: "Ah, finally, the last whale died."

We pushed each other for the first position,
pounding down the hill as if trying to crush
pebbles beneath our sandals with our feet,
we went down to the valley,
but as we were about to say,
"finally, the last whale ..."
on the cobbled path in the dark valley,
"What on earth was a Whale?"
the child asked us in an innocent voice.

I tried to explain to him about whales,
but since I didn't remember a thing about whales
myself, I clammed up.
And then I realized with a sense of fathomless
annihilation that the old man of just now
was the "me" of the past
and the child none other

than the "me" of the future.
The face of the child,
looking up silently at me,
distinct in the evening light,
was crumbling away.

In that same piece Ōe writes, "I now realize that McVay, the tender-hearted poet from America, who brought us an international control plan for whale-fishing, had not come armored as a rugged protester against our bloody huntings ... I feel as if McVay had been drawn to Japan, dreaming of the 'Saint' who would save the whales and *Homo sapiens* as well. Now I find myself longing desperately for the advent of the 'Saint' as I listen at midnight to the crying of the whales on the recording McVay left us."

In the late 1970s, Ōe sent me a four-page, handwritten letter in English, wherein he said two of his books arose from our conversations. In ink he drew a tree in the middle of the letter.

Scott with Ōe Kenzaburō at Princeton in 1966.

After our home burned to the ground on February 6, 1981, a lawyer said we should make a list of what we lost with the estimated values. At the very top I put this letter from Ōe, followed by a penciled postcard from John C. Lilly in 1964 ("from falling hand I pass the torch …"), followed by our Hans Wegner furniture and art. Our lawyer, Tom Campion, said the written items were "goose eggs."

In 1994, I carried the *New York Times*'s front page to the lawyer where it was reported that Ōe Kenzaburō had been awarded the Nobel Prize in Literature for creating "an imagined world, where life and myth condense to form a disconcerting picture of the human predicament today." He said, "Oh, oh, oh …"

"No," said I, "Ōe, Ōe, Ōe …"

*From *Whales: A Celebration*, edited by Greg Gatenby, Little Brown & Co., 1983.

IF KNOWLEDGE OF THE UNIVERSE WERE A LADDER OF ONE HUNDRED RUNGS

In August of 1970, en route to Japan, we paused in Hawaii near the end of a weeklong conference on the future of Hawaii in the year 2000. It was organized and planned by Professor Glenn Paige, an old friend and classmate, political scientist, Korean studies specialist, and today the lead proponent of nonkilling through a book and a not-for-profit. Paige had organized the conference with the governor, and he included some prominent futurists.

One afternoon, August 6, I gave a talk on the discovery and documentation of the six-octave song of the humpback whale, which became the anthem for whale conservation and conservation writ large.

Afterward, Arthur C. Clarke (1917–2008), author of *2001, Childhood's End*, and other works, asked if we could have breakfast the next day since Warner Brothers had taken a one-year option on *Deep Range*, his book about dolphins, and he had some questions.

Over a long and fascinating breakfast, he peppered me with questions about whales and then asked if I had any for him.

I asked the good man from Colombo, Sri Lanka, one question: "If knowledge of the universe were a ladder of one hundred rungs, what rung do you think *Homo sap* is on now?"

Mr. Clarke's reply astonished me. He said, "Either ten or ninety; we have either the rough scaffold or most of the picture."

I was surprised since the entire point of his *Profiles of the Future* (1962) was that we as a species were notoriously bad at looking ahead. His lead example in the book was H. G. Wells, our most prominent foregazer. Wells said he saw no future whatsoever for submarines because of the extreme pressure in the depths of the seas. Submarines would simply implode.

Also, in his book *The Exploration of Space* (1951), Clarke wrote, "If we have learned one thing from the history of invention and discovery, it is, that, in the long run—and often in the short run—the most daring prophecies seem laughably conservative." (p. 111)

I don't know much, but I wouldn't put us above rung three. One rung would be for language. Another rung is for scientific observations (such as those made by Confucius, Nicolaus Copernicus, Johannes Kepler, Charles Darwin, Alfred Russel Wallace, Marie Curie, Sigmund Freud, Carl Jung, Rosalind Franklin, Albert Einstein, Rachel Carson, Barbara McClintock, Jane Goodall, and Sylvia Earle). A third rung is for mathematics (which is a different type of language), and music— Bach, Beethoven, Mozart, and the fellows who play the slit drums in Melanesia.

With Stanley Kubrick, Arthur Clarke wrote the screenplay for the science-fiction film *2001: A Space Odyssey*, released in 1968. Near the turn of the millennium, Gus Speth, then dean of the School of Forestry and Environmental Studies at Yale, mentioned over the phone that Paul MacCready—maker of the human-powered aircraft Gossamer Albatross—thought the most memorable line of the twentieth century was uttered by the sentient computer HAL 9000 in Kubrick's film *2001*, "Just what do you think you're doing, Dave?" as Dave was reaching to pull HAL's plug.

THE OLD MONKEYS

Scott and Denzaburo Miyadi, a lead biologist, on his
Monkey Mountain in Kyoto, August 15, 1970.

In August 1970, we visited Denzaburo Miyadi, primatologist (and uncle by marriage of Ōe Kenzaburō) in Kyoto and founder of the Primate Research Institute. He was renowned as the lead biologist in Japan.

He was seventy-five years old and walked us up Monkey Mountain on a hot steamy day—zack, zack, zack in swift strong strides—to see his macaque monkeys, now grown to two troops, Alpha and Beta, busy grooming one another.

We were with him a couple of days. On the second day, he introduced us finally to our driver—his son!

Dr. Miyadi invited me to give a talk on the six-octave song of the humpback whale. I passed out paper and pencils so that his colleagues and students could trace out the sequence of the songs they heard as they listened to the recording.

I played the audiotapes and some eagerly transcribed what they heard the frequencies to be. Some did not. Later, I asked Dr. Miyadi what was going on. He said the young students eagerly traced the highs and lows, the gutturals and the squeals over time—and the senior faculty as well. The junior faculty did nothing since "they were afraid of making mistakes and endangering possible promotion."

On his desk Dr. Miyadi had a tall stack of monographs in Japanese recounting his observations of the macaques over the prior twenty-five years. None were available in English or in German.

So I asked him what he had learned.

He summarized his life's work: "Oh, the old monkeys learn more slowly than the young monkeys!"

Hella connecting with Japanese
macaque monkeys.

DOESN'T THE INTERNATIONAL WHALING COMMISSION TAKE CARE OF THIS?

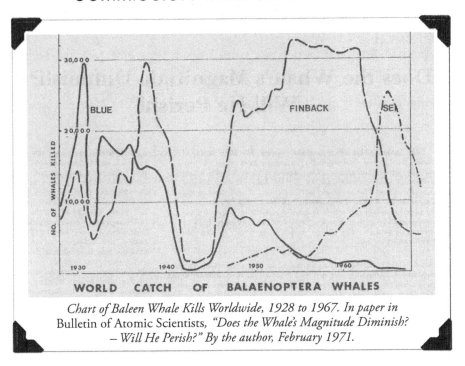

Chart of Baleen Whale Kills Worldwide, 1928 to 1967. In paper in Bulletin of Atomic Scientists, *"Does the Whale's Magnitude Diminish? – Will He Perish?" By the author, February 1971.*

The year was 1970. The predecessor of 1973's Endangered Species Act, the Endangered Species Preservation Act of 1966, had been passed by Congress. Walter J. Hickel (two-time governor of Alaska) was named US Secretary of the Interior by President Richard Nixon. I was receiving mail and telephone calls from Michael Frome, a dedicated environmental writer who often traveled with Wally Hickel, informing me that he was briefing the secretary on the plight of the great whales.

Thanks to Frome's persistence, Secretary Hickel placed most of the great whales on the endangered species list: the blue, fin, humpback, right, sei, and Bryde's whales, which was justified by their severely reduced numbers. But, to my astonishment, the sperm whale was also listed, which could not be justified since it was still a comparatively abundant species, with numbers estimated at 600,000 worldwide.

On the preceding page is a chart from my 1971 paper in *Bulletin of Atomic Scientists*, showing the precipitous decline of one species after another in the first two-thirds of the twentieth century.

At that time, an American company in the Midwest used the spermaceti oil from the massive head of sperm whales that were taken by the Japanese. It was used for a high-grade engine lubricant of unparalleled quality under stress and heat.

That company, wishing to continue using the oil, retained the esteemed law firm of Covington & Burling in Washington, DC, to challenge the listing of the sperm whale as endangered.

A review of the matter was scheduled by the Department of the Interior. Roger Payne and I were invited to defend the listing. The attorney from Covington & Burling wore a pink shirt with a white collar—the first one of its kind I had ever seen.

The conversation lasted three hours. Roger had tossed a recorder on the table. At no point did we try to defend the listing. The turning point in the discussion occurred when the lawyer asked, "Doesn't the International Whaling Commission take care of this?"

I asked him, "What do you think the annual budget of the IWC is?"

He said, "I have no idea."

I said, "Make a guess."

He said, "I don't know—maybe $300,000 to $400,000 a year."

I said, "It wouldn't even take care of your carfare for a month. It is only $16,000 a year. The IWC is a voluntary association without capacity for enforcement of quotas."

When Roger and I left the meeting, he returned to his home in New York City (he was employed by the Rockefeller University as a biologist at the time) and dropped off the audiotape at WBAI, where they scrapped the scheduled program that evening and aired our conversation on the radio from seven until ten o'clock.

The sperm whale was not delisted. I note here the critical role played by E. U. Curtis "Buff" Bohlen, assistant to Wally Hickel and later Deputy Assistant Secretary for Fish and Wildlife and Parks. Buff was instrumental in drafting the Endangered Species Act and in carving out 102 million square miles of federal land in Alaska to be protected as parks and/or wildlife refuges. The total acreage is more than twenty times the size of New Jersey.

After Hickel was fired (November 25, 1970) for challenging Nixon on the Vietnam tragedy—which led to four Kent State students being killed by the National Guard—Bohlen let the presses run the listing of the great whales that weekend in spite of being told to stop them.

When, in 1975, the IWC put a ban on the killing of bowhead whales that year, I was invited to be the first to testify in an open hearing in Washington. I was followed by twenty Inuit who protested the ruling based upon the scientists' best estimate of the depleted stocks. After the Inuit, a dozen conservation groups spoke in favor of the ban on killing for one season. One outlier was a woman with the Sierra Club who said she had been with the whalers near Barrow and felt that they should pursue their annual harvest (the whalers are largely from Anchorage and Fairbanks, and they come up to the northwest coast for a couple of months' vacation). I called David Brower, "The Archdruid" and founder of the Sierra Club, and asked if he stood by her testimony. He said he did, but what could he say—otherwise a champion of the land and all her critters.

Postscript

It is interesting to recall, as well as a trifle ironic, that when our daughter Cynthia was working at the World Wildlife Fund in 1984, largely in

Mexico and Guatemala, she had a major exhibit of her cutout art on the ninth floor of Covington & Burling, in a space kindly offered to young artists. It was a splendid show, and Cynthia sold most of her artworks.

EVEN IF YOU CHANGE YOUR CLOTHES, THE KILLER WHALE WILL REMEMBER YOU

Two bowhead whales, almost belly to belly, cover of American Scientist, *January–February, 1973.*

On May 13, 1971, during the first expedition I organized and led to the Alaskan Arctic to study, film, and record the majestic bowhead whale, we chartered a plane to travel from Point Barrow to Point Hope, 315 miles away.

We were not destined to reach Point Hope, however. The blizzard that had begun that morning gathered in intensity as we flew south, and we did not spot any whales as we tried to follow the edge of the shore-fast ice. We put down in Wainwright—ninety miles southwest of Barrow—because the winds had reached fifty miles an hour, and weather reports indicated that conditions were even worse around Cape Lisburne and Point Hope. We could not return to Barrow until the storm subsided twenty-four hours later.

Our disappointment at that moment could in no way have anticipated the privilege we would have of getting to know a few of the friendly people of Wainwright. It so happened that our unexpected visit coincided with the end of anthropologist Richard K. Nelson's stay. At this village, he had gathered some years earlier much of the material for his book, *Hunters of the Northern Ice*, and he had come back to Wainwright expressly for the whale hunt. While the snow swirled around our hut and huskies occasionally yelped at passersby, whalers Raymond T. Aguvluk, Sr., and Homer Bodfish shared some of their experiences with us. Homer is the grandson of Hartson Bodfish, the Yankee whaling captain who whaled for thirty-one years in the Arctic and in his dotage reminisced for a book, *Chasing the Bowhead*.

In response to a question about whether the bowhead whales are recovering from their precarious situation of fifty years ago, when the last whaling vessel to steam to the Arctic returned home "clean," Raymond replied, "Well, my grandfather and my dad used to tell me that a long time ago there were less whales than now. The schools (of whales) that used to come up (along the coast), they almost killed them all off, those old-time whalers. The whale is coming back, I think, getting a little thicker."

The reason I can offer exact quotes is that I recorded our conversation in Raymond's home between 9:00 p.m. and 3:00 a.m. Dick Nelson was present throughout. Raymond was then forty-four years old, a father of eight children, and reputed to be the most knowledgeable man in the village about the bowhead.

Raymond's estimate of the then-current population in the western

Arctic was between one and two thousand whales, but he cautioned that his estimate is rough and unsubstantiated.

Shades of *Moby-Dick* were invoked when Nelson told us that during a prolonged period on the ice, where they had been hunting whales without success, they saw a "creamy-colored" whale. It was seen through binoculars about three quarters of a mile away near the first run (of three) of many whales. Every time the whale rolled to the surface to blow, Raymond's crew saw that it had no black pigment on its back or sides. It was the only albino bowhead the men had seen, and the knowledge of its existence provided an added incentive for us to return to the Arctic.

My primary impulse in mounting this trip was to try to record the voice of the bowhead whale. On our first day of recording on the shore-fast ice four or five miles due west of Point Barrow, Mark Konishi and I obtained some fine recordings of the most prominent, ubiquitous sonic phenomenon along that coast, the springtime song of *Erignathus barbatus* (the male bearded seal). It is some two minutes long, consisting of a strong rising onset and then slowly descending warbles that follow a predictable sequence.

We also picked up the sounds of every footstep in the vicinity—a circle with a radius of at least 100 yards—recorded through six or seven feet of ice at a depth of eighty feet. The "crunch, crunch, crunch" of anyone walking was plainly audible through the hydrophone, and it is not unreasonable to assume that a marine mammal in those waters, with highly sensitive hearing, could hear such steps as well.

Raymond Aguvluk recalled, "Our father used to tell us not to hit a sled or anything else out there when the whales were near. I've noted many times that when the whales start coming up that if somebody hits something, the whales sink rapidly from sight."

Raymond also recalled the time when he and his companions heard the voice of one bowhead: "It was just like a guitar playing inside the water. It was so nice to hear it, just like the guitarist playing something. I don't know how they do it."

When asked if he had put his ear to the bottom of the boat or had listened through a wooden paddle in the water, he said, "We could hear the sounds just standing there; they vibrated a long ways. I have heard it only one time."*

The largest bowhead whale that the renowned Scottish whaling captain William Scoresby captured in the early 1800s south of Greenland was fifty-eight feet, according to his iconic two-volume work published in Edinburgh (1820).

Raymond gave us a description of the largest bowhead taken in recent years near Wainwright by his whaling crew, a sixty-three-foot whale:

"Homer (Bodfish) was there with me the day we shot that whale about a mile away from our camp, up north alongside the ice. Then we started chasing it. We had a float already attached to the whale, and when we shot it again, the whale went down and took the whole float with him. We didn't know where he went. About twenty minutes later, he came up. He went south this time. We used seven bombs, and with the last one we got him. The float got stuck underneath the ice so he couldn't go any place after that. We used three boats with kickers (to drag the whale back), and then we went and got all the people to help us. We cut it up in four days. It took the whole village—about 300 people. We started pulling him up by the flukes. We cut the head off because it was too heavy for our block and tackle. You know that a sixty-three-ton whale is pretty heavy. The whale was about nine feet from eye to eye."

In the corner of the room I saw a piece of baleen from that whale and measured it myself. It was an astonishing twelve feet one inch. Remember the blue whale, the largest of baleen whales, has baleen of only three or four feet. Baleen is a horny substance found in two rows of plates attached along the upper jaws of baleen or rorqual whales. In the bowhead, the baleen hangs down from the giant mouth, and the hairs along the fringes strain small organisms such as copepods and euphausiids (krill) for nourishment.

Another enormous whale, alleged to have been sixty-seven feet, was taken by Simeon Patkotak's whale crew in the spring of 1970 at Barrow. Photographs and moving pictures exist, which tend to support the claim of its size but are not definitive.**

We discussed beluga whales at length, especially since a symbiotic relationship seems to exist between the bowhead and the beluga. In fact, Raymond said that the bowheads seem to surface often in a pod of belugas, "a halo of belugas," if you will. That phenomenon was captured definitively in a film by the National Film Board of Canada on my second expedition two years later.

We also spoke of the 8,000-mile California gray whale migration.

Well after midnight, one other member of the whale tribe, the killer whale (Orcinus orca) was discussed, since it figures prominently in Eskimo legend and experience.

Raymond told us that he had never taken a killer whale, or *araluk* in Inuit: "Our granddad told us not to bother them at any time, because if you bother them, they go after you and turn your boat over. We just let them go. We never hunt them." Thus, while the Eskimo have been oriented for centuries to hunt for every land and sea creature, the killer whale is not among them. Homer explained:

"We are very superstitious about killer whales up here. We know from our ancestors from way back that they once tried to kill a whale like that, a killer whale, and they hardly wounded it. It is known that the whale capsized the boat and chewed up both human beings who were in the boat. It is said that these whales have a good memory and even after many number of years pass, they always know which human being had been shooting at them."

At that point in the conversation, a little girl who had sat quietly in the corner for six hours spoke for the first time. "Yes, even if you change your clothes, the killer whale will remember you!"

Scott holding Inuit carving of bowhead whale, acquired during first bowhead expedition in 1971.

* Fine recordings of the bowhead whale were made by Christopher Clark of Cornell University during the migration of the spring of 1985. Chris had a four-hydrophone array that recorded some 35,000 vocalizations over a seven-week span. Oddly, and amazingly, only nineteen overlapped—as if the whales were unduly courteous and attuned to a sequence of calls of which we haven't the slightest understanding. That is one of the single most interesting facts I know about whales, and it remains inexplicable today.

** Within the past ten years, the heads of spears have been found in the carcasses of bowheads taken by the Inuit. Because the art of making these sharp instruments evolved continuously, we have a pretty definite idea of the approximate dates when those old spears were first thrown. They are old, some over 100 years, and one nearly two centuries old!

Postscript

The nine-person crew I assembled two years later, including Bill Mason, who had filmed wolves after living among them for six weeks and done another trilogy on white water canoeing, had presumed that Raymond Aguvluk would be with us. Sadly, he died, but Homer Bodfish was with us and can be seen in the National Film Board of Canada documentary, *In Search of the Bowhead Whale.*

The primary source for this narrative is the cover article in *American Scientist*, "Stalking the Arctic Whale," by Scott McVay, January–February 1973, Volume 61, Number 1.

CAN WE GO TO DINNER NOW?

In June 1971, the International Whaling Commission met in Washington, DC, a singular occasion since in those days the annual meetings typically took place in London.

On the first day, a young gregarious gentleman from the Mexican Embassy in Washington, Eduardo Jiménez González, approached me and said, "Scott, if we in Mexico can be of any help in efforts to save the whales, please let me know."

I said, "Are you serious?"

He said, "Yes, anything we can do to be of help, we shall do."

I said, "How about dinner this evening?"

"Fine."

That evening at the hotel I explained to him that Scammon's Lagoon along the Baja California coast was under severe threat, and that it was a nursery for the California gray whale near the end of its southern migration, among other sites. I suggested that the Mexican government create the first whale sanctuary on Earth to protect this place. Eduardo said it was a good idea, and he would pursue it. Now can we go to dinner?

First, I drafted a detailed proclamation explaining that the gray whale, through over-exploitation, had been reduced to a few hundred in the 1890s because of whalers like Charles Scammon, and the same thing had happened again in the 1930s. The stocks were now rebuilding nicely toward an optimal 21,000–22,000, but needed protection from several kinds of industrial assaults. The document was written with a "Whereas" series of historical and current points leading to a "Now therefore," for the signature of Luis Echeverría, the president of Mexico.

Eduardo said that looked good to him, and he would work on it. Can we now go to dinner? I suggested that he might want to write out the proclamation in Spanish first. He did so and then asked if the president of the United States, Richard M. Nixon, would write his president a note of congratulations if this is accomplished. I said such a letter could easily be arranged. I would draft it.

After the IWC meeting in the course of the summer and fall, I called Eduardo many times, maybe three or four times a month, to see how things were progressing. He said, unfailingly, that things take time. When it happens, will the US president write a letter to President Echeverría? I assured him that this would happen.

Eduardo never called me until October or November, when he reported that the proclamation had been approved and would I come down for the ribbon-cutting ceremony. I said I could not get away, but would see to it that President Nixon wrote a congratulatory letter on the occasion of the creation of the first whale sanctuary on Earth, even if it were not yet then adequately protected. The draft letter I submitted was sent essentially as written.

To the best of my knowledge, this was the first of several whale sanctuaries and refuges on the planet and a start on seeing that other lagoons down the coast and in the Sea of Cortez gained some degree of protection.

In December 1977, our family took a cruise out of San Diego with cetologist Ted Walker, where I was his assistant, and visited all the lagoons along the coast of Baja. We saw gray whales galore at a time of recreation, play, courtship, mating, and calving. Hella and I returned two more times with the board of the World Wildlife Fund, ever marveling at the wonders of Baja, especially the spyhopping gray whales.

HE LOOKED ME RIGHT IN THE EYE!

In June 1971, in Washington, J. Lawrence McHugh, the US commissioner to the International Whaling Commission, asked me, a member of the US delegation, if I would like to meet Colonel Charles Lindbergh, the first person to fly across the Atlantic in 1927. I said I would be honored.

Being apparently aware of my efforts to address the plight of the great whales, Lindbergh said, "Look, McVay, you don't have to worry about the blue whale."

Why not? The blue whale had been taken in the Antarctic since 1903–04 in growing numbers every year until the greatest kill of more than 30,000 was taken in 1930–31. Then the numbers declined precipitously until 1965 when only 112 were taken. The numbers fell even with better technology and greater effort.

Lindbergh said, "Don't worry about the blue whale. I met a Japanese whaling captain, and he said there are plenty of them in the Antarctic. He looked me right in the eye!"

I asked, "Where are they, the blue whales in the Antarctic?"

Lindbergh seemed uncomfortable with the question but said, "They are under the ice."

I pressed, "How do they breathe?"

Lindbergh seemed flustered and annoyed. I said I could not fathom what he was telling me. It didn't ring with available evidence of a highly decimated species and a severely reduced catch. Would he please write me the details? He said he would. Within the week I received a three-page handwritten letter with the same malarkey that the Japanese whaler told him while looking directly into his eyes.

I normally reply to all correspondence, but in this case, what can one say, particularly when Lindbergh was widely regarded as a hero of the twentieth century for his flight across the Atlantic.

LOCHNESS MONSTER

The "Lochness Monster," in 2013, Lochness, Scotland.

In the early 1970s at the annual meeting of the International Whaling Commission (IWC) in London, Sir Peter Scott sometimes asked me to read his opening remarks to see if there were any factual errors. I did so gladly. Peter was a prominent biologist, prolific author, artist, a founder of the World Wildlife Fund and designer of its logo, creator of Severn Wildfowl Trust in Slimbridge, champion glider pilot, sailor, and an eloquent voice for conservation.

In 1975, the last year I served on the US delegation to the IWC, Peter was driving me across London, a terrifying experience in itself, when he asked if I had seen the remarkable enhanced underwater photographs by some Japanese of the Lochness Monster.

I said, "No."

He instructed me to reach under my seat and pull out an envelope containing these recent images. Peter was excited. He invited me to look at them closely.

"Sure, if you will keep an eye on the road," I replied.

For the life of me, the photographs were no more than a blown-up blur—even when I squinted and tipped my head. I reflected how interesting science is when you have an artifact to study and wondered why we were so stirred by stuff that did not seem to have a basis in reality—like Bigfoot or the Yeti.

Some months later, I was asked by a semi-scientific journal to review a huge tome of unexplained natural phenomena, with the lead example being the Lochness Monster. I respectfully declined.

THAT TIE!

In August 1997, *US News and World Report* said that Alexey Yablokov, a Russian biologist, supplied the International Whaling Commission with figures showing that between 1959 and 1972, one Soviet whaling ship killed 73,773 whales when only 32,000 were officially reported. Included in the tally were endangered humpback and blue whales.

This was a fearless and courageous act since Yablokov had been blocked by the Russian fisheries ministry. The Russian general prosecutor demanded that Yablokov be charged with passing state secrets. Michael Tillman, US representative to the International Whaling Commission, said, "He's a one-man conscience for his country." Yablokov also released records of thousands of whales taken off the coast of Africa traveling to or from the Antarctic. By this time he was the scientific adviser to President Boris Yeltsin.

I met Yablokov in January 1973 in Moscow when a dozen American biologists met with Soviet counterparts to work on nineteen endangered species projects. I walked into a room with a number of people, where from across the room Yablokov, standing tall and erect, was immediately apparent to me. My plan was for him to codirect with me my second Arctic expedition to study, film, and record the bowhead whale in the Alaskan Arctic.

Yablokov had earlier lived on Wrangel Island off Siberia for five weeks with walruses and wrote a book on what he learned. He was also the most prominent Russian biologist on whales. My expedition was to be the first of nineteen discrete projects that were formally approved after two weeks of deliberations and careful planning.

At the conclusion of this work, I was in Yablokov's home for supper, and I gave him all my publications, the *Song of Humpback Whales* album, and a copy of *Mind in the Waters*, and he reciprocated with a stack of his stuff.

"I wish there was something more I could give you," I said.

"*That tie!*" he replied and reached over for it.

It was one of white sperm whales on a blue field, a Princeton Nantucket tie someone had given me. I gave it to him with pleasure.

The USSR did not let Yablokov leave the country. I met with Philip Handler, president of the National Academy of Sciences who was soon meeting in Spain with Millionshekov, his Soviet counterpart, but to no avail. What I learned later was that Yablokov was not "politically unreliable"—it appeared that he was simply cussedly independent. This was brightly borne out by this story of the release of previously unknown whale kills when the Soviets were second only to the Japanese worldwide.

When I sent Alexey the film made by the National Film Board of Canada of the expedition, *In Search of the Bowhead Whale*, his response was excited with a sad twinge that he was not a part of it.

BUT I DON'T DO THIS

In January 1973, I was part of a team of biologists who traveled to the USSR to explore the possibility of working with our Russian counterparts on endangered species research projects.

The mission was a result of a bilateral agreement Russell Train had negotiated a year earlier.

The lead whale biologist, Alexey Yablokov, I hoped would become codirector with me of a project to study, film, and record the bowhead whale in the Alaskan Arctic later that spring. I had just published the cover paper in *American Scientist* on my first bowhead whale expedition in 1971.

After some ten days of discussion in Moscow with outdoor temperatures often at 25 degrees below zero Fahrenheit, some nineteen projects were approved. The leader of the Russian team, a Dr. V. V. Krinitsky, maintained a large colony of beavers in a reserve six hours by train south of Moscow. Krinitsky also spoke fluent German, so he and I could speak past the pretty KGB agents.

We traveled by train south of Moscow to the aforementioned reserve, which also had many wild boar that were being trapped and transported elsewhere in the Soviet Union.

When Dr. Krinitsky showed us his beaver colony, which had been built and studied over decades, he explained, "Beavers mate for life, and if you separate them, they cry real tears and never mate again."

I had published two op-eds in the *New York Times* in 1972, one on the whales' plight and the other breaking the story of "The Great Porpoise Massacre," which detailed the unassailable fact that five million spinner dolphins were caught and killed in tuna nets in the Pacific in the 1960s, unbeknownst to the general public.

Upon our return to the States, I wrote an op-ed piece for the *Times*, leading with the beavers-mate-for-life story—a comparative rarity in the mammalian world—as a metaphor for this hopeful thaw in the Cold War we had experienced.*

The piece on our plans for research on endangered species with Russian biologists was rejected by the *Times*.

On April 1, 1973, I was in Washington for three site visits for the Dodge Foundation. After lunch, I went over to the *Washington Post*.

Someone got out of a car. A person in the car said, "Bye, Ben."

I walked into the *Washington Post* building with that gentleman. He entered an elevator, as did I. He rode to the sixth floor and stepped off, as did I.

I asked him, "Would you please take a look at this?"

He read my op-ed piece, walked down the hall, and came back, saying, "It will be in tomorrow's paper. But I don't do this."

It was Ben Bradlee, executive editor of the *Washington Post*, the editor behind the investigation of the Watergate scandal.

In August 2013, Ben Bradlee, ninety-one, received the Medal of Freedom from President Obama.

Ben Bradlee died on October 21, 2014, at age ninety-three of natural causes. A long obit beginning on the front page of the *New York Times* the next day said he "presided over the *Washington Post*'s Watergate reporting that led to the fall of President Richard M. Nixon and that stamped him in American culture as the quintessential newspaper editor of his era—gruff, charming, and tenacious."

"Just get it right," he would tell his reporters.

*On the topic of monogamy in mammals, in an article in the *New York Times* on July 30, 2013, it was reported by biologists Dieter Lukas and Tim Clutton-Brock of Cambridge University that 9 percent of mammal species are monogamous. Their paper in *Science* looked at 2,545 species of mammals, about half of those known to science, tracing their mating evolution from a common ancestor 170 million years ago. The article by Carl Zimmer begins, "The golden lion tamarin, a one-pound primate that lives in Brazil, is a stunningly monogamous creature. A male will typically pair with a female and they will stay close for the rest of their lives, mating only with each other and then working together to care for their young."

In a cartoon from Asahi Weekly, *November 6, 1970, the author is shown astride a whale, garbed in the stars and stripes, protesting the volley of harpoons that seemed aimed at him.*

WHAT WILL IT TAKE TO MAKE SURE
THERE ARE NO DEMONSTRATIONS?

Whale Eye: Of 26 sperm whales brought to a whaling station at Ayukawa, Japan in August, 1970, the eye of only one remained open; the lid never closed; the image of the assailant remained on the retina, and we wonder what we have done.

In the early 1970s, the International Whaling Commission became somewhat more responsive as the cry against the slaughter of whales grew. Actual quotas for given species were assigned, eliminating the blue whale unit that had allowed the killing of whales to proceed unimpeded with the kill tallied at season's end.

In June 1972, in London, Russell Train, US ambassador plenipotentiary, arrived fresh from the Stockholm Conference on the Human Environment and blew the charade wide open by talking to the press, to the fury of Chairman Inge Rindal of Norway—who said the meeting was to be held *in camera* and a press release would be available on Friday at three p.m.

The quotas set that year were renounced by the Japanese and the

Soviets in the fall, who then took 85 percent of the catch worldwide.

That led Tom Kimball, president of the National Wildlife Federation, to call for a boycott of Japanese and Russian goods. (I did participate in his press conference on the condition that six Japanese news outlets were present including the *Asahi Shimbun.*) The board of National Audubon Society followed suit, after I met with them in Ohio, which led the Society not to buy any Japanese cameras, binoculars, cars, et cetera for two or three years.

In 1975 (my sixth and last IWC meeting, fifth on the US delegation), I walked in on Monday morning to get a cup of tea when I was approached by a well-featured Japanese gentleman who stood 6' 5" tall. He was listed as "ambassador plenipotentiary" (and had, I learned, served as Japanese ambassador to Saudi Arabia the prior five years). He said, "We are having dinner this evening."

"Oh, and where are we dining?"

He smiled, "Scotty's restaurant."

That evening, over dinner, he said that later in the summer the prime minister of Japan was coming to the United States, followed a couple of weeks later by the emperor.

He asked me, "What will it take to make sure there are *no* demonstrations?" (As if I were in charge of demonstrations!)

In a nanosecond I replied, "A quota of 1,300 for the sei whale in the North Pacific." The Japanese had been arguing vociferously for 3,300 despite the recommendation of the IWC Scientific Committee of 1,300 as the maximum kill that the stocks could bear.

On Wednesday, the "ambassador plenipotentiary" left. On Friday, at 2:55 p.m., the Japanese commissioner said, "We accept quota of 1,300 for the sei whale in the North Pacific." Our U.S. commissioner, Robert E. White, whom I had informed of the Monday evening conversation, blinked … and smiled.

In August, an advance man for the Japanese prime minister Takeo Miki came to our home. He asked what the prime minister should say about whales on his visit. I had prepared three pages, which began, "In Japan we think about the whale the way you think about the domestic cow …"

The day before the prime minister's press conference at the National Press Club in Washington, Christine Stevens, founder and president the Animal Welfare Institute, called. She said, "You are coming down, of course."

"No, I am working."

She said we should prepare questions for the prime minister, and we came up with eighteen of them.

The next day, I understand, the prime minister opened his remarks pretty much as I had written them and then went on to other matters, according to Christine Stevens.

Written questions were passed forward. The prime minister returned to the podium irate, saying he received twenty-five questions and eighteen (!) were on whales! He said he had already spoken on that topic at length.

A few weeks later, Emperor Hirohito arrived, and a luncheon at the White House was planned. The White House is National Park number one, and Christine Stevens had gotten permission for a small plane to fly over the White House with a trailing banner, "EMPEROR HIROHITO, PLEASE SAVE OUR WHALES."

That evening a welcoming reception for the emperor and his wife was held at the Japan Society in New York. Hella and I were invited.

We were no sooner in the door of the Japan Society than an aide to the emperor said to me, "Mr. Macaway, the emperor did not see the plane nor the banner."

"What banner?" I asked. He repeated three times what the banner said.

Thank you.

That exchange occurred three more times with three other aides during the evening.

When one's goal is the full cessation of whale killing, one uses science, the arts, and other means to try to change minds and hearts.

Whale poster with Scott's poem.

Postscript

Leafing through a flyer selling whale knick-knacks, I spotted a dramatic photo by Paul Chesley of upended humpback whale flukes, breathtakingly beautiful, with two chaps in a kayak in the foreground. Below the image were chicken scratches that I couldn't make out. So I called the company in Baltimore and asked the woman who picked up the phone what was written there. She said a poem, which she read, noting that it was by "a distinguished and frail poet, Osaka."

"Well", I said, I hate to disappoint you. I wrote the poem in Osaka. How many posters had been printed?"

"10,000."

She put on her boss. He said: "The next edition of 10,000 will carry your name."

A check for $500 came in the mail as a surprise.

THE MAN WHO SKIED DOWN EVEREST

Cranes at Umezawa Manor in Sagami Province, *number 31, in Katsushika Hokusai's iconic series of* Thirty-Six Views of Mount Fuji, *1830–35.*

In April 1977, three Save the Whales concerts were scheduled in Tokyo for sold-out audiences of 10,000 each on Thursday, Friday, and Saturday nights. Some ninety-five musicians, including Odetta, Louisiana Red, Richie Havens, Jackson Browne, Lonnie Mack, J. D. Souther, Peter Rowen, Rolling Coconut Revue, and David Darling, were recruited by clarinetist, bandleader, and impresario Paul Winter, and they all flew from California to perform and participate.

Paul invited me to speak to the whale issue between sets, as he did young California governor Jerry Brown.

A competent, well-spoken young woman informed me that she would be translating for me. She wanted to have my script in advance so that she could do a precise exact translation. She said she was aware that *Moby-Dick* was "my bible." Her father had translated the work into Japanese, a rigorous undertaking, and she wanted to get my remarks right.

I explained I would speak freely, and she should do the best she could.

I recall my initial remarks when I put up an image of Mount Fuji on the screen. Then I overlaid an image of the magnificent arctic bowhead whale whose head is one-third of its body and is capable of producing a large variety of utterances, some construed to be songs.

With a smile I said we knew Mount Fuji was revered throughout Japanese history and celebrated by artists and musicians and poets as the iconic symbol of the country. It was mysterious, elusive, majestic, unknowable, typically shrouded. Mount Fuji was held sacred—think only on the thirty-six woodblock depictions of the mountain from as many angles by Katsushika Hokusai (1760–1846), begun at the age of seventy when he was at the peak of his creativity and artistic vigor.

For many of us in the West, the whale is mysterious, elusive, majestic, unknowable, and glimpsed only fleetingly and incompletely. That fact, that situation, impelled some of us to view the whale's diminishing presence as a challenge, vowing to do what we could to make sure that these behemoths of the sea were not extirpated but rather celebrated and understood better for what we could learn from them. (For example, what are we to make of the resident orca pods along the north Pacific Rim with brains three times as large as ours, who are matriarchies with little violence among them?)

In another presentation, I spoke of the six-octave song of the humpback whale, which is sung by all the males in a population, but evolves over four, five, or six years into a completely different song. We know today of fourteen different song cycles found in different oceans.

Close to midnight on Saturday, Paul Winter asked me to invite anyone in the audience to join us in climbing Mount Fuji the next morning to meet Yuichiro Miura, the Japanese alpinist who in 1970 had skied down Everest, skiing 6,600 feet in a little over two minutes and falling 1,320 feet from the steep Lhotse face.

Muira used a large parachute to slow his swift descent and came to a full stop 250 feet from the edge of the crevasse. The event was captured on film, which won world acclaim. He had also, just that week, founded the first school of ecology in Japan. We were to gather at a spot in the main train station at six o'clock. As I recall, only five or six of the 10,000 showed up and joined us on the bullet train to Fujijama.

Typically, folks who climb the mountain start the evening before with a staff that is branded with a hot iron at each of ten stations as one circles upward. We began at station five where below us was just bare scree and above just snow. We trudged upwards for a couple of hours until we met Yuichiro Miura coming down on skis. His father was with us, sporting two cameras, clicking proudly away. We gave Yuichiro a shirt, designed by Steve Katona, with the notation "Stop Whaling," in Japanese, Russian, and English. We also gave him a book, *Mind in the Waters*.

Yuchiro Muira, wearing a T-shirt we had given him that reads
"Stop Whaling" in Japanese, English, and Russian and holding our gift of
Mind in the Waters, *with Hella at the eighth station atop Mt. Fuji, 1977.*

WHAT DO YOU KNOW ABOUT THE COURTSHIP AND MATING OF WHALES?

After I published an article in *Natural History*, January/February 1973, called "Can Leviathan Long Endure so Wide a Chase and so Remorseless a Havoc?" (a line from Melville), Arthur Godfrey invited me to go on his radio program. My mother and hundreds of thousands of others felt that Godfrey had a touch on radio that connected intimately with the individual listener at home.

After doing the Lipton "flow-through" teabag commercial, Mr. Godfrey asked me, "What is an endangered species?" In looking about the studio, with a male vocalist, a female vocalist, and a nine-piece band, I replied that he was an endangered species. Of course, as a founder of the World Wildlife Fund, he knew the answer to the question, but he laughed.

We talked about the plight of the spinner dolphins in the Pacific. Five million had been killed in tuna nets in the 1960s without any awareness by the general public. We also talked of the great whales who were continuing to be decimated by whaling fleets in the Antarctic and North Pacific.

Time flew, and at the end of the hour, I was heading for the door to get back to work, but Mr. Godfrey said he usually taped three hours of radio at a time, and the third hour was going to come up on February 14, Valentine's Day. He asked me what I knew of the courtship and mating of whales. I said very little, but perhaps enough to go for an hour.

When the third session was taped, I was getting up to leave, and he invited me into his office. He was relaxed, friendly, and conversational. He had a big checkbook with sheets of checks, like my father, and he wrote me a check for $225—$75 for each hour, a lot of money in those days.

Maybe I never should have cashed it but rather framed it as a memento.

A couple of weeks later, I received in the mail three audiotapes of the program sent by a retired gentleman, an audio guy, who said that folks rarely had any record of radio interviews, and he did this as a voluntary service. If I wished to send him $20, fine, if not, please keep the tapes. I sent a check pronto.

CETUS: THE SIGN OF THE WHALE

In Berlin, my last year and a half there, Bob Kausen was a fellow caseworker and friend. He was married to Linda, the daughter of Chuck Jones, a renowned animator and cartoonist (Looney Tunes, the Road Runner, and Wile E. Coyote), second only to Walt Disney. Often on a Sunday, Hella and I would sail with them on the Wannsee, sometimes to the French Officers' Club for lunch. Bob was my best man when Hella and I married on August 9, 1958. He was also a good photographer, who offered to take pictures that day. Owing to the singularity of the event, he borrowed a better camera than his own, and the flash was out of sync with the shutter, so that an iconic image of us toasting one another is a black silhouette.

Bob and Linda Kausen on the day of our wedding in Berlin, August 9, 1958.

Bob Kausen was a graduate of the California Institute of Technology, a genial engineer, and a problem solver. When he and Linda returned to the States, he took a job with a company in Boston for a few years, and then they returned to their native California.

Years slid by. In 1970, we visited them. The Kausens had three children and were living in a house with another couple who had three kids, too, in what was described as an "open marriage." In fact, some Brits made a film with that title about their living situation. What troubled us a little was that the other couple did not seem to be quite as alive as our friends.

We slept for the first time in a waterbed. Hella said it made her feel seasick. The place had a swimming pool, and all the kids went skinny-dipping. Our girls thought it was a hoot. When Bob came home from work, he sat cross-legged, erect, in a kind of yoga trance to mitigate the general din around him.

I have never had the slightest interest in astrology. There we were in California at the height of the flux and exploration, and somehow or other a new book fell into our hands by Stephen Schmidt, *Astrology 14*, describing a zodiac system with two new signs, Ophiuchus and Cetus. To my surprise, my birthday, June first, fell in the middle of the Cetus—that is—Whale, dates.

It turned out that the other man in the house, another Gemini like me, took this news badly. He rushed to the phone and called his guru, saying he had become what he understood to be the true nature of a Gemini. He was flummoxed by this new scheme and asked, "What can I do?"

Stephen Schmidt's new astrological lineup with Cetus neatly fitting my own date of birth gave me a moment's amusement and delight. Maybe this explains my passion for whales. Maybe not.

An Arduous Process of Wandering

The modest person learns not to trust
one paradigm. Most of what he knows
accumulates through a long and arduous
process of wandering.

— David Brooks
The Social Animal

HOLY WATER

As a young man, serving as assistant to the president of Princeton University, I had small appreciation of the importance of ritual. In the late 1960s, President Robert F. Goheen was working hard to bring about coeducation at Princeton, integrate the student body on campus, and not be deflected from the university's mission during the agonies of the Vietnam War.

Hundreds of claims were made on his time from every corner of the university community and beyond. He organized his time well, but still often went home evenings laden with books by professors being considered for tenure or to be hired.

During spring break one year, Goheen wrote Foster Jacobs, who was in charge of the grounds, to suggest that a tree planted outside his window might be transplanted elsewhere. He said that when he dictated at that window, he saw that the tree, perhaps a silver beech, had not dropped its leaves all winter long. Goheen noted he met his deadlines.

One day, perhaps in 1966, I had prepared a few suggested remarks for opening three events on campus, one after another. When he returned to the office, head down focused on the next thing, I asked him: "How did it go?"

He lifted his head while moving along, and said, "A little holy water here, a little holy water there."

This stood me in good stead, years later, when I took on the presidency of the Chautauqua Institution, a place rich in ritual and ceremony.

No campus in America has the abundance and variety of major sculptures by masters than has Princeton. Why? It's a story that is little known, but astonishing. A gift of stock worth $10,000 had been made nine years earlier, with the suggestion that it be held. When the donor suggested it be sold, the sale produced one million dollars. When Goheen wrote to the donor to consider endowing a couple of professorships, the donor replied that $100 million had been spent on construction and buildings, why not put one million into art.

Patrick Joseph Kelleher, director of the Princeton University Art Museum, recruited an advisory group of three. They chose Henry Moore (*Oval with Points*), Jacques Lipchitz (*Song of the Vowels*), Isamu Noguchi (*White Sun*), Gaston Lachaise (*Floating Figure*), David Smith (*Cubi XIII*) and twenty-two other pieces of note and grace.

In 1966, Lady Bird Johnson visited the Woodrow Wilson School of Public and International Affairs (WWS) as part of her planning for the LBJ presidential library in Austin, Texas. Only three of us knew in advance of her visit: President Goheen, dean of the school Marver Bernstein, and me. My assignment was to intercept young Philip Bobbitt, a freshman who would be emerging from the School of Engineering and nephew of President Johnson.

Secret Service men were on the roof of Frick Chemistry Library next to the WWS. Lady Bird moved rapidly through the School, designed by Yamasaki, peppering Goheen and Bernstein with questions.

Philip was wearing torn jeans with holes at the knees and asked, "Why didn't you give me a heads-up?"

Philip Bobbitt, class of 1971, went on to earn a law degree at Yale and a PhD at Oxford and to become a celebrity professor of law at Columbia as an eminent scholar of the Constitution. He is also the sponsor of a national poetry prize in honor of his mother.

After the tour of the School, the party repaired to Prospect, the Goheens' home. Lady Bird quizzed young Charlie Goheen on what he was doing with a small boat in the reflecting pool by the school. He said brightly that he was studying the angle of declination of the sail in reference to the movement of the wind and was about to elaborate when Mrs. Goheen said, "Thank you very much, Charlie."

During my first summer at Chautauqua in 2001, I received a letter from Bob Goheen in which he said his mother had taken him to Chautauqua when he was ten years old. He remembered two things: one, he became acquainted with baseball (which he loved); and two, he became acquainted with Presbyterianism (which he endured).

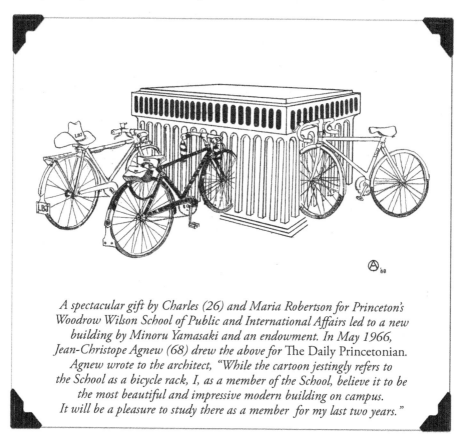

A spectacular gift by Charles (26) and Maria Robertson for Princeton's Woodrow Wilson School of Public and International Affairs led to a new building by Minoru Yamasaki and an endowment. In May 1966, Jean-Christope Agnew (68) drew the above for The Daily Princetonian. *Agnew wrote to the architect, "While the cartoon jestingly refers to the School as a bicycle rack, I, as a member of the School, believe it to be the most beautiful and impressive modern building on campus. It will be a pleasure to study there as a member for my last two years."*

Another event is worth noting. One day in 1966, Goheen mentioned that Ethel Jadwin, widow of alumnus Stanley P. Jadwin, had died, and he thought she may have remembered Princeton in her will. I cleared my throat and asked how much. He said it could be two or three million. It turned out to be $27 million unrestricted. I was impressed by the trustees' decision, at the president's recommendation, to use the bequest to create the Jadwin Complex, the physics building and the math tower on the lower campus, plus endowments. Also, the Jadwin Gym was erected nearby.

Mrs. Jadwin had, years earlier, created a scholarship in honor of her husband, Stanley, a track star, and every year she received a couple of letters from student recipients. She invited them for lunch in New York and kept up with things at the university through these students. The university did not particularly court her then, as they now court potential benefactors. It was her unquenchable interest that led her to keep current through the students.

In 1999, Hella and I came from an event on campus to the Garden Theater to see the movie *The Cider House Rules*. We arrived a little breathless at 6:29 p.m. for the 6:30 showing. Only one person was in the audience— Dr. Goheen, halfway down on the left on the aisle. We seated ourselves opposite him on the right and chatted for a while. At 6:45, when the film

Nassau Hall, illuminated from Cannon Green where a roaring bonfire celebrated football victories over both Yale and Harvard.

was still not yet shown, Goheen quipped, "I wonder if they are waiting for this place to fill up."

When Dr. Goheen died, the memorial service in the University Chapel was filled with jazz, something he had specified as part of the service, but something which came as a surprise to many who thought of him as energetic but not exuberant.

Yet, at that moment, I looked up at the last completed stained glass window in the upper reaches of the place on the south side. It is by far the most luminous and glorious of them all, catching the morning light during Sunday services and throwing a bright glowing image to the pews and the floor below. It is called The Poetry Window and contains Virgil, Dante, Shakespeare, Emily Dickinson, William Blake, and T. S. Eliot, among others. This window was suggested by Robert Francis Goheen, reminding us of yet another facet of his vitality.

UNDER NO CIRCUMSTANCES...

In 1966, when it was clear that William D'Olier Lippincott, dean of students at Princeton (and raconteur of "Down Maine" stories), was stepping down, President Goheen asked me to draw up a list of possible candidates for the position. "And," he said, "don't neglect the Rhodes Scholars."

I prepared a list of ten or a dozen prospects, and Goheen put a crisp arrow beside the name of Neil Rudenstine and asked me to invite him down from Harvard for a visit. When I reached Neil to convey the invitation, he replied, "Under no circumstances." He was happy with his teaching and scholarship as an assistant professor of English and as a tutor at Adams House.

I asked if he would be willing to do the president the courtesy of traveling briefly to Princeton to meet with him. Neil said that he was not interested in administration and politely declined.

I pushed the courtesy angle, and Neil finally relented. A date was set, he traveled to Princeton, and after a meeting with Goheen, signed up for a five-year stint as dean of students. He served in that job from 1968 to 1972. Then he became dean of the college from 1972 until 1977 under President William Bowen, and then became provost from 1977 to 1988.

Bowen and Rudenstine went on to the Andrew W. Mellon Foundation as president and executive vice president. Then Neil took on the presidency of Harvard for ten years from 1991 to 2001, chosen in part because of his administrative experience. And so the day follows the night.

Postscript

"(Christopher) Eisgruber reports being 'startled' when then-President Shirley Tilghman asked him to be provost in 2004, worrying that the responsibilities of the job—the provost serves as chief academic and chief budgetary officer of the University, under the president—would take him away from the teaching and writing he was very happily engaged in. His passionate belief in Princeton University's ethos, particularly its commitment to providing a strong liberal arts education, along with a conversation with colleague Neil Rudenstine convinced Eisgruber to take the job.

"Rudenstine, a fellow Rhodes Scholar, pointed out that the 'beauty' of university administration lies in the fact that 'your bookshelf becomes broader, rather than just deeper.' Rudenstine was right: as a result of becoming provost, Eisgruber says that he 'learned what I might not have learned if I had focused only on my field.'" (*Princeton Magazine*, August/September, 2013, p. 22.)

Neil Rudenstine is author of the book *The House of Barnes: The Man, The Collection, The Controversy*, about the Albert C. Barnes art collection and its controversial recent move from its original site in Merion, Pennsylvania, to Philadelphia. In 2014, Farrar, Straus and Giroux published, to academic and popular acclaim, Neil's latest book, *Idea of Order: A Close Reading of Shakespeare's Sonnets*.

WE ARE EAGER TO HEAR FROM YOU, BUT ...

It was in 1966, I believe, when the Class of 1909 invited me to speak at their dinner at the Nassau Inn. I was working in One Nassau Hall, and the gentlemen wanted a little update on life at the university.

I looked at the sign-up list and quaked at the illustrious list of classmates, led by Judge Harold R. Medina, Sr., renowned for presiding over trials of eleven leaders of the Communist Party charged with advocating the violent overthrow of the government. Pictured on the cover of *Time* magazine (October 24, 1949), he also ruled in the Investment Bankers Case (1951–52), an antitrust case against seventeen prominent Wall Street banking firms. The Class of 1909 is luminous in the annals of Princeton University, with nine members having served on the board of trustees (as many as the Class of 1922, led by Adlai Stevenson, who ran for president twice on the Democratic ticket against Dwight Eisenhower).

The list that evening also included the renowned Dodge twins: Cleveland, vice president and director of the Phelps Dodge Corporation; and Bayard, who was president of the American University in Beirut for twenty-five years (1923–1948). It also included Frank Laubach, who founded and led Laubach Literacy, an organization that enabled millions to become literate; Henry Fairfield Osborn, president of the New York Zoological Society; and Norman Armour, former ambassador to Venezuela.

As the dinner was winding down, Judge Medina said, "Mr. McVay, we are eager to hear from you, but may we go around the table and catch up on each other's activities?"

"I am here at your pleasure," said I, noting one gentleman, not on the list, a seemingly ordinary chap, whom I thought I could identify with.

They went around the room of perhaps twenty to twenty-five classmates, eventually coming to the one I noted. He said, "I'll pass."

Someone said, "But weren't you at the White House last week?"

"Yes, but who would be interested?"

The first envoy from China had come to have lunch with the President and had requested that this chap and his wife be included, owing to his work in China years earlier. To this day I do not know the gentleman's name, since I could not find it while scouring the Class of 1909's forty-fifth yearbook on those then living.

The meek shall not only inherit the Earth, they are the Earth.

ON THE OCCASION OF TWENTY-FIVE YEARS WITH PRINCETON

Who would venture to add one whit
to what the President has already writ
of Mr. Mestres's contribution
to this learning institution.

If another were to try quietly
to etch the imprint of his energy
get beyond the gritty nitty
that would be "an exercise in futility."

Seeking then a lighter turn
recall a few phrases that burn
as shrapnel from skirmishes past
that have left our resources intact.

Which committees "labored mightily and delivered a mouse"?
Which of "our ducks are not swans" in this house?
We have repeatedly been spared the double bind
knowing "consistency the mark of a small mind."

How many deliberations into words ride
but often turn out "a long climb for a short slide"?
With tangential results when words should sing
we are punching a pillow or pushing a string.

Of our rich and gaudy ways absurd
the Treasurer was not always heard
without sacrificing what we shall hold most dear
still we can't stop "choking on cream right up to here."

Far better than "carrying coals to Newcastle" (in kegs)
is "like teaching my grandmother to suck eggs"
(I'm not sure what that may mean,
but it's been said to good effect to a dean.)

If once in a while we boot it, and spirits sink
recognize first "Murphy has had his drink."
On which occasion, having done all off-to-put-it
did we have to be willing to bite the bullet?

In plain clear English, without a wand,
who was to the right of Ghengis Khan?
When it comes to the grounds, let's not get frilly,
we'll pursue a policy of "shabby gentility."

When it comes to parking and things fold-blinded
we tend to be "mashee-minded,"
and proposals will be unread-ed
if their authors be "fuzzy-headed."

For anyone who dices distinctions too thin,
the exercise may be tossed in the bin,
for we shall have less interference
when not making "distinctions without a difference."

To what circle lower in Hell could one be confined
than to have a given proposition aligned
with a cant described by Forrestal brightly
as "feeling deeply and thinking lightly."

What was that about the consultant?
who makes his role less than exultant?
(the comment offered and offered gratis)
he borrows your watch to tell you what time it is …

If you still can't sort out the good from the bunk,
then don't get into "a wrestling match with a skunk!"
or wasn't that a euphemism for the ladies for a duel
just after we'd been served "mighty thin gruel."

A few watchwords kept the Treasury secure
but must not for a moment obscure
the hard thought, care, and compassion
that went into denial of proposals impassion'd.

(I would like to add that this rhyme
was not written on University time.)

November 25, 1971

Postscript
During his quarter century as Princeton's chief financial officer, Ricardo
Angelo Mestres was the one within the administration who found one
hundred different ways of saying "no," when ideas were bursting all about
to spend money. The above got a laugh when read at a luncheon honoring
his service given by President Goheen. Mestres was an indispensable
mentor to me.

IT'S MY MOTHER

*John Gardner, "the leader's leader," met with the first leadership group
of the Partnership for New Jersey at the close of their training in 1987.
He is flanked by Tom O'Neill (left), the Partnership's executive
director, and Alan Bildner, Jr., a member of the first class.*

In 1966, when John W. Gardner (1912–2002) came to Princeton to
receive an honorary degree, he was then Secretary of Health, Education,
and Welfare. Working in the president's office, I was assigned to him
for his visit that day. Yet I blurted out in the first minute, "What, Mr.
Secretary, are the ten great issues facing humanity?"

My interest in the staggering challenges, even then, was keen.

To my surprise, he reached into the breast pocket of his shirt and
pulled out a three-by-five card on which were neatly written his top ten,
numbered in order of priority. Wow. He noted education and health of
course, but also the nuclear threat, population, and poverty. Climate
change and energy had not yet surfaced.

When I entered the foundation field six years later, I read all of Gardner's essays at the front of the Carnegie Corporation's annual reports during his years as president.

I also read his books on excellence, self-renewal, and leadership.

Once I was invited, along with a dozen grant-makers in New York, to spend a day with John Gardner. Three months later I was called and asked how that day affected my work. "The day was fascinating, but," I explained, "he had been a guide to me for years."

In 1987, Tom O'Neill asked me if I might invite Mr. Gardner to speak to the first graduating class of Leadership New Jersey, an initiative of the Partnership for New Jersey. Gardner in the meantime had founded Common Cause and Independent Sector. He also presided over the creation of the Corporation for Public Broadcasting.

He was a good speaker, even though he acknowledged not speaking easily in public before he was fifty-five years old.

In driving him to the Trenton train station afterward, I asked why he seemed a little down.

He said, "It's my mother. She turned ninety-five, and I was trying to ease her into entering a retirement community. She went out and bought a red roadster!"

Some time later, Stanford University was celebrating the hundredth anniversary of its first graduation. The university could choose any speaker from the entire alumni body, and the choice was Mr. Gardner.

It was a beautiful day in Palo Alto on June 16, 1991, as Gardner took the podium in an outdoor ceremony. His opened with the thought, "There can't be many in this audience who were alive one hundred years ago when the first commencement occurred. But I do know of one alert and vital woman who meets that description and is here today. She supplied you with your commencement speaker, and she put me through Stanford, so I want to acknowledge the presence of my one-hundred-year-old mother."

"Mother, stand up and be recognized."

In the front row, she stood up and waved her arms in the air, smiling.

Postscript

On January 6, 2015, David Brooks's column in the *New York Times* references this speech by John Gardner. Below are a few of David's favorite lines from John's speech, which he describes as "chockfull of practical wisdom":

"The lessons of maturity aren't simple things such as acquiring information and skills. You learn not to engage in self-destructive behavior, not to burn up energy in anxiety. You learn to manage your tensions, if you have any, which you do. You find that self-pity and resentment are among the most toxic of drugs. You conclude that the world loves talent but pays off on character.

"You discover that no matter how hard you try to please, some people in this world are not going to love you, a lesson that is at first troubling, and then really quite relaxing.

"You build meaning into your life through your commitments— whether to your religion, to your conception of an ethical order, to your loved ones, to your life work, to your community."

WHOM DO YOU LOOK UP TO?

During a dinner prior to his lecture at Princeton in the late 1960s, Isaac Asimov, the science and science-fiction writer, inscribed one of his paperbacks to Hella and another to me. He said he had just completed his 199th and 200th books. His wife had left him, saying she could not compete with his two typewriters.

Over dinner I asked him, "Dr. Asimov, whom do you look up to?"

"No one," he said.

The table fell silent.

"Is there someone whom you look across at?" I asked.

"Perhaps one," said he. No one spoke.

"Who might that be?"

"Maybe Marvin Minsky?"

A year or two passed, and we were at Woods Hole at a lovely outdoor event sponsored by the National Academy of Sciences. We were about to leave when Hella spotted a nametag with "Minsky" scrawled on it stuck on a beige turtleneck jersey.

She said, "Go ask him whom he looks up to."

I walked over, and Minsky, the so-called father of artificial intelligence with a big mass of wiry hair, was in animated conversation.

I edged in, not wanting to pop the question too abruptly, and said I was worried about the rapid depletion of tropical rain forest in the Amazon at so many football fields per hour.

Minsky said not to worry.

Why?

"We'll take care of it."

"But how?"

"Robotics. We'll put a sheet over the Amazon."

"Before or after it is cut?"

"That doesn't matter," said Marvin Minsky.

At that point I didn't give a hoot about whom Minsky looked up to or across at.

FOR FRANK AT FOUR SCORE

When the doggerel is flying,
Snapping, sizzling in the pan,
Let go of all other minstrels
Frank E. Taplin, Jr. is your man.

When George Kennan turned ninety
Anna Hall Jerome became eleven
Dicky Dilworth touched seventy-five
all had yeasty Frank their bread to leaven.

So when Frank waltzes across the line
of three score and twenty, true,
you want him there with a Steinway
playing Gershwin, *Rhapsody in Blue.*

If you plan a beguiling trip from the fog
(where you might find one as joyous as Hella)
to the heart of old Europe, say Prague,
Bring that Frank fella to keep you from quella.

Or if cosmic inquiry is your bent,
about hydrogen clouds you do wonder,
you're torn between Peebles who sees pebbles
and the Zeldovich pancake, let Frank be your seer.

But we're straying, baying, not quite saying
what's suddenly upon us so freighty,
this timeless chime, Peg's dear Frank,
who toasted us all, prime numbers too, is eighty!

How toast the host?
How not the Rhodes not remote?
Who caught with finesse
In other a certain largesse?

In a few words or on the ivories
their loves, their unending birthdays
their peccadilloes, their joys, their toys
the rains they knew, the sun's strong rays.

Stuff and nonsense, piff and poo
What ever can we do?
Let's reach far and wide, within and beyond the tribe
to try to catch this gent a little ... sans diatribe.

Poet, scholar, tooter, rooter
music-maker, wag and wit
observer, friend, card-carrier
(union four), master of the exquisite.

Vermonter, Clevelander, Tiger, Tiger
burning brighter, Peg delighter,
giver, getter, for music, the Met
on who better than Frank can you bet?

Or be it global warming, company leader,
or Nassau Hall greeter,
the rare compleat angle, er,
ever for the greater good, sir.

E'er, too, with élan, n'er down nor dour
a gardener sowing sweet diversity
pace-setter in life's little run
Yet, heh, the day's just begun.

What, though, is the central chord
with this delightful troubadour?
The boost to soar, the spark through life
came from Mother then dear dear Peg, his wife.

Peg's top word for Frank
is forth-coming, yes, forthcoming
her first thought of him before they
joined forces lightly drumming.

Bright apples in their twelve eyes,
their children produced some little guys
who are not so little any more
and theirs are on the rise.

We salute you, Frank Taplin
Forthcoming, civic, ever cordial
Among all penitents in this skin
On being unbelievably octogenial

June 22, 1995

Postscript

Frank Taplin, a Rhodes Scholar from Cleveland and predecessor of mine as assistant to the president at Princeton, was president of the Metropolitan Opera and the key mover in saving 600 acres of the Institute for Advanced Study woods from rampant development—a bon vivant and transformative philanthropist.

I was privileged to speak—between Robert F. Goheen and George Kennan—at Frank Taplin's memorial service in 2003 in the Princeton University Chapel.

UNEXPECTED JOURNEY

In 2005, on May 14, the Princeton University Art Museum organized a symposium and exhibition in honor of Gillett Good Griffin called "Unexpected Journey."

It was exciting to hear a dozen persons speak on that Saturday, including Gillett, briefly, at the top of the day.

Since Gillett had opened Mexico, the Mayan and Olmec worlds, to our family in 1969 when our daughters were nine and eight years old, we came to marvel at pre-Columbian civilizations. In our first three days, we explored with Gillett the Aztec Pyramids of the Sun and the Moon, located thirty miles northeast of Mexico City at Teotihuacan, two millennia ago the largest city of Mesoamerica. He took us to meet a family who lived and worked there making superb replicas of artifacts from centuries past.

Continuing visits to Central and South America made us appreciate the history and heritage of Mesoamerica on the continent where we live, in contrast to our typically Euro-oriented view. Why do 1,000 planes fly to Europe for every one to South America?

In the summer between freshman and sophomore years at Harvard, Cynthia did a study with Professor Evon Z. Vogt, a Mayan ethnographer, of the enchanting town of San Cristóbal de las Casas in the state of Chiapas. Our older daughter Catherine, as an engineering student at Princeton, took Gillett's course on Mayan life and art. She recalls vividly playing some of Gillett's small ancient vessels as flutes in his home.

Before that day, May 14, 2005, I wrote a poem, "Some Lucky Few Do," that sought to capture a bit of this Johnny Appleseed for the Mayan, whose bright face looks like the essence of the Olmec, renowned for their massive head sculptures. Hearing closely the speakers that day, many of whom made study of the Mayan their lifework in the wake of Gillett's inspiration, I wrote a second poem, "The Next Day," seeking to catch the essence of their admiration.

After that celebratory day in 2005, I sent Gillett the two poems, asking which he might prefer. He wrote back in elegant penmanship, "I was deeply moved by your two poems—before and after. They may be the most meaningful expressions I received. It was a joyous event, and I am still stunned by so much love." At the top of his ivory paper is an ink drawing of him, comfortably perched on a cloud with a graceful number 9 on it.

The year 2005 also marked the centennial of Albert Einstein's discovery of relativity and the fiftieth anniversary of his death. It turns out that Gillett, as a young man who had moved to Princeton after graduating from Yale, was a good friend of Einstein. They had dinner once or twice a week because their repartee was unending. Puns, then and now, are seemingly of low repute, but they both delighted in them. Gillett had not mentioned their friendship until fifty years after Einstein's death. His Christmas greeting that year had a drawing of Einstein waving and Gillett bidding him good-bye, noting simply:

50 years ago
I waved and said goodbye
to a friend
— Albert Einstein —
and 2005 celebrates
the Einstein year.

Now one can visit the basement of the Princeton University Art Museum and wonder at the breadth and grace of the pre-Columbian exhibition, lovingly built over decades by Gillett and friends. One of our favorites, *A Master Teacher and Apprentice*, occupies a cherished spot. Since the Dodge Foundation, at its core, was about the cultivation and encouragement of teachers, I put a photograph of this iconic work in one of our annual reports.

A Master Teacher and Apprentice, *terra cotta figurines from Xochipala, Mexico, dated before 1500 BC. The delicate dialog of the older and younger learner reaches across centuries.*

When Hella and I traveled to Honduras in 2009, our first stop was at the great Mayan site of Copán, southern anchor of the Mayan empire and the site of the monumental hieroglyphic stairway. We had the good luck to hear a ninety-minute talk by the lead archeologist there over the prior quarter century, David Sedat, a professor from the University of Pennsylvania. He packed much of what he knew, including an insatiable curiosity, into that talk about the discovery of three royal tombs, one of which held the remains of Yax K'uk Mo, Copán's dynastic founder, and another which held the remains of Yax K'uk Mo's wife, "the Lady in Red." She was accompanied by jade, ceramic art, and extremely valuable mother-of-pearl necklaces and was wearing a skirt made of thousands of jade sequins. The culminations of these discoveries and insights are the stuff of a poem called "Copán."

SOME LUCKY FEW DO

What is life
but an Unexpected Journey?
We arrive, unscripted, trying to discover
our role in this play.
Some lucky few do.
The passionate few are ever awe-struck
full of wonder at each new discovery.

Like Jefferson, Gillett Good Griffin is an encourager,
building a field of study, understanding the Mesoamerican
so that their works and deeds stand tall as the Romans,
the Greeks, the Egyptians.

Laughing like one of those two on the edge
in Chinese art, amused and bemused
at human foibles, cradling a singular ceramic piece,
then, using it for a whistle or flute,
toodling our family to climb
Pyramids of the Sun and the Moon,
to meet the real family who makes the real good fakes,
turned loose to visit 18 other sites, including
Monte Albán in Oaxaca, imprinting us and our girls
with enchantments which led to Tikal, Coba, Machu Picchu,
the Amazon, Pantanal, even Pablo Neruda, mapping the
sonic repertoire of two kinds of capuchin monkeys.

Forty years ago two tasks were seen of equal moment:
decoding the Mayan glyphs
and cracking the whale code.
The first was done by a nimble lad
before he entered Princeton.
The second is but a surface scratch so far.
Soooo ... our chortling, cajoling, piffle fluter,
we follow and learn from a master at life
and other civilizations who has
an astonishing eye for beauty and a deft hand
for depicting it
a heart as big as a jaguar.

May 14, 2005

THE NEXT MORNING

Yes, that's it, by jove
you wanted to give people
a sense of beauty and you did.
Michael Coe says, "Gillett taught me to see."

In *The Mouse's Tale* (1951)
we see drawings that hint
at what is to come
the forms, the dancing forms,
the master and the apprentice
conveying the spell of
mentor on learner
or the Moon Goddess
sketched as deftly, lovingly,
observantly as da Vinci would (if he could),
the democratic faith in an object's
capacity to teach us about
the common humanity of the Mayan.

Yes, if you don't understand it,
draw it. And, yes, wow,
the rediscovery of Temple B
at Río Bec—what a roll of the jaguar's eyes
but the capper is that
Gillett far from his claim of the periphery,
the edge, was in the middle

making it happen and encouraging
the tempted, the curious
to make the Mayan world their lifework.

Our dear good G, not smoking, good teeth,
the ripples, the waves of this pounding heart,
the boundless enthusiasm and awe
the unbounded friendship down the years.

The friggin' rabbit,
whiskered, bemused, observing, scribbling,
the Codex of community
the glyphs now known.
We cherish Gillett beyond this treasure trove
of thousands of objects
which whistle the dream.

May 15, 2005

COPÁN

To me it is no mystery
that the soul of the site
at Copán is occupied
by a woman, a matriarch,
now a beloved skeleton
lying on a bed of jade
& mother-of-pearl jewelry
body painted and repainted
bones reverently painted
and repainted
in the red essence
carrying the idea of resurrection
profoundly linked to the first
of a dynasty of lords—
wife?
giver of five births,
buried in this deep holy of holy
places
who was she?
whence her authority
and grace?
apparently old at death
are all suppositions about her
turned again on their ear?
Hella posits the possibility
she was in charge,

the chief who may have
beckoned the young consort
to her court and
over time
he won favor
and became the first of
sixteen Copán kings.

What thinkest thou Gillett?

Honduras
January 15, 2009

YOU'RE THE BEST

*Princetonians from miles around gathered for a lecture
by Princeton president Shirley Tilghman and a festive
luncheon afterward at the Atheneum at Chautauqua.*

On the Saturday morning of Princeton Reunions, the university's president, Shirley Tilghman, spoke to alumni in Richardson Auditorium. This was a cherished hour for us, since Hella and I were eager to hear from her on the highlights of the year, ever fresh and compelling even though we live here and visit the campus regularly.

As an able neuroscientist, lover of the arts, a natural leader with élan, discernment, and esprit, she spoke for half an hour without notes and then did a meticulous and gracious Q and A.

On May 28, 2011, she mentioned first the wildly successful She Roars gathering which drew some 1,400 women alumni including Sonia Sotomayor, Associate Justice of the Supreme Court; Lisa Jackson, head of the EPA; Wendy Kopp, founder and president of Teach for America; and outstanding women on the faculty.

Shirley Tilghman, president of Princeton University, speaking in Chautauqua's historic amphitheater, opening a week on science in society in 2003 by explaining the reasons for stem cell research.

She next noted the completion, occupation, and dedication of the new state-of-the-art Frick Chemistry Laboratory, costing $450 million, paid for entirely by royalties from Eli Lilly. Why? It was thanks to research by Princeton chemistry professor Ted Taylor on a cancer drug called Alimta. How did it work? Taylor used a substance from the membrane of a butterfly wing.

She greeted Malcolm Warnock of the Class of 1925, in the first row, the oldest living alumnus who would be 106 years old in a few weeks.

Before the session, I had a chance to talk briefly to Robert Rawson, Jr., the chair of the board when Tilghman was named the nineteenth president of Princeton. Rawson, it turned out, was to receive an honorary degree in three days at commencement. He confirmed the story below as I remembered it.

Tilghman said, "I find it deeply paradoxical that the United States has without a question the finest colleges and universities in the world, but a

K–12 education system that is leaving vast numbers of students behind." She charged all graduates to give some time and talent to strengthening public schooling.

Back at the alumni session, she said she was impressed that 15 percent of the senior class applied to Teach for America, noting that the quality of teaching was "the civil rights issue of our day."

When Shirley Tilghman was chosen as Princeton's president, Hella and I were away at Chautauqua. Tilghman traveled the country meeting alumni and parents, drawing crowds of 800 in large cities like Los Angeles and New York. We had a first chance to hear her speak in spring of 2002 in Cleveland before about 400 folks where Mr. Rawson gave her a wonderful introduction. She smiled as she took the microphone, saying how much she appreciated the support and encouragement of the board. Indeed, when she awoke in the morning, she said she felt that the chair was right beside her. I looked over at him and his wife, and both laughed heartily.

The next summer, 2003, we had a week at Chautauqua devoted to Science and Society, and President Tilghman had kindly accepted my invitation to give the opening lecture in the 5,000-seat amphitheater. We had a dinner in her honor the prior evening and a lunch after the lecture for Princetonians from miles around. First, she took questions on the day's topic and then questions about life at the university. At the close, I mentioned that there were over 1.5 million not-for-profits in America and that folks should keep in mind the comparative need of a given institution when they made gifts. Shirley said she wanted equal time. I thanked her and closed the meeting.

When we returned to Princeton in 2004, we went in June to Summer Intime on a Thursday evening for a student play and were told that it was sold out—contrary to being only half full on Thursdays for decades past. How so? President Tilghman bought all the tickets and gave them away. Her love of the arts prompted Peter Lewis, a classmate, to commit $101 million for the Lewis Center of the Performing and Creative Arts, a big idea intended for realization in the McCarter Theatre neighborhood.

Perhaps four years ago at Reunions, following a precise and eloquent disquisition on achievements of Princeton's students and faculty, and replies to questions, a well-clad, well-spoken Asian American asked why not reinstate the charming tradition of a run in the buff at midnight by sophomores in response to the first snow. He said a school in Cambridge had no trouble with it. Shirley paused, smiled, saw that time was out and said, "Nice try. Our meeting is concluded." (Harold Shapiro, her predecessor and fellow Canadian, later explained to me that the seemingly innocent event was fraught with dire consequences, since copious drinking often precedes this run in the buff and unwanted things happened afterward, and that was why he banned it. Oh.)

In 2010, Tilghman said that thirteen sports teams triumphed in the Ivy group. She was ticking them off, got to twelve, forgetting for an unlikely moment the last. "Well, moving on …" A few minutes later she remembered and said, "Women's tennis!"

In 2012, Princeton topped the Ivies in fifteen sports, an all-time record for any of the schools. When asked how she felt about a liberal arts education these days, she said "That's the topic of my remarks to graduates on Tuesday," noting concisely, "a liberal arts education is the best vaccine against early obsolescence." She also noted a phenomenal 86 percent acceptance rate from the newly reinstituted early admission acceptance practice.

On March 27, 2013, President Tilghman spoke in the Fields Center to the Old Guard on "Reflections on Princeton: Lessons Learned in Nassau Hall," and I had the joy of introducing her to the huge crowd. It was impossible, and inappropriate, to try to note the rich tapestry of her presidency. I touched on a few highlights, and brought her up, recalling: "A few years ago an old duffer in the front row at Richardson struggled to his feet, leaning on a cane, looked up and rasped, 'I have heard Harold

Dodds ... Bob Goheen ... Bill Bowen ... Harold Shapiro ... and now you—you're the best!'"

Her first lesson, she said, was her surprise that whatever she said, it was scrutinized. For example, in her first few weeks, she said, "What we need around here are more students with green hair." Well, that one went viral. What she meant, of course, was that she wanted to see more diversity in the student body. Yet, several years later, the top undergraduate student, the winner of the Pyne Prize on Alumni Day, turned up in green hair and a mohawk. She smiled, oddly and wonderfully vindicated. She thought the green hair comment might wind up on her tombstone.

Later, in the Q and A, she was asked, "What do you want on your tombstone?"

She thought a moment and offered, "She is resting."

Shirley spoke of a dozen lessons, noting that recruiting and retaining faculty are at the core of the job, since the quality of the faculty attracts excellent students, that diversity and excellence go together, and the necessity for Princeton to be a part of the global marketplace.

She was asked, in a piece in the Summer 2013 *Princeton Magazine*, "What do you consider your greatest achievement as president of Princeton University?"

She replied, "The question is like asking Sophie to choose among her children. There is no single achievement that stands out above the others, so perhaps the simplest answer is to say that my greatest achievement is to leave the university stronger and more vibrant than I found it."

In no way can I convey our admiration for Shirley Tilghman's leadership at Princeton over her twelve years there, but can only hint at it through small details of a masterwork in progress.

President Tilghman completed her part of the long race of leading the university with energy, ingenuity, and integrity.

Each Word Suggests

There are so many ways for speakers of English to see the world. We can glimpse, glance, visualize, view, look, spy, or ogle. Peek, watch, or scrutinize. Each word suggests some subtly different quality: looking implies volition; spying suggests furtiveness; gawking carries an element of social judgment and a sense of surprise. When we try to describe an act of vision, we consider a constellation of available meanings. But if thoughts and words exist on different planes, then expression must always be an act of compromise.

— Joshua Foer
Utopian for Beginners
The *New Yorker*, December 24 & 31, 2012

FORTY UNDER FORTY

Sometime in 1974, when I headed the Robert Sterling Clark Foundation, Brooke Astor (1902–2007), a doyenne of New York philanthropy, called to invite me to a day focused on critical issues.

After being elected to four terms as governor of New York, where he set national standards in education, the environment, and urban policy, Nelson Rockefeller established the Commission on Critical Choices for Americans that addressed six study areas, including energy and its relation to ecology and food, health, world population, and quality of life. Rockefeller sought to strengthen his policy hand in a run for the White House.

Brooke Astor explained that the Commission's work had been pursued by an older crowd, and it needed a breath of fresh air from "Forty Under Forty," that is forty persons under the age of forty from forty different fields. For example, John Adams of the Natural Resources Defense Council was chosen for the environment; Peter Berle, a New York state assemblyman (later president of National Audubon Society) from public life; and she wanted me to represent philanthropy. I had been on the job as the founding executive director of the Robert Sterling Clark Foundation only a year and was pulling our random giving into a coordinated strategy.

Within the foundation field, then and for years to come, Brooke Astor was one of the few who understood, among many topics, the need to identify bright kids and provide them with intellectual and personal nourishment to enable them one day to be contributors to our society. I also liked her.

I explained, however, that I had turned forty-one and was therefore ineligible to participate in this very special forum. She gave a hoot, said that she wouldn't tell, and instructed me to make myself available for what turned out to be a fascinating day.

In our subgroup on the environment, John Adams argued that the plutonium breeder reactor was a doomsday machine, for plutonium 239 has a half-life of up to 24,000 years. I described the plight of the great whales whose numbers had been tragically decimated by whaling in the twentieth century and the continuing slaughter, now mainly by the Japanese and the Soviets. Peter Berle, chair of our group, reported out over lunch that we recommended "a breeder reactor for whales." That was a light touch in a serious day of grappling with issues looking ahead.

That day was not a springboard for Nelson Rockefeller to become president, but he was named vice president by Gerald Ford, also unelected.

FOR SALE: A LARGE PRICELESS HIGH MOUNTAIN TRACT IN NEW MEXICO

In 1972, Herb Mills, then executive director of the World Wildlife Fund, asked me to assist him in securing $15 million to purchase the vast Vermejo Park Ranch in New Mexico, 5 percent of which poked up into Colorado. This immense tract of 591,000 acres was up for sale for a mere $30 million. He believed Vermejo to be the only large tract of land left in the West that would qualify as a national park.

Mills said the Ranch had been in the hands of a single family, William Bartlett (1902–1948), and then W. J. Gourley. It was the place where hunters from Los Angeles, Houston, and Denver came to bag the big four: bear, bison, elk, and mountain lion. It had eighty mountain lakes. The mountains rose over 13,000 feet. Mills personally saw fifty bald eagles and forty-five golden eagles his first morning there.

Mills had gotten a commitment of $5 million from each of three donors and needed to raise the remaining $15 million. Did I have any ideas?

I arranged for a meeting with Roger Kennedy (1926–2011, years later director of the National Park Service), the chief financial officer of the Ford Foundation whose office, along with that of the Foundation's president McGeorge Bundy, was on the twelfth floor of the building.

Roger, padding around in slippers, listened to Herb's earnest pitch for this rare, exciting conservation opportunity. Roger said he would refer the proposal for analysis to a consulting firm, Sweet, in Philadelphia.

Sadly, Roger was shortly thereafter hurt riding a bicycle in Central Park, hospitalized, and laid up for weeks. And I became enmeshed in my new job heading up the Robert Sterling Clark Foundation and did not pursue the matter further.

The remaining $15 million was not raised. The property was purchased in 1973 by Pennzoil, a company built and led by the Liedtke brothers, Hugh and William, both graduates of Amherst.

When I served on the board of the National Park Foundation in the 1970s, chaired then by Lawrence Rockefeller, Bill Liedtke sometimes came to meetings to learn about how national parks were managed.

Years passed. Major conservation groups sought to acquire the land, including the Trust for Public Land and The Nature Conservancy. None were successful.

In 1996, Ted Turner bought the property, and I thought that news was welcome since he had acquired large tracts in Idaho and Montana and had two sons who were foresters. I saw him at a foundation conference shortly thereafter and congratulated him, noting my relief that he would do the right thing by the property, which was still a "sportsman's paradise."

He said, jocularly, "I plan to mine it, graze it, and exploit it every which way."

Nineteen years have passed, and I just read the elegant website inviting sportsmen, fishermen, and nature enthusiasts to partake of the splendors of the Vermejo Park Ranch today. While the gorgeous mountain scenes scroll by, the website describes the long history and current amenities, conservation of close to 100 mammals—bison, mule deer, black bear, pronghorn, elk, mountain lion—and 200 species of birds, hiking, and horseback riding, all while gorgeous mountain scenes scroll by. This is the largest component of Turner's two million acre ranch empire.

Turner seems to have used edges of this priceless high mountain tract for moderate exploitation, but an underlying conservation ethic appears to drive this enterprise. This mirrors what he has done in other endeavors, such as distributing environmental guru Lester Brown's books to leaders in commerce, government, and the nonprofit sectors.

IT HAS BEEN SUGGESTED BY SOME ...

A highly touted event for grant-makers was held in the deeply carpeted lower-level meeting room at the Ford Foundation. It was a gathering for New York funders to meet and hear from the first president of the Robert Wood Johnson Foundation, David E. Rogers, after a year on the job in 1973. When he was only twenty-eight, Rogers had been chosen dean of the Johns Hopkins University School of Medicine.

Howard Dresner, treasurer of the Ford Foundation, gave a florid introduction of Dr. Rogers, a tall, nimble, Ichabod Crane figure who bent over the microphone. The Johnson Foundation had recently become a very large foundation dedicated entirely to health care. It was second only to the Ford Foundation in size and capacity.

Dr. Rogers, a friend and exemplar, began by saying, gently: "It has been suggested by some that the building in which we meet is inward-looking and that petitioners may feel a little intimidated when they enter."

He understood that it takes $3 million a year to maintain the building. He said, softly, he would like to associate himself with that view.

A book, *The Big Foundations* (1972), had been written by Waldemar Nielsen (1917–2005), an informed critic of a sometimes-arrogant line of work. The "Big 33" foundations were taken to task for being unresponsive to the needs of society and the planet, and showing timidity and lack of imagination concerning wise deployment of their giving.

The Robert Wood Johnson Foundation, with assets exceeding $1.2 billion at that time, was beginning to define a fresh set of strategies for improving health care by creating immediate citizen access to emergency medical care through the 911 phone system, as well as central control of communications and a prompt and appropriate emergency system capacity.

Noting that he was new at the job, David Rogers said the only way he knew how to understand what was really going on in health care in America was for his program staff to be out there three or four days a week. Meetings in the office are less productive than those in settings devoted to improving health.

In 1985, Nielsen updated that critique with another book, *Golden Donors*. The Robert Wood Johnson's philanthropy came out smelling like a red rose at its peak in summer. The imagination, energy, and wisdom of their grantmaking won Nielsen's applause. The bulk of the large foundations were still seen as timid, inert, and lacking courage, but as potentially a force for public good.

David Rogers was a splendid artist and woodworker, shaping long before the sun rose amazing depictions of animals or women in motion. A few of these, on a mother-infant theme, can still be seen in the offices of the foundation today.

In his last years, David Rogers (1926–1994) was a national spokesman in responding to the HIV virus crisis at the national level. Beloved to all who were lucky to feel his courage, leadership, and sensibilities, he transformed health care in this country and created a pattern for giving going forward to this day.

Postscript

When thinking about David Rogers's commitment to getting his staff out into the field, I was reminded of a detailed article about Pope Francis, who had been on the job just nine months when he was named *Time*'s Person of the Year (December 23, 2013). It read: "To Francis, poverty isn't simply about charity; it's also about justice. The church, by extension, should not reflect Rome; it should mirror the poor, which helps to explain why he has turned the once obscure Vatican Almoner, an agency that has been around for about 800 years and is often reserved for an aging Catholic diplomat, over to the dynamic fifty-year-old Polish Archbishop Konrad Krajewski and told him to make it the Holy See's new front porch.

"You can sell your desk,' Francis told Krajewski. 'You don't need it. You need to get out of the Vatican. Don't wait for people to come ringing. You need to go out and look for the poor.'"

SCIENCE BOOK OF THE YEAR?

At a dinner some time in 1972 I was sitting next to René Dubos (1901–1982), who coined the dictum, "Think globally, act locally," when he said his mother showed him a book of 400 famous persons when he was a boy. That inspired him to aim high in his own life. Dubos was a renowned microbiologist, conservationist, and author of many books.

Dubos also mentioned that he chaired a small committee that chose *The Blue Whale* (1971) by George Small as the "Science Book of the Year."

I asked him why? He replied it was based on a review of the book in *Natural History* magazine, which, it turns out, I had written.

I said the book was not well researched nor was it well written, and it was unworthy of this recognition. Had he read the book? The answer was "no."

Dubos said that a "boxed" paragraph from the book was in the review, and it was clear and cogent. I replied it was the most quotable paragraph in a book written by a New York geographer.

He asked, why did I give it a relatively good review? I replied that I did not. The book made a case for conservation of whales but not a strong one.

Is there any substitute for actually reading the book, especially if one gives it such an august acclamation?

PLEASE LOWER YOUR EXPECTATIONS

It was a bitter rainy night
but a fever gripped the crowd
assembled
high above Central Park
for Uri bend-the-spoon Geller
was about to perform.

I looked over the wet folks
piled into that apartment
and felt they were divided
pretty evenly
between believers and …
skeptics. Yah, about
fifty-fifty.

Uri's Ed McMahon
said our star had had
a hard day in
Phila-del-phi-a
under the scrutiny
of social psychologists
from SRI
calibrating if his mind
had bent
anything that day …
so we would be seeing
Uri not at the top
of his game.

When Uri appeared,
tall, charming, curly-haired, spare
a rush ran through the crowd.

(We're sitting down
front to espy any
odd moves up close.)

Uri said, you know,
It's hard to do the
ineffable
if someone in the group
is working against you.

So, as a single organism
we wheeled about
to see
one tough guy
in the back
arms massively folded
glowering with doubt.

We glowered back,
give poor, tired,
strength-depleted
Uri a chance
to strut his stuff.
So now folks
we're 99% with Uri
but we weren't blinking
for fear of missing
some sleight of hand.

Well, Uri did so-so.
He bent Hella's
silver hair piece
and stopped a watch.

but forget not,
Uri trained
as a magician.

Mind his roots!

1974

Postscript

This was at height of Uri Geller's celebrity or notoriety, when his abilities to perform paranormal phenomena were under scrutiny by scientists. The arc of his life since suggests a prowess couched in stage tricks.

CHRISTO!

Pont Neuf wrapped by Christo. Paris, 1985.

When the Council on Foundations moved from New York in 1974, where 40 percent of the foundations were located, to Washington, DC, a lacuna prompted us to create gathering opportunities for grant makers. The Foundation Luncheon group was formed for monthly luncheons where we heard from such folks as Nelson Rockefeller and Ralph Nader, both big draws.

When it was my turn to invite a speaker, I recruited and introduced Philip Morrison, a distinguished theoretical physicist from MIT who was of international stature and, reputedly, a dynamic speaker. Morrison was a member of the Manhattan Project who went on to become a vocal critic of the nuclear arms race. He had been a reviewer of science books for *Scientific American* for years.

Some 150 of us gathered in May 1975 on the lawn at Rockefeller University to hear what he had to say about where philanthropy might go in the next twenty-five years. Well, this consummate man of science spoke only of the arts.

Morrison began by talking about the renowned glassmaking in Murano, Italy, across from Venice, as early as the eighth century and moved swiftly on to our own day. The last part of his remarks was devoted entirely to Christo, a young artist who worked out-of-doors who had not done too much up to that time. Only four of his twenty-two projects—*Corridor Storefronts* in Kassel, 1968; *Wrapped Coast*, Sydney, 1969; *Valley Curtain*, a 400-meter cloth stretched across Rifle Gap, Colorado, in 1971; and *Running Fence*, 1973, in California—were done. Still to come, too, were the wrapping of Pont Neuf bridge in Paris (1984) and the Reichstag building in Berlin (1995), which Hella's classmates later described as a jubilant day for Berliners.

So, in the mid-1980s when we were invited to hear Christo speak at the School of Visual Arts in Summit, New Jersey, and have dinner with him and his partner, Jeanne-Claude, afterward, the event took on added meaning. In the auditorium, Christo was introduced before a large crowd, but before he could speak a loud voice interrupted him: "Christo! Don't talk without the slides. Talk about something other than the projects!"

For Time *magazine, Christo created a wrapped work of art,* Endangered Earth, *which was the Planet of the Year, January 2, 1989.*

After this eruption, Jeanne-Claude ran to fetch the slides.

The executive director said to me, "They didn't request a slide projector."

I said, "Get one, pronto."

Fifteen minutes later, Christo told their story with a series of strong slides showing exactly what he meant. It is interesting and not implausible to reflect on the fact that Christo and Jeanne-Claude were *born on the same day the same year*—June 13, 1935—he in Bulgaria, she in Morocco. They both were Gemini. It is as though there were four of them coming at you all at once.

They financed their projects by selling the detailed drawings that seem architectural in nature.

In 2002, we had a week devoted to the visual arts at Chautauqua. When I called, Jeanne-Claude picked up the phone.

"How did you get this number?"

"You gave it to me," I said.

I pitched for them to come to Chautauqua for a day, offered a decent honorarium, and Jeanne-Claude said they were working on a big project for Central Park, *The Gates*. Christo was working seventeen hours a day, she thirteen hours. But, she said, taking three days out would be good for them, and they would enjoy the drive up and back along the Finger Lakes. She accepted my invitation. But she called back three minutes later to say Christo said, "No!" The deadline was looming, so they had to decline.

Actually, the deadline was later pushed back a year to February 2005. Hella and I flew up from St. Petersburg to see *The Gates* and walk for hours with our family, with a break for lunch at the Metropolitan Museum of Art, thanks to our daughter Catherine.

We were transported by the rippling orange banners—drawing attention to the beauty and singularity of Central Park—against a cobalt blue sky and snow shimmering all about.

Cynthia, our other daughter, took scores of photos of *The Gates* from many angles during their two-week run that February. She made a major work of art with thirty-six images—tight punchy verbal takeaways, with one panel in a natural color where orange predominates, one in blue, and one in black and white.

Christo once reflected on the nature of his large outdoor art by saying, "Do you know that I don't have any artworks that exist? They all go away when they're finished. Only the preparatory drawings and collages are left, giving my works an almost legendary character. I think it takes greater courage to create things to be gone than to create things that will remain."

Philip Morrison was right—Christo and Jeanne-Claude were a phenomenon of surprising imagination and invention and execution that touches a fresh common chord of human aspiration.

Our family under one of 7,503 gates installed in Central Park in New York City by Christo and Jeanne-Claude, February 2005.

DID THEY FIND ANYTHING?

In 1974, at the Robert Sterling Clark Foundation in New York, we created a program for support of liberal arts colleges called "Building Bridges Across the Moats," which aided colleges whose resources contributed to the learning and enhancement of their local communities.

In the course of reviewing proposals, I visited perhaps seventy-five colleges and met with their presidents and others to discover programs that merited funding. At this time, I got a call from John R. Coleman, president of Haverford College, saying he was coming to New York and asking if he could see me.

"I'd be honored," I said. I had read his book, *Blue-Collar Journal* (1974), which he—a labor economist—wrote about his experience working as a ditch digger, sandwich maker, and garbage man during his sabbatical. In each case, he left to return to chair meetings of the Mid-Atlantic Federal Reserve Board. He was seeking to understand the life of blue-collar workers, but he was under no illusion that he could inhabit the shoes or the circumstances of a worker, since he knew he would return to the full span of life as a college president after these temporary stints.

When Coleman arrived in my office, he explained that he took the Haverford job after ten years at the Ford Foundation, since he wasn't sure he could trust himself to continue in that work without his hat size growing larger. Also, in accepting the Haverford post, he told the trustees it was on the condition that his leadership must be evaluated at the five-year mark. After four years, Jack asked the trustees what they were doing about his performance review. They said, "Nothing. You are doing fine."

At Jack's urging, a committee of faculty, staff, and students was formed. They rendered a detailed report eighteen months later. Dr. Coleman asked if I would like to see the report, bending over to fish it out of his briefcase. I said, "No thanks, but did they find anything?"

Coleman acknowledged that the report was generally favorable, but the review picked up on one thing: the faculty felt individually that he did not understand nor fully appreciate their work.

Isn't that the human condition—who feels understood or appreciated?

Not too long after this, Jack Coleman returned to the world of philanthropy by becoming president of the Edna McConnell Clark Foundation. He and I then worked to help found NYRAG (the New York Regional Association of Grantmakers, known today as Philanthropy New York) so that grantmakers in the New York area could be in regular touch with one another.

In 1986, Coleman pursued a long-held dream by acquiring and running an inn in Chester, Vermont, which he called The Inn at Long Last. I understand he is well at the age of ninety-three!

On Our Earth

On our earth, before writing was invented,
before the printing press was invented,
poetry flourished. That is why we know
that poetry is like bread; it should be
shared by all, by scholars and by peasants,
by all our vast, incredible, extraordinary
family of humanity.

— Pablo Neruda

THE FIRE

Houses are very important. Describe your house and I'll tell you who you are. Your world is there. It's what covers you, like a bird's feathers.

— Marcela Serrano, *Ten Women*

In a major catastrophe, experts say, the psychological world collapses just as resoundingly as the physical one. The most prominent casualty is the sense of invulnerability with which most people manage to face the risks of daily life.

— "The Emotional Impact of Disaster: Sense of Benign World Is Lost" by Daniel Goleman, the *New York Times*, November 26, 1985

When I left Princeton University in May 1972, to head up the Robert Sterling Clark Foundation in New York City, we had to leave our university house at 40 McCosh Circle. This meant we would buy a house of our own.

Hella and I designed a one-page form for assessing every house we looked at—strengths and weaknesses. We looked at twenty-five houses in this rational way and didn't like any of them—not to mention we could not afford most of them. Then, one Friday evening at a party, we heard of a home at 4566 Province Line Road that was going on the open market the following Wednesday. We left the party at once to see the place and, upon arrival, the checklist was tossed to the winds.

We fell head over heels in love with this house between two streams, built by Colin Fry, a Scotsman, with his own hands. He had used gorgeous doors from an old Trenton church. Our future neighbor and a colleague at Princeton, Tony Maruca, said the place had "oceans of charm."

The next morning, Saturday, we took the girls, then twelve and eleven, to see the place in the daylight. We explained to them we would be negotiating, feigning mild interest and asked them to show their "usual restraint."

Well. We entered the house, and Catherine and Cynthia sprinted into a den to the left where Colin Fry had lived while building the rest of the house. The girls squealed from the small loft, "We love it, too!"

We loved our place, where the girls created a village across the main stream called Megapteraville, and they discovered critters under the rocks in the stream, replete even today with small fish, water striders, and abundant frogs. We have a great blue heron in residence for several months every year, abundant deer, and a flock of wild turkeys who fly to the tops of big trees deep in the woods out back, as well as a glorious albino squirrel.

On a Friday the first week in February 1981, with Catherine and Cynthia at Princeton and Harvard in engineering and biology, respectively, our home burned to the ground shortly after a serviceman sent by the oil company came for a routine maintenance call.

Friday was one day of the week when Hella did not teach until eleven and was home. She let the serviceman in and offered him a cup of coffee. He was taciturn. When he left later, he sat in his car for minutes before driving away. Within the hour, the furnace room was ablaze and soon the entire house. Hella ran to a neighbor's house to call 911 and then me.

Our first attorney, Jerry Stockton, had the furnace hauled out with a backhoe. Close inspection revealed that the nozzle through which the oil fed had not been screwed back in place, so the oil flowed freely on the floor. When the furnace next fired, the spilled oil caught fire, and the room became a rotisserie.

Our dachshund, Curio, took off and did not turn up for three days.

*Cynthia and Catherine sorting through
the shards of house fire in February 1981.*

It was so cold the water in the streams was frozen. No fire hydrant was nearby. So there was no way to put out the blaze. The story of the fire lit up all the newspapers in the area. Hella was photographed wringing her hands.

That evening we had dinner with Bill and Sylvette Krause. Bill said, "Your house was a museum." How true, thanks to Hella's aesthetic touch and delight in beauty.

The weekend after the fire, Cynthia came down from Harvard and Catherine from Princeton to sift through the charred rubble, tears in their eyes.

For a fortnight, we had dinner with friends, the last joined by a couple who had lost their home to fire, too. That couple spoke slowly, drank a lot, and left early. We asked, "Is that what a devastating fire will do to you?" Our hosts said, "No, they were alcoholics before the fire."

I checked up on the serviceman. He had had eighty "callbacks" because of unsatisfactory service, and he had been fired three times.

Years later, in March 1987, our suit against the oil company by our insurance company and us was "settled" at a nominal amount, with eight lawyers sitting around the table, in Middlesex County. We had been worn down, physically, mentally, and emotionally, by the process.

Through Hella's hard work and diligence after teaching each day, the site was cleared, and plans went forward to build a new home, environmentally attuned, on the old site. For Hella, this was the second time she had lost everything—the first when her home in Berlin was firebombed in February 1943.

Thanks to architect Bob Hillier's suggestion, we hired Cyril Beveridge to design a new house on our beloved site. Cyril had just won a statewide competition for affordable housing with a house costing $33,000.

We were out for fifteen months, staying at a place on Hodge Road in the winter through the kindness of a classmate of Catherine's, Fred

Woodbridge, and then at Victor and Frances Lange's home on Jefferson Road in the summer.

We paid property taxes on our nonexistent home. The township said that our payment was in their budget. In this difficult period, the bank where we had our mortgage tried to raise the rate. It went all the way to the esteemed president of the bank. When Hella met with him and explained our plight, the decision was made to keep the rate the same. That gentleman has been a friend in the intervening decades.

When the new house was roofed out, we threw a party, a picnic for all the workers hired by our terrific builder, Jim Potts, their families, our neighbors, and friends with plenty of music and good food. This celebration is called a *Richtfest* in Germany.

On October 25, 1982, we wrote our attorney Tom Campion a long letter on "The Nature of the Loss," which began: "It is an odd thing but true. When someone says to us, 'I can imagine how horrible it is to lose your home,' the thought, however genuine, has a hollow ring. Often the expression of sympathy is followed by a query about the adequacy of insurance, or a comment that he has recently taken pictures of every nook and cranny of his home's interior and locked away their prized possessions in a vault somewhere.

"The person who is likely to understand is one who has had a similar experience. Then the conversation takes a different turn: 'Were all the family pictures lost?' 'What about the children's letters, artwork, poetry, and compositions?' 'How much unpublished stuff did you have?' 'How many outfits had your wife sewn by hand?' The conversation is of a different character as it must be with refugees where both home and homeland, and maybe family, were lost."

To this day, our hearts go out to folks affected by this awful kind of loss.

VALENTINE'S DAY

After our beloved home in the woods burned to the ground, we were gypsies for fifteen months. In May 1982, we returned to our new home. We had lost almost everything, at the twenty-three-year mark in our marriage, and we realized that a more enduring aspect of life is the relationship with others. That prompted us to organize a Valentine's Day party for couples whom we liked and whom we thought to have good marriages. Each was invited to bring a poem or song that meant something to them. The first year was such a success that it became a tradition.

Those were memorable evenings—ever crowned with Hella's superb cuisine and the telling choice of poems or the singing of songs.

Barbara Boggs Sigmund, the vibrant mayor of Princeton, spoke aloud her poem, apparently for the first time, about the loss of her father, Louisiana Congressman Hale Boggs, on a flight with a bush pilot in Alaska. It was called "Mount Boggs: Elegy for an Unburied Father."

> In October of another year,
> He disappeared.
> His plane was swallowed up, so
> *Newsweek* said.
> The gaunt land gulped him down
> And nothing has been found.

Everyone present wept. Congressman Boggs was never found, and Barbara's mother, Lindy Boggs, came to be elected to his seat from New Orleans in Congress. She was a champion of appropriate education for bright students, among other causes. In her vibrant eighties, she was named United States Ambassador to the Vatican.

Some years later, we were driving Barbara back to Princeton from Northern New Jersey. She had contracted cancer of the eye six years earlier and wore various spiffy eye patches to make light of the anguish. Already weak from cancer of the second eye, she said she would like to put together a little book of her poetry. Would we help her?

Barbara Boggs Sigmund,
mayor of the Borough of Princeton,
1990.

At that time her sister Cokie Roberts, a journalist for NPR and ABC, had a daughter, Rebecca, studying at Princeton (Class of 1992). She gathered poems from behind the dresser, under the bed, here and there—pulling together, too, the wrenching poetry Barbara wrote during this fatal illness.

Working with Anne Reeves of the Arts Council of Princeton, we had a budget of $6,000 for the book. I approached Bill Sword and read to him two of the poems. He wept and offered to give the full six thousand. I said I would accept one thousand. Then I talked to Susie Wilson, our neighbor, and she said he would give the remaining five. I said we would accept one. The sixth person I asked was Tommy Boggs, a younger brother of Barbara who lived in Washington. Yes.

The handsome book, *An Unfinished Life*—in purple and red, Barbara's colors—was printed. The book signing occurred on September 19, 1990, at the Institute for Advanced Study, where Barbara inscribed hundreds of copies at a festive event the vision of which lingers yet in the heart.

The inscription to us read, "To Scott and Hella, who had the vision this book needed to come to birth, the persistence to see it through, and the love to do it all. Much love and many thanks, Barbara."

She died at fifty-one less than a month later on October 10, 1990.

When her beloved husband and scholar Paul Sigmund died on April 27, 2014, at the age of eighty-five, his life was celebrated by his family in the Princeton University Chapel. In the program was this poem from Barbara's book:

Breath of Life

Paul breathed so sweetly
on me last night.
Dear mate of half my life,
Purveyor of knowledge and love,
Always giving me room
　to grow
　　　to soar
　　　to breathe.
We have been one flesh, one mind,
Would that we could also be one breath.

POETRY HEAVEN

Octavio Paz, poet-diplomat, at the Dodge Poetry Festival in 1988,
who said, "The mission of poetry is to give eyes to mankind in order that
the simple acts of life can establish their interior dignity and mystery."
In 1990, he received the Nobel Prize in Literature.

Where did it start? Poetry has ever been part of the human experience, part of every language and culture on Earth. The oral tradition, honored on every continent, is where it started. For untold centuries, the singer, the poet, the sage carried the history, lore, and mythology. No language is better or worse for the making and saying of great poetry—whether an epic like the Old Norse Edda or a Japanese haiku.

In seeking to make the case for poetry with our capable board at the Geraldine R. Dodge Foundation, I showed a wheel of philanthropy in America in fall 1985, revealing 7 percent devoted to the arts. We were then giving 21 percent to the arts. Our other areas of giving were education at the high school level, public interest/critical issues, the welfare of animals, and local projects.

I showed a second wheel of the national breakdown within the arts, where only 2 percent went for "writing and poetry." The assumption perhaps is that poetry, like mathematics, can be done with a pad and a pencil. Our thought was that, underfunded and undervalued, poetry might be an interesting niche, if strategically engaged.

I approached two people I had in mind to take on this initiative part time. They were unavailable. Alicia Ostriker suggested I talk with Jim Haba, who taught at Glassboro State College (now Rowan University). I met with Jim in his comfortable home in Hillsborough on the last day of December 1985. As the sun was slipping from view in the west, his wood-burning stove warmed the room. Jim and his wife Erica's cats purred nearby. I offered him the charge of elevating poetry and poets through a major festival—and lifting the role of teachers of poetry in the schools—a seemingly impossible tightrope which Jim, it turned out, was able to pull off with devotion and élan.

Howard Nemerov conversing with Scott and Hella at
Dodge Poetry Festival, Waterloo Village, New Jersey, 1990.

We wrote every high school English teacher in New Jersey to get their thoughts on how we could be of help to them in teaching poetry. We received a mailbag of enthusiastic responses to our questions. Emily Style of Madison High School wrote, "I want to encourage you to present poetry and its connection to thinking and teaching, so those who attend [the planned Dodge Poetry Festival] can envision the classroom as a poetic place." Jim and I chose fifteen teachers whom we invited to our home on a Saturday in spring 1986. Each teacher brought a poem close to his or her heart. The first hour was given to hearing those poems of fantastic reach and grace. Hella prepared a delicious salmon lunch for all.

We had already met in New York with Stanley Kunitz and Galway Kinnell, who were excited by the idea of a poetry festival and urged us to create something beyond what was out there then. From the first I felt we should be in a rural location (away from the coiled left-brains of academia), namely Waterloo Village, which was shaped and nurtured by Percy Leach and Lou Gulandi, interior designers who created this enchanted place over many years, in northern New Jersey.

Stanley Kunitz and Lucille Clifton relishing each other's company at the Festival.

The Dodge Foundation invited poets of immense range and originality from the outset. The joy, energy, and laughter of the festivals at Waterloo Village was reflected in crowds of up to 20,000 for the four-day biennial festival and in three film series by Bill Moyers—*The Power of the Word*, *The Language of Life*, and *Fooling with Words* (the first two with David Grubin)—and *Poetry Heaven* with Juan Mandelbaum. Those PBS programs reached over 50 million people, and that may be part of the reason that poetry is flourishing (comparatively speaking) in our culture today.

Jim ran engaging workshops every spring, "Clearing the Spring, Tending the Fountain" (a line from Robert Frost) for English teachers, some of whom were becoming published poets. Dodge poets visited schools statewide on a regular basis. With the assistance of a teacher advisory committee, Jim wrote the teacher guides prepared by WNET 13 to accompany the Moyers poetry series.

In the packed big green tent at Waterloo in 2002, Billy Collins said it was supposed that poets came readily to the Dodge Festival for the camaraderie, but, in his view, it was for Jim's ineffable introductions that somehow, inexplicably, floated the poet to the podium. These introductions, without a note, revealed Jim's innate grasp of the poet and the nature of his or her work.

Kurtis Lamkin, poet, singer, musician on the kora: "If you treat us like equals, we will treat you like kings." Dodge Poetry Festival, 1996.

These introductions are one of his signatures. Another is the choice and courtship of the poets themselves. That correspondence will one day be of interest to scholars.

Although Bill Moyers did three major series on PBS from the Dodge Poetry Festivals, in none of the titles is the word "poetry."

In 1996, filmmaker Juan Mandelbaum put a microphone in front of one festival participant, Philadelphia poet Nzadi Keita, and asked, "What is going on here?"

"Oh, this is poetry heaven!" she replied.

That became the title of his three-hour series and this vignette.

Bill Moyers begins his book, *Fooling with Words: A Celebration of Poets and Their Craft* (1999) as follows:

"Praise the bridge that carried you over," advises a character in *The Heir-in-Law*. So I wish to thank the many people whose collaboration brought this book to safe passage. Scott McVay and the trustees of the Geraldine R. Dodge Foundation head the list, because without them

Journalist Bill Moyers greets Bettye Spinner, a teacher-poet, at the gala launch of The Power of the Word, *a six-part series on poetry on PBS, 1989.*

there would have been no Dodge Poetry Festival, and without the festival there would be no book. Scott has now retired as executive director of the foundation, but if the poetry world could afford twenty-one-gun salutes for its heroes, there would have been no end of deafening praise in his honor when he stepped down after twenty-three years."

On October 24, 2014, at the fifteenth biennial Dodge Poetry Festival in Newark—the day when 4,000 high school students from fourteen states embraced poetry—Richard Blanco was asked by one student, "When did you feel you were a poet?"

Blanco, who was born of Cuban parents and was chosen as the poet for President Obama's second inauguration on January 8, 2013, replied that it was when he read William Carlos Williams's "The Red Wheelbarrow." Interesting! At the first festival in October 1986, shortly after Blanco graduated from high school, that poem was written in white on a red T-shirt, now a rare item. A few weeks later, I was wearing that shirt as Hella and I walked across a meadow in Madagascar when we came upon a home where a red wheelbarrow stood glazed with rain water with white chickens scurrying about. A woman was tossing the chickens some grain. I peeled off the shirt and gave it to her. She knew some English, but the small gift may have surprised her.

Scott at enchanted podium, Dodge Poetry Festival, 1988.

Poetry heaven can occur almost anywhere.

LOOK FOR A SIGN

Joseph Bruchac, Abenaki poet and storyteller, who said, "Sometimes, I say, just trust your heart/and if it's right, a sign may come." From "On Lenape Land," 1992.

A young man, John Kraft, who worked at Waterloo Village in northern New Jersey, had over several years built a little village reminiscent of the Lenape Indians who used to live in those parts.

John was not uninformed since his father, Herbert C. Kraft (1927–2000), had been the lead scholar on the Lenape for years and a professor at Seton Hall University. Yet the young man worried that the village might be less than authentic.

Therefore, when Joseph Bruchac, a poet and songwriter who is part Abenaki, came to the Dodge Poetry Festival in 1992, John asked me if Joe might accompany him on a one-mile walk to the site near the lake.

"By all means."

We were walking along, and John explained that thousands of school kids came every year, and he was eager to do the right thing by the Lenape and by the children.

Upon arrival and first glimpse, John asked Joe Bruchac what he thought.

"Look for a sign," he replied.

At that moment a black dot formed on the horizon, and it grew in size as it hurtled through the air toward us. That dot became a bird. The bird grabbed a limb of a sandalwood tree and spun around so rapidly that it flipped off and landed on a branch of a tree beside us.

It was an osprey, rarely seen in this inland area.

The next day, just before I introduced Bruchac in the big green tent, I asked if I might mention what had happened the day earlier.

Joe said he had written a poem called "On Lenape Land," and he read it before a spellbound audience. He began:

> Sometimes, I say, just trust your heart
>
> And, if it's right, a sign may come.

Eighteen years later, Hella and I created a Poetry Trail in Princeton on the rolling fifty-five-acre tract of the former Robert Wood Johnson estate, which had been saved from McMansion development through efforts by the D&R Greenway Land Trust and is known as Greenway Meadows. It is directly behind the renovated barn that serves as the Trust's headquarters.

At the dedication in October 2010, six of the poets on the trail of forty-eight signs—half of which are poems by women—were present to read their poems, which saluted some aspect of the natural world. Other of the poets later walked the Poetry Trail: Naomi Shihab Nye, Coleman Barks, Rita Dove (whose husband Fred Viebahn made a touching video of her walk), and Jane Hirshfield, who came on the day of her reading in the Princeton University Chapel with the Paul Winter Consort.

Joseph Bruchac and his son, Jesse, who is fluent in Abenaki, walked the trail with flutes and drums, other poets, and waves of neighbors and friends on April 15, 2011. Miraculously, David Kelly Crow captured the entire event on a video called *Transplanted Trees*. That evening as Joe and his son spoke to a packed crowd at D&R Greenway, Joe said something that will ring in our hearts until our last day: "The poems here are like transplanted trees—they will continue to grow."

In a way, one of Joe's poems, "Prayer," found early on the trail, captures the essence of the respect and mystery and awe of the natural world that we sought in choosing the poems, each placard's design, and the sighting and sequence of the poems.

The Poetry Trail was one of five trails described in *WLT (World Literature Today)*, January–February 2013, in a section called "Finding Poetry Under the Open Sky," organized by Pattiann Rogers.

Therein is quoted Diane Churchill, an artist and master teacher (who created *Guide*, the artwork that graces the cover of this book) who wrote: "The Poetry Trail stands out most strongly for the understated beauty and homage to both the word and the land. They were married so well. While reading each poem, the words seemed to flow out and into the landscape, altering it slightly. The long gazes seem to attach to thoughts about the poems. If I lived nearby, I would be there often and it would be like an ongoing liturgy of experiencing the sacred."

WHERE ARE THE WOMEN POETS?

It was a time when the only good poet was a dead poet. Dead poets were safer. After all, you did not know what a living poet might do next.

A British filmmaker, Lawrence Pitkethly, managed to get a large sum of money (some $13 million), mainly from the National Endowment for the Humanities, for a thirteen-part PBS series titled *Voices and Visions*. It was seven years in the making. Each hour was devoted to a major (deceased) American poet: Robert Frost, Ezra Pound, Langston Hughes, Walt Whitman, Hart Crane, William Carlos Williams, Emily Dickinson, Marianne Moore, T. S. Eliot, Wallace Stevens, Elizabeth Bishop, Robert Lowell, and Sylvia Plath.

I asked Pitkethly if he would consider making a one-hour film of the first Dodge Poetry Festival in October 1986, at Waterloo Village. He said yes. I asked how much he would charge for the task. Being awash in money, he said, $25,000. I said I thought our trustees might be willing to contribute $50,000 to do it. It turned out to cost $75,000, and Pitkethly absorbed the difference.

The first Dodge Poetry Festival, generously encouraged by Stanley Kunitz and Galway Kinnell, turned out to be a resounding success over a three-day period.

When Pitkethly invited Jim Haba and me to see the rough cut of the documentary at the New Jersey Network studios in Newark, both of us watched in dumbstruck amazement. When the hour was finished, neither of us spoke. The rough cut lacked a single woman poet. Maybe three minutes went by. Jim had recruited some top-flight women poets, but they were wholly absent from the proposed film. Among them were Gwendolyn Brooks, Ruth Stone, Sharon Olds, and Sonia Sanchez.

When we finally found our voices, we asked that the women's voices be heard too. From the cutting-room floor, Pitkethly dredged up three, who were given cameo appearances in a film called *Poets in Person*.

Afterward, I suggested that Jim scour the New York area for the finest filmmaker he could find. That turned out to be David Grubin, who in turn recruited Bill Moyers for the Dodge Poetry Festival in 1988 that led to *The Power of the Word*, *The Language of Life*, and *Fooling with Words*, PBS series over the next dozen years that featured scores of amazing women poets.

A SMALL SCRIBBLE ON
A FORMIDABLE WOMAN POET

today's *New York Times* contains
the fuller story of Adrienne,*
her father raising her
as a literary prodigy
who climbed from formalist constructions
to battering the wall of oppressions,
800,000 books sold,
no mention of the galloping
west coast sea shell poem,
cramming her vibrant life
into a compact pulsing obit
is an art, too,

yet what I remember is
that morning on the stage
in the big green tent at Waterloo
when she perched on
a large wicker throne chair,
and a lanky preying mantis
moved about its rounded top
& the clever filmmakers
were trying out the long arching
spidery new camera which
they worried might intrude
on the poet's delivery ...

well, Adrianne played to it,

cosseted it,

flirted with it,

did a little dyad,

smiled sweetly,

while saying her smiting stuff

railing at the inequities,

yes, a preying mantis

& a subtle new amplifier

for a face and heart

of trenchant grace.

March 29, 2012

*Adrienne Rich

*Adrienne Rich at Dodge Poetry Festival in 1994, said, "I have never
believed that poetry is an escape from history, and I do not think
it is more, or less, necessary than food, shelter, health, education,
decent working conditions. It is as necessary."*

WHEN ONE HAS LIVED A LONG TIME ALONE

*Galway Kinnell, poet and guide, reading at first Dodge
Poetry Festival in the church at Waterloo Village, 1986.*

It was, I think, at the third Dodge Poetry Festival in 1990 when
Galway Kinnell stood at the podium in the big green tent at Waterloo
Village. It was a glorious day. Not only was nearly every one of the 2,000
seats occupied, but the crowd had also spilled generously out across the
lawn.

Galway stood there smiling. A hank of his hair hung down. His
shoelaces were untied. He said he was going to read a poem from his new
collection, *When One Has Lived a Long Time Alone.* He held up the book
with its beautiful front-of-jacket painting detail of *Orchard* by Gustav
Klimt, an inviting expanse of meadow and orchard leading to hills.

I looked around the tent and thought that perhaps one hundred
women were thinking, "Well, the poor fellow, I could be such a comfort
to him."

Galway cleared his throat, saying again he was reading a poem from *When One Has Lived a Long Time Alone*, called "Oatmeal."

I eat oatmeal for breakfast.

I make it on the hot plate and put skimmed milk on it.

I eat it alone.

I am aware it is not good to eat oatmeal alone.

Its consistency is such that it is better for your mental health if
  somebody eats it with you.

That is why I often think up an imaginary companion to have
  breakfast with.

Possibly it is even worse to eat oatmeal with an imaginary companion.

Nevertheless, yesterday morning, I ate my oatmeal with John Keats.

Keats said I was absolutely right to invite him: due to its glutinous
  texture, gluey lumpishness, hint of slime, and unusual willingness
  to disintegrate, oatmeal must never be eaten alone.

He said that in his opinion it is perfectly OK to eat it with an
  imaginary companion,

and he himself had enjoyed memorable porridges with Edmund
  Spenser and John Milton.

The poem concludes:

For supper tonight I am going to have a baked potato left over from
  lunch.

I am aware that a leftover baked potato is damp, slippery, and
  simultaneously gummy and crumbly,

and therefore I'm going to invite Patrick Kavanagh to join me.

Patrick Kavanagh? Hmm. There's a clue perhaps to why we were
ever surprised to see Galway with his shoelaces untied. In spring 2004,
we traveled with a group of Princeton alumni through Ireland with
Paul Muldoon and Michael Cadden. Every morning, Paul or Micheal
offered a sterling talk on one Irish poet or writer or another—John Keats,
George Bernard Shaw, Samuel Beckett. One day we saw the tombstone of
Patrick Kavanagh, and it read something like, "You will see me along the
hedgerows playing with the children, shoelaces untied."

Galway does connect with an audience, whether reading Whitman,
whom he sometimes seems to embody, or Rilke, whom he has translated,
or his own work.

But I don't think the dear women who would provide some solace
to this pied piper should think he has in any way led a lonely life. See his
2005 poem on Shelley, which begins:

When I was twenty the one true
free spirit I had heard of was Shelley,
Shelley who wrote tracts advocating
atheism, free love, the emancipation
of women, the abolition of wealth and class,
and poems on the bliss of romantic love,
Shelley, who, I learned later, perhaps
almost too late, remarried Harriet,
then pregnant with their second child,
and a few months later ran off with Mary,
already pregnant herself, bringing
with them Mary's stepsister Claire,
who very likely also became his lover,

and in this malaise a trois, which Shelley
had imagined would be "a paradise of exiles,"
they lived, along with the spectre of Harriet,
who drowned herself in the Serpentine …

On the first page of the *New York Times* of October 30, 2014, is a three-column photo of Galway Kinnell, reporting his death at eighty-seven on October 28 in Sheffield, Vermont. Inside is a full-bodied obituary that honors his life and work. So many thoughts pounce to mind. I remember in the late 1980s suggesting in a detailed letter that Princeton University award him an honorary degree. The secretary of the university, enthused by the reminder of his standing in the world of poetry, had him appointed to the board of trustees. That was an idea that did not recognize who he truly was, and Kinnell quit after a couple of years. I remember, too, his devotion to Walt Whitman was so acute that not only did he memorize long passages of *Leaves of Grass*, but he even went so far as to "improve" on Whitman's own text. Finally, Hella and I recall his kind invitation to celebrate at his home in New York City Stanley Kunitz's birthday in his nineties. Lastly, he was the moderator of an evening saluting Stanley's hundredth birthday at an event sponsored by Poets House, at which Stanley recited two of his poems.

As mentor, guide, poet, and pathfinder, few have done more in our time for poetry and its infinite possibilities than Galway Kinnell.

SORRY, THIS IS A PRIVATE PARTY

Gwendolyn Brooks, beloved poet from Chicago who encouraged children to write poetry, 1986.

The year was 1996. The place was Waterloo Village, New Jersey.

Through great good luck, Gwendolyn Brooks (1917–2000) accepted our invitation to return to the Dodge Poetry Festival, where she was again a hit. She was an American Poet Laureate at the time when the post was called Consultant in Poetry to the Library of Congress. She also encouraged and welcomed the poetry of children and often sent them a check for $25, $50, or $100 from her home in Chicago.

I had invited her to a small luncheon with a couple of trustees and other poets in the Meetinghouse.

As she approached the door by the kitchen and started to enter, an assistant cook went over and told her—a small black woman—"Sorry, this is a private party."

The renowned poet turned and walked away. I ran after her, apologized, and invited her to come back please. She said, politely but firmly, "No thanks."

A few months later, Brooks was back in New Jersey for a reading at the Montclair Art Museum. Over dinner, a white foundation person described at length what it was like to be a black person in the city of Newark. Brooks, who had chronicled with immense originality the African American experience in poetry, listened.

My heart sank a second time.

At the festival, Gwendolyn Brooks was one of the star attractions when she spoke her poetry in a compelling rhythm. "We Real Cool" goes like this:

The Pool Players
Seven at the Golden Shovel

We real cool. We
Left school. We

Lurk late. We
Strike straight. We

Sing sin. We
Thin gin. We

Jazz June. We
Die soon.

And "The Mother," which begins:

> Abortions will not let you forget.
> You remember the children you got that you did not get,
> The damp small pulps with a little or with no hair,
> The singers and workers that never handled the air.
> You will never neglect or beat
> Them, or silence or buy with a sweet.
> You will never wind up the sucking-thumb
> Or scuttle off ghosts that come.
> You will never leave them, controlling your luscious sigh,
> Return for a snack of them, with gobbling mother-eye.

Among hundreds of memorable lines is her thought, from *Windy Place*:

> To be in love
> Is to touch things with a lighter hand.

THEY DID NOT ASK AGAIN

Between 1979 and 1998, Hella and I traveled to Washington, DC, every June for the Presidential Scholars, 141 graduating high school seniors, a boy and a girl from each state, fifteen at large, six from overseas, and twenty in the arts, theater, dance, music, writing, and visual arts. The high point of the week for them was going to the South Lawn of the White House where the president welcomed and spoke to them, their parents, and a beloved teacher.

We were there because the Dodge Foundation gave every Presidential Scholar $1,000 to pursue a dream of their choice. Typically, one of my trustees accompanied us, and, when presenting the checks, spoke to the scholars along with myself. It was an exhilarating week punctuated by a carefully choreographed series of encounters.

Working closely with the Commission on Presidential Scholars, I was asked for suggestions of speakers. I recommended Rita Dove, who was named Poet Laureate of the United States in 1993, the youngest ever (she had read at the 1992 Dodge Poetry Festival). Dove, a professor at the University of Virginia, read in 1994 to the scholars who were thrilled, and she personally inscribed a copy of her book *Selected Poems* to each one.

The Commission staff was pleased, too, and asked, "Whom do you recommend for 1995?"

"Another African American," I said, "Lucille Clifton, hailing from Buffalo, mother of six who taught, among other places, at St. Mary's College of Maryland."

Clifton was the only poet invited to every Dodge Poetry Festival from 1986 until her death in 2010. This, too, was a blockbuster success, as

Clifton's words, line by line, connected with this new crop of Presidential Scholars. Clifton inscribed a copy of her book *The Book of Light* to each in turn.

Somewhat eagerly, my suggestion for 1996 was awaited. I suggested Sharon Olds, an audacious, soft-spoken poet who was a colleague of Galway Kinnell at New York University in the writing program. We shipped off a carton of her latest collection of poetry, *The Father*. In Washington, apparently the first book fell open to her poem "The Pope's Penis," and the carton came sailing back like a boomerang.

They did not ask again.

Sharon Olds received the Pulitzer Prize for Poetry in 2013.

STAG NIGHT

In 1975, I accepted an invitation to speak at the Explorers Club in New York about my second expedition to study, record, and film the rare bowhead whale in the Alaskan Arctic. The highlights of that expedition were captured in a documentary by Bill Mason for the National Film Board of Canada, *In Search of the Bowhead Whale*.

A fortnight before the date, someone from the Explorers Club called to say that the evening would be a "stag night"—that is, no women were allowed.

I was upset since Judy Collins had recently completed a film about her piano teacher in Denver in homage to her influence on Judy's life and career. She had kindly given me a private screening and was looking forward to seeing the bowhead film at the Explorers Club.

I said I would cancel the event since word of a male-only audience was unappealing in principle, and it was counter to an invitation I had made.

The caller said that the club was in the process of eliminating the stag lecture, and this was to be one of the last. I demurred, saying I would prefer not to give the talk. The caller then proposed that I give the talk twice, a couple of weeks apart. This seemed an acceptable solution, and the second date was one that worked for Judy's calendar.

The next time I spoke at the Explorers Club was on December 17, 2012, when I read eighteen poems about natural history from *Whales Sing and Other Exuberances* (2012). Since a fair chunk of the contents of that book celebrates both the sciences and the arts, traditionally separated in universities yet incredibly alive and exciting at their intersections, the event provided a happy echo across forty years.

Thank goodness it wasn't a stag night, since all the books sold that evening were bought by women.

Postscript

Judy Collins used Frank Watlington's tapes of humpback whale songs recorded off Bermuda in her rendering of the traditional "Farewell to Tarwathie" in 1970.

THAT WHICH IS ALIVE I PRAISE*

*William Durden and Scott on day of Bill's inauguration
as president of Dickinson College, 1999.*

For sixteen years, William Grady Durden led the Center for Talented Youth (CTY) at Johns Hopkins University—the most comprehensive effort in the country to develop and nurture the academic talents of youth in America. Throughout his tenure, from time to time, the Dodge Foundation assisted path-breaking research on the identification and nurturance of talent at CTY, perhaps the most neglected segment in schooling. For example, it turns out that a child should move ahead scholastically in line with her proclivities, not in the rote sequence of grades.

During the last eleven years of that time, Durden served as a representative of our Department of State, advising many governments on developing programs for bright youth from Germany to Argentina, Brazil, Japan, Malaysia—sixty countries in all.

Dr. Durden is the senior author of a book, *Smart Kids: How Academic Talents are Developed and Nurtured in America*, with the late Arne Tangherlini, which I reviewed at length. The book examines the lives of nine youth and the predicaments that their particular talents and personalities posed for their parents, their schools, and themselves.

Consider five telling, topical sentences:

- Starting with the first indefinite gropings, a child's business is to learn.
- For the child, the drive to mastery is as keen as the need for food.
- By nature, all children are intellectuals, in that they are perpetually concerned with making new discoveries.
- A talent will rarely come to fruition if the environment is not geared to its unfolding.
- Schools must be willing to adopt flexible policies which allow students to forge ahead at their own pace, especially in the areas where their capabilities and interests are greatest.

In 1999, Bill Durden became the twenty-seventh president of Dickinson College in Carlyle, Pennsylvania, where he had graduated in 1971. He invited me to speak before him at his inauguration—a true honor.

In 2013, Dr. Durden—a Fulbright Scholar to Freiberg University with a PhD in German Literature from Johns Hopkins University— joyously relinquished the helm of his beloved alma mater. He is in demand as a speaker here and abroad.

Beyond his recent affirmation of Malcolm Gladwell's powerful critique of college ranking ("The Order of Things" in *The New Yorker* February 14, 2011), is one on "Notes to a 21st Century Student":

• Attempt to meet and speak with the great people of your time—approach them civilly and in an informed manner. Ask them to share their advice about how to live an engaged life professionally and personally. Ask them about their passion and motivation for what they do.

• Never underestimate or belittle any experience you have had in your life. Think about the knowledge and skills you have gained. You never know what might come in handy in another context.

• Don't worry about having a life plan—rather be prepared for chance and when it occurs, recognize and engage it.

• Seek a tough mentor—not a "yes-person" who artificially builds up your self-esteem. And in general beware of sycophants offering you unearned praise.

• Leadership is often narrative—storytelling—with a protagonist, a plot, and a foil.

• Boredom and repetition are essential parts of leadership, as leadership consists primarily of telling a story again and again and in such a compelling manner that others want to be a part of it. Each repetition must sound as if it is being delivered for the first time with passion and urgency.

• Do not underestimate the role of passion in your profession—you must believe strongly in what you pursue, and it must be far bigger than yourself.

I am convinced that the most undervalued and neglected segment of the school population are the bright, probing, questioning kids. They need to be challenged, guided, and encouraged. In my experience no one has done this with greater élan and success than Bill Durden. He was the lead apostle for the gifted, building on Julian Stanley's founding of the program at Johns Hopkins dating back to the 1970s.

Perhaps it is not overstating the matter to cite George Bernard Shaw:

"This is the true joy in life ... being used for a purpose recognized by yourself as a mighty one ... being a force of Nature instead of a feverish selfish little clod of ailments and grievances complaining that the world will not devote itself to making you happy... I am of the opinion that my life belongs to the whole community and as long as I live it is my privilege to do for it whatever I can."

Das Lebendige will ich preisen.
— Goethe, *"Selige Sehnsucht,"* from *Selected Poems,*
    Princeton University Press, 1983

WHY REACH FOR EXCELLENCE?

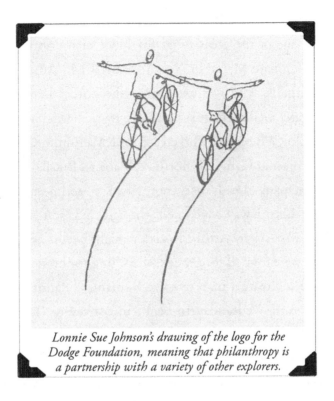

*Lonnie Sue Johnson's drawing of the logo for the
Dodge Foundation, meaning that philanthropy is
a partnership with a variety of other explorers.*

I should have expected nothing less than something singular from Edwin Schlossberg, the author of *Einstein and Beckett: A Record of an Imaginary Discussion between Albert Einstein and Samuel Beckett*, each of whom broke the mold for science and literature, respectively. His book *The Philosopher's Game* is arrestingly original about the turning point in the lives of 100 thinkers. The reader is invited to choose the pivotal quotation by these individuals.

In the late 1970s, Schlossberg proposed the idea for a retreat covering the question "Why push for excellence when some say let's go for a beer?" Ed and I planned it at his home near Becket, Massachusetts, and invited ten brilliant young achievers to wrestle for three days with the nature of the quest for excellence.

Hella and I drove Joni Mitchell, the singer-songwriter-artist, up from her home in a warehouse of Lower Manhattan and came to feel her questing spirit. (Her lilting "Big Yellow Taxi" song was hailed by Bill McKibben as one of the great songs for biodiversity on the eve of the huge People's Climate March in New York in 2014.) Among the group was Lynn Margulis, who was examining the border between non-life and life; Margaret Geller, the first person to map a swatch of the cosmos; and Tom Lovejoy, a biologist who created the Minimum Critical Size of Ecosystems project at Camp 41 north of Manaus, Brazil.

Each participant already had more than a lifetime's achievements behind her or him. I was concerned, though, that something like the story of *The Call-Girls* by Arthur Koestler might occur. Ten high-priced globe-trotters were invited for a week, according to the story, to a chalet in Switzerland to create a map to solve humanity's daunting problems. It took them until Wednesday to begin to convey to the others their "specialness." So in advance we mailed to every participant a copy of *The Call-Girls*, as well as a dossier of background data on each of their fellow participants, to deflect that possibility. That little worry was unwarranted

It was as engaging as any meeting I can remember, but it was the better, far better, for the presence of Joni Mitchell. She was so frank, guileless, and unabashedly revealing about a man who stalked her for months that she made the rest of us peel off the carefully encrusted persona with which we confronted the world. Each participant described the nature and character of their motivation (or joyous obsession).

That gathering of ten young accomplished pioneers in ten different fields reminds us that individuals can and do transform our thinking and patterns of perception. Therefore, early schooling is important. Allowing youth to proceed at their own pace and among peers who read and do and are full of questions creates a world attuned to solving problems and making music.

In the sphere of philanthropy, one seeks to back persons and not-for-profit organizations who are reaching for excellence. By hearing from young accomplished achievers across a span of fields, our mission was informed and reinforced. This exploration enabled me to convey more vividly to my board the nature of projects by gifted scientists, artists, and others.

Postscript

Jacqueline Kennedy Onassis kindly invited us to Ed's wedding to Caroline Kennedy on July 19, 1986. We were then in China with the first cohort of Chinese language teachers and were sorry to miss the happy occasion.

WHAT A GIFT!

So many points on the trajectory of Renaissance man Edwin Schlossberg's life are interesting.

For instance, the choice and explication of his dissertation at Columbia on Albert Einstein and Samuel Becket (published as *Einstein and Beckett: A Record of an Imaginary Discussion between Albert Einstein and Samuel Beckett*) was a master stroke.

Or, consider the gloriously provocative book, *The Philosopher's Game* (1977), containing one-page accounts of the lives of 100 individuals from the river of human history that focused on the turning point in each of those lives. At that juncture, whether it was Jesus or Mohammed, St. Joan of Arc or Margaret Sanger, Copernicus or Darwin, Sappho or Sojourner Truth, Bach or Lao Tzu, Ed offered three quotations for the reader to consider. One turned the page and found "CORRECT!" beside the right one, and the other two citations were also correctly attributed.

Or, who came to greet René Magritte (blue sky, clouds, homburg …) when he arrived at the New York airport? Ed—no one else, just Ed.

But I will zoom in here on one event, the eightieth birthday of Buckminster Fuller in 1975, whom Ed chose to honor with a singular and elegant gift. Bucky was broke and out of favor. Ed had worked for him after graduate school and admired his energy, imagination, and application. Fuller was undeniably one of the key innovators of the twentieth century.

Well in advance of the date, Ed sat Bucky down to sketch the evolution of the cosmos all the way to the tetrahedron.

When Bucky was young, he wanted to be a cartoonist, but that path was not encouraged. Yet he drew with force, grace, and grit. Bucky's version of how things spun out was done in twelve panels.

Ed had secured commitments from fifteen museums nationwide for $15,000 each to receive one of a limited edition of these drawings.

Ed then arranged to have the twelve works printed on superb triangular paper (chosen by lithographer Tatiana Grossman) plus a thirteenth containing a poem called "Epilever" by Ed in homage to his mentor. Ed said he didn't want to call it "Epilogue" since that would seem too close to the end.

We were lucky to be present on Bucky Fuller's eightieth birthday for the exhibition of the thirteen triangular panels at a gallery on 57th Street. Ed presented Bucky with a birthday check for $225,000. Bucky spoke forcefully and at length.

I said quietly to Ed afterward, "He didn't thank you."

Ed said, "I was thanking him."

Postscript

In 2010, at the Shanghai World Expo, Ed Schlossberg and his team created a $2 billion structure inspired by the reverberating thought of Chuang Tzu (369–266 BC):

"I do not know whether I was then a man dreaming I was a butterfly or whether I am now a butterfly dreaming I am a man."

The vast interactive exhibition engaged folks while walking through a sonic and luminous environment inspired by the mystery of a thought older than two millennia.

I'M PERFECT!

Sometime in 1976, a woman called from Dobbs Ferry, New York, and said: "Not since da Vinci ..."

I asked, "What?"

"Not since da Vinci has there been such a one as our son."

"How so?" said I. She said her husband and she had a child of immense gifts, though only six months old, and could I come by for a visit? I suggested we stay in touch.

Since she was somehow aware of my long-standing interest in bright kids, the mother called periodically, every year or half year, to report on Marnin's growing precocity.

Finally, at about the five-year mark in 1981, she said he was using Omar Khayyam Moore's talking typewriter and taking a course at Columbia and another at MIT. She repeated her plea, "When are you coming for a visit?"

I said, "How about this Sunday—does that work for you?"

"Yes! What time?"

"How about noon?"

We were returning from Harvard, where our daughter Cynthia was studying, and could drive through Dobbs Ferry about that time.

The mother had mentioned that both she and her husband had curtailed their professional lives by half so that each of them could give forty hours a week to their son. They had turned their living room into a floor-to-ceiling library with all kinds of prompts and tools for learning.

At noon we tapped on the door. The woman greeted us and ushered us into her home.

Hella, who by then had been teaching mathematics for over two decades, greeted the little curly-headed fellow with a smiling "How are you?"

"I'm perfect!" he replied.

Well, it was downhill from there. He sat in the middle of the living room. He interrupted our conversation, minute by minute. He pounded on O. K. Moore's talking typewriter for a minute or two and then abandoned it.

The way the device works is that if you happen to hit, say, three letters such as C-A-T, in sequence, the word "CAT" appears on a screen and a reassuring voice says "CAT!" The keys are color-coded so that the toddler learns to touch-type as he learns to read and write.

Hella then engaged him in number games, since in arithmetic and mathematics there is a general trajectory or sequence of learning. After an hour there, we politely took our leave. I asked Hella how far along the boy was in math. "About the second grade."

Three or four years later, the Dodge Foundation put a little money ($12,500) behind a course for unusually precocious kids in Metuchen public schools that was taught by Lisa Garrison, who later served as a program officer at the foundation.

The course had eight or ten children from the area, plus one from out-of-state—our Westchester lad.

Lisa reported that working with these inquiring kids was a thrill—with one exception. This spoiled kid, ever craving attention, constantly disrupted the class with his "acting out" and attention-seeking antics.

We are still waiting for his name to turn up in the newspaper.

I'M NO BETTER THAN THE REST OF THEM

One meets some unforgettable characters when engaged in giving money away. Early in my tenure with the Robert Sterling Clark Foundation in New York City, perhaps in 1972 or 1973, a gentleman appeared on my doorstep by the name of Freddie Jonas (George Edward Jonas—1897–1978). The Clark Foundation made grants in the New York City area, and I undertook an initiative to support liberal arts colleges that made resources available to their local communities, which we called Building Bridges Across the Moats.

Jonas had become wealthy through his father's felt hat business and wished to channel his capacity on behalf of promising disadvantaged youth. He established in honor of his father the Louis August Jonas Foundation and founded a camp in Rhinebeck, New York, by the name of Camp Rising Sun in 1930.

Freddie Jonas radiated the spirit of giving, the spirit of philanthropy. His mission was to develop in promising young people from diverse backgrounds a lifelong commitment to sensitive and responsible leadership for the betterment of their communities and the world. His approach was to invite bright poor students from abroad and an equal number from this country. Those from abroad came from many different countries. Prior campers from a given country helped determine who came next.

"What is your role at the camp?" I asked.

He said, "I am the janitor. I am not important, but the idea of fostering an appreciation of diversity and friendship across boundaries of color, religion, gender, culture, and nationality matters."

He was also interested in expanding intellectual horizons and heightening artistic sensibilities. Among the alumni of the camp is singer-songwriter Pete Seeger; Neil Rudenstine, president emeritus of Harvard; Sidney Lumet, filmmaker; and a host of luminaries from abroad, including Tina Gharavi, an Iranian American filmmaker, and Roxanne Krystalli, a conflict management professional working in Egypt, Uganda, Colombia, and Guatemala. The compelling idea of Camp Rising Sun lives to this day, propelled by the spirit of Freddie Jonas.

He explained that the new campers gathered in the summer on a Sunday evening. One Sunday, there was a kid who seemed a bit full of himself. So, on Monday morning, Freddie took the kid aside, noting that this was a camp for promising kids but that he seemed special beyond the rest. Hmm, thought the camper. As a result, Freddie explained, he was being given a special assignment to peel a mound of potatoes for supper. That took all day.

The next day, Tuesday, Freddie took the lad aside, explaining that they were having salad that evening, and a heap of onions needed to be sliced and diced. The lad went at it, weeping all the way. On Wednesday, Freddie approached him again, and the young man declared, "I'm no better than the rest of them!" and joined the other campers.

IS THIS IDEA PLAUSIBLE? WILL IT WORK?

In her senior year at Princeton in spring, 1989, Wendy Kopp called me and asked if we could meet to explore an idea she planned to pursue full time. Her senior thesis proposed the idea of creating Teach for America. She told me her application for a job at Morgan Stanley was declined, and she was pursuing the implementation of her thesis as plan B. The irony, it turned out, is that Morgan Stanley later provided ample office space gratis to Teach for America.

At our initial meeting, Wendy wondered if many of her generation who were looking for a way to make a difference in the world would choose teaching over more lucrative opportunities. If a prominent teacher corps existed, the idea looked plausible to me, and the Geraldine R. Dodge Foundation was among the early and regular funders.

As a twenty-one-year-old, Kopp raised $2.5 million in start-up funding, hired a skeleton staff, and launched a grassroots recruitment campaign at the top colleges and universities.

The youngest recipient of the Woodrow Wilson Award, Princeton's highest accolade for an alumnus of the undergraduate college, was Ralph Nader (Class of '55) at the age of thirty-six. In the intervening forty-two years, no one younger than Wendy Kopp, at age twenty-six, has received that award. And, truth is, Teach for America has grown in influence and clout since then, strengthened its summer training, and become recognized for building a pipeline of leaders committed to educational equity and excellence.

Twenty years after its founding, Teach for America had 28,000 alumni, 65 percent of whom are still engaged in education. For the academic year 2010–2011, TFA received 50,000 applications and accepted 4,500 of them to work in low-income communities.

At the quarter-century mark, Kopp has expanded her mission in schools across the globe. "We saw 1,000 people come for Teach for Pakistan's first forty spots and 2,400 compete for Enseña por Colombia's sixty spots," Kopp said. Teach for All, started in 2007, works with social entrepreneurs in other countries to recruit teachers. Today it is a network of thirty-three independent organizations around the world.

The lesson: A painful rejection may provide an opportunity to pursue something of consequence for our society.

Postscript

Two days after the 2014 midterm elections, when Republicans took over the US Senate, Nicholas Kristof wrote in the *New York Times* in a piece titled "America's Broken Politics":

"I'm in the middle of a book tour now, visiting universities and hearing students speak about yearning to make a difference. But they are turning not to politics as their lever but to social enterprise, to nonprofits, to advocacy, to business. They see that Wendy Kopp, who founded Teach for America in her dorm room at Princeton University, has had more impact on the educational system than any current senator, and many have given up on political paths to change." (November 6, 2014)

*The Sleep of Reason Produces Monsters,
number 43 of 80 prints in this evocative
series,* Caprichos, *1798, by Francisco Goya.*

Caprichos

The author is convinced that it is as proper for painting to criticize human error and vice as for poetry and prose to do so, although criticism is usually taken to be exclusively the business of literature. He has selected from amongst the innumerable foibles and follies to be found in any civilized society, and from the common prejudices and deceitful practices which custom, ignorance, or self-interest have made usual, those subjects which he feels to be the more suitable material for satire, and which, at the same time, stimulate the artist's imagination.

— Goya's expectations for his *Caprichos*,
the first paragraph from an announcement
n the *Diario de Madrid*, February 6, 1799,
as quoted by Robert Hughes in his book,
Goya (Albert A. Knopf, 2003)

GOD IS ON OUR SIDE

President Ronald Reagan addressing Presidential Scholars,
their parents, and favorite teachers, 1985.

With an event in life, it usually happens only once, and it's gone.

What I describe here occurred in eight successive Junes during the administration of Ronald Reagan on the South Lawn of the White House, pretty much word for word. It was the greeting of the President of the United States to the 141 Presidential Scholars, two from every state, a boy and a girl, twenty in the arts, fifteen at large, six from overseas, and their families.

When President Reagan stepped out of the White House, he strode athletically across the lawn to the microphone, beaming radiantly.

After welcoming the Presidential Scholars and their families warmly, the president said he felt a little embarrassed by the scholars and their accomplishments since he himself had not been a very good student.

In fact, he said, when he received recently an honorary degree from his alma mater, Eureka College, he quipped, "I thought the first one was honorary!"

In 1986, we were in China with eighteen of the initial Dodge Foundation Chinese language teachers who—thanks to the good efforts of Professor Timothy Light of Ohio State University—gathered to learn for a month at Beijing Language University.

When the teachers' studies were concluded, they traveled a bit, and we with them. When in Shanghai, Hella and I traveled to meet with the president of Fudan University, Xie Xide (aka Hsi-teh Hsieh) (1921–2000), who had a PhD in particle physics with a focus on semiconductors from MIT. She was a highly regarded diminutive woman who was a member of the Central Committee of the Communist Party of China in charge of education for the country and foreign educational exchange programs. She helped revive the physics culture in China, and still used a typewriter (a friend later got her a computer).

President Xie Xide said President Reagan had been in China recently, and he addressed the leadership of the country. In his remarks he said, "We are so successful in America because God is on our side."

Dr. Xide said she excised that sentence from the President's speech "for your sake and for our sake" when it was transmitted across China.

I mentioned what President Reagan said annually to the Presidential Scholars. She said he told the same story, and we did not know what to make of it.

ONE GOOD DEED

Sylvia Earle, marine scientist and aquanaut,
Charlie Rose *show, October 26, 1993.*

The agony and the anguish of eight years of George W. Bush, Dick Cheney, and Donald Rumsfeld led me to wonder what a memorial would look like that might encapsulate this presidency.

Few lines of work do I admire more than the cartoonist who can, in one image, often with a punch line, skewer a particular folly or foible. Herblock (1909–2001) was near the top in nailing the absurdity of the day. Our own Jimmy Margulies in New Jersey (*Bergen Record*) comes through on an almost daily basis.

My own "dream" embodiment of those bumbling Bush years would be an inflatable, portable room containing the most tellingly accurate takes by cartoonists during those eight years. The cartoonists nailed the phony allegation of WMDs (weapons of mass destruction) in

Iraq that "justified" the invasion to the strutting, swaggering "Mission Accomplished" speech on the aircraft carrier *USS Abraham Lincoln* on May 1, 2003. Truth be told, the vast majority of the casualties, both military and civilian, have occurred since that inappropriate declaration of "mission accomplished."

How many cartoons—100 or 1,000 or 10,000? No idea. The number of cartoons in the exhibit should be governed by their penetrating character and relevance. I had pulled together an album of such cartoons from the first four years. During that period, when we traveled abroad, folks excused us since Al Gore had actually won the 2000 election, although he didn't fight for it. After the second election, when Bush won after four years of governing by fear and intimidation, people in Europe or South America or Asia were mystified why this bumbler, who had lost some mental and empathetic capacities through addiction and had a "missing" year in his life when he might have been serving his country, could possibly be re-elected on his wretched record.

On June 15, 2006, the front page of the *New York Times* sported a photograph of President Bush signing a proclamation establishing the Northwestern Hawaiian Islands Marine National Monument. This area of 4,500 square miles contains wild coral reefs that are among the healthier and more extensive in the world and other pristine forms of aquatic life. This came about through the thoughtful and timely efforts of Dr. Sylvia Earle, pictured beside the President.

She is a friend and colleague since 1974 when she saw my documentary on the Arctic bowhead whale as a member of the board of the Environmental Defense Fund. Sylvia has been the lead scientist in America regarding conservation of the oceans for several decades. She has spent more time underwater than anyone and that earned the appellation "Her Deepness." I spoke with her at length the following week and learned that a couple of months earlier she had been at the

White House for a screening on the fish, mammals, and coral in the area and, directly thereafter, had an extended conversation with President Bush.

The creation of the Marine National Monument in Hawaii stands as a true accomplishment beside the still-rubble-wracked and anguished peoples of Iraq and Afghanistan.

One good deed indeed.

Postscript

On June 17, 2014, President Obama said he was using his executive authority under the Antiquities Act of 1906 to create the world's largest marine protected area in the south-central Pacific Ocean (*New York Times*, page A17), building on the action of his predecessor, described above.

The *New York Times*'s editorial on June 17 was rapturous and accurate in describing "Mr. Obama's Ocean Monument." "They are seven sand-and-coral dots in the middle of the Pacific Ocean, far west and south of Hawaii," it read. "If you said they were among the most inconsequential bits of United States territory, who would argue? But the 21st century has brought a greater appreciation of Howland, Baker, and Jarvis Islands; Johnston, Wake, and Palmyra Atolls; and Kingman Reef. It's because the waters around them are an unparalleled wildlife habitat… covering nearly 782,000 square miles."

In actuality, in late September 2014, some 491,000 square miles were protected—since tuna fishing interests protested, and that caused the shrinkage of still the most massive marine park on Earth.

GOD BLESS AMERICA!

The occasion was a meeting of the national board of the Smithsonian on a weekend in 1974 in Washington, DC.

That Friday evening, Hella was seated next to Joseph Hirshhorn (1899–1981). He was not a voluble dinner companion, but from time to time he jumped up and said, "God bless America!"

He had made a fortune, first in mining and oil, then in gold and uranium. In 1966, after being courted by several museums, he contributed 6,000 paintings and sculptures to the Smithsonian along with a $2 million endowment. After his death, another 6,000 works of art and an additional $5 million for endowment were bequeathed.

To this day I remember the stunning movie shot from the air and on the ground of sculptural works of art by Rodin, Picasso, Giacometti, Calder, and Moore being hoisted by a crane into a cavernous truck for transport to Washington. Seeing those iconic works arcing noiselessly through the air was a rare sight.

On Saturday the board had luncheon in The Castle prior to the formal dedication of the Joseph H. Hirshhorn Museum and Sculpture Garden, the highlight of the weekend. This time I was seated at Mr. Hirshhorn's table but not next to him. S. Dillon Ripley, the secretary of the Smithsonian, spoke to me quietly and asked me to make sure that Hirshhorn did not make his little speech over lunch but rather, as planned, in the building early that afternoon.

When the appetizer was served, Mr. Hirshhorn stood up. I ran around and sat him down. When the entrée was served, he rose, and again I persuaded him to sit down. When dessert was served, again he stood, and I was too late in trying to stop him. He read slowly from penciled notes on the back of the formal invitation we all had received from the secretary and the regents: "Ladies and gentlemen, I am glad to welcome you to the museum bearing my name …"

Dr. Ripley shot a glance at me, boring two holes in my heart. I had let someone down, whom I greatly admired, indeed revered. Sadly, I shrugged my shoulders.

After we walked over to the soon-to-be-blessed Hirshhorn Museum, designed by Gordon Bunshaft, and took our seats, the dedicatory program began, skipping over the spot for the donor's remarks.

WHAT SHOULD I ASK HIM?

Governor Tom Kean and Scott.

It was near the end of Thomas H. Kean's impressive eight years as New Jersey's governor in late 1989. Michael Aron, the lead reporter at New Jersey Network, called. He said he was doing an exit interview with the governor in a month and wondered what he should ask him.

My relationship with the governor goes back to his first weeks in office. He had named someone from Pennsylvania as his Commissioner of Education. I was sitting with him at dinner when he was told that this man had a bogus PhD. He asked me, "What do you suggest?" I mentioned Saul Cooperman, the superintendent of education in Madison, who had given me a two-hour presentation of what he would do if chosen. Saul was on the short list, and he was then appointed. His views on education meshed beautifully with the governor's, who was a teacher himself.

Later, Governor Kean asked me to organize the top business leaders of New Jersey into a partnership to make the Garden State a better place to live and to work. I did, and we had a long run. Also, I worked with the governor or his representatives on eighteen issues in education, the arts, and the environment. The governor spoke at the first Dodge Poetry Festival and at a major event in Newark celebrating the work of Mel Levine with kids struggling to learn.

I suggested to Michael Aron, "Don't ask if he is running for president." (His wife is not keen for him to go to Washington, nor to play the First Lady role, which she abjured in New Jersey.) "Instead, ask about how he overcame difficulty in reading, stuttering, so-so performance in schools when he was shuttled back and forth to Washington when his father was a congressman."

The day before the interview Michael called again, saying he called me first, and he was calling me last. I repeated what I said before.

The morning of the interview at Drumthwacket, the governor's official residence, Michael, a confident, poised, informed, well-prepared, and well-versed journalist, greeted the governor by saying he had lain awake all night reviewing his questions, possible answers, and follow-ups, and said he was a wreck.

The governor, who had lifted the arts, education, and the environment, reassured Michael that he rarely went into a meeting fully prepared because he was not a good reader.

Michael asked, "Would you talk about that on camera?" Yes, he would.

Kean mentioned that he went to a camp in New England where he was a camper year after year. Then he became an assistant counselor, later a counselor, discovering his vocation as a teacher.

After college, he taught for three years. His father decided to run for the Senate. Tom came back to New Jersey and was asked to go to a nearby gathering for his father the candidate.

"As long as you remember, I-I-I do-ah-oh-n't speak."

At the gathering someone asked Tom to say a few words. Forgetting himself, he did. The applause has not stopped.

Kean said that he was still a poor reader. That was why he listened so closely.

The hour with Michael Aron was one of the finest in NJN's history.

Subsequently, Tom Kean was president of Drew University for fifteen years, chair of the 9/11 Commission, and has served on many boards, including chairing the Robert Wood Johnson Foundation and the Carnegie Corporation.

IS THAT IT?

At Princeton reunions, June 2000, some luminaries from the Classes of 1940 (Goheen), 1945, 1950, 1955 (Nader), 1960, and 1965 (Bradley), were part of a panel in McCosh 50, the largest lecture hall on the campus, addressing a packed house.

Senator Bill Bradley was a couple of minutes late. He explained that while he was walking across campus, a woman had run up to him to say her daughter had named her pet guinea hen for him. Bill said he was touched by the thought and to please convey his regards to her daughter.

As Bradley hurried on, he wondered, "Is that it?"

Here is a man who as a student in 1964 led the American men's team to triumph over the Soviets' basketball team in the Olympics. He was a star player with the Knicks, too, for ten years (1967–77), and was elected US Senator from New Jersey for three terms (1979–1997). In 2000, he challenged Al Gore for the Democrats' choice for president and graced the cover of *Time* (October 4, 1999).

Recently, he gave a talk about his many intersections with the USSR, beginning when he was a Rhodes Scholar at Oxford. Some of his fellow students and he rented a hearse and drove to the Soviet Union. Later, much later, he was involved in meetings with Soviet leaders, including Mikhail Gorbachev regarding *Perestroika* (reconstruction) and *Glasnost* (openness).

He told the story of that defining final basketball game with the Russians by noting he had gone to a Russian professor to learn how to say, "Hey, big boy! Watch out! Back off!" in Russian.

Early in that game, a big bruiser banged into him, and Bradley barked in Russian, "Hey, big boy! Watch out! Back off!"

That player, in shock upon hearing colloquial Russian, went back to his teammates, seeming to say, "They all speak fluent Russian." Good basketball is also a head game.

One personal interaction with the senator was in the early 1980s when he conducted an all-day leadership development session every year with as many as 150 high school students, one from every school in North Jersey, addressing a half dozen issues confronting elected officials at the national level and looking toward their resolution. This was a rigorous exercise requiring an analysis of the plusses and minuses attached to working on each issue.

Senator Bill Bradley table-hops among high school students attending his leadership seminar at William Patterson College, 1981.

Bradley explained to the students that public service was ranked thirty-seventh among career choices—that is, off the charts on the low end. It lacked standing and esteem in the culture. He sought to lift its stature among these students, whom he hoped would be the future leadership of New Jersey, the nation, and maybe the world, as they wrestled with seeking solutions to tough questions.

The formulation of the problems and the way Bradley personally conducted the sessions, engaging every student, was impressive.

"I'm making hard choices now as a United States Senator," he told the students, "and I want you to help me. Let's not go for cliché answers or easy solutions. I'm not a senator in Washington making decisions that affect your lives and not caring what you think. What you think and say is important to me. Today we are all United States Senators."*

On the second and third day, he met with another 150 students from schools in Central and South Jersey.

Bradley did this every year for a number of years, and the Dodge Foundation provided modest support through educational improvement centers to cover the cost of lunch in the hope that more capable young people would pursue public service as part of their lives.

*From a two-page essay in the 1981 Geraldine R. Dodge Foundation annual report.

WHAT DO YOU THINK?

In 1985, Queen Beatrix of the Netherlands asked Pieter Winsemius, a director with McKinsey & Company, to lead the Green Plan efforts within the low-lying country in light of global warming and the prospect of rising sea levels.

Pieter's first move was to meet with the head of Royal Dutch Petroleum, a friend. They met face to face, flanked by aides across a long narrow table. Winsemius laid out the issues and the urgency of the matter. Before the ranking CEO in Holland could respond (Pieter had put a cautionary finger to his lips), he then walked around the table, stood behind the CEO, and offered an appropriate response supporting his pitch for collaboration. The CEO smiled in agreement.

In August of 1993, marking our thirty-fifth wedding anniversary, we were traveling around Turkey by bus. One day we stopped for lunch where other busses stood. I spotted one with "The Netherlands" on the front and walked over to where a group was eating lunch. I asked who among them was familiar with the Dutch Green Plan. Every hand went up. I asked if and how they were engaged in reducing carbon emissions and in other things. Every one, whether in business, the not-for profit sector, or government, explained what he or she was doing at work and at home.

At about that time, Dr. Winsemius kindly agreed to fly to New Jersey to meet with our then-governor Christine Todd Whitman. The idea was to try to lift her understanding of crucial environmental issues we were confronting here in New Jersey. With half the population of the Netherlands (8 million versus 15 million), we are the most densely packed of the fifty states. Winsemius did fly over on his dime. I had arranged the meeting, and Winsemius graciously and thoroughly outlined several aspects of the Dutch Green Plan. The governor gave us more time than promised.

In 1998, when the board of the W. Alton Jones Foundation— devoted to sustaining biodiversity on Earth and reducing the nuclear threat—traveled to Europe, our first stop was the Netherlands. We had a crowded three-day program, but Monday morning over breakfast at the Hotel Pulizer in Amsterdam was open. I called Dr. Winsemius on Sunday and asked if perhaps he was free. He said yes. Well before 7:30, our agreed-upon meeting time, I was standing outside the hotel. At 7:29, he appeared on an old woman's bike he had found at the office.

With joy I welcomed him. Incidentally, for years he led the leading conservation group in the country, and he had written a book of animal fables about conservation illustrated by a noted Dutch artist.

As I ushered him in, he asked me to please sit down. He was carrying a battered briefcase. As he opened it, a massive old tome emerged written by his ancestor, Pieter Winsemius, going back sixteen generations and four centuries. The book contained his ancestor's account of the state of human knowledge at the time after visiting the sixteen universities on the continent.

Winsemius had inherited the book from his father upon his death. He asked, "Should I have it recovered? What do you think?"

I said "Yes, but keep the cover—now let's go in." The briefing was sterling in all respects. Pieter explained that they regularly met on the security of the dikes, so he shifted the emphasis to global warming and what we can do to reduce carbon emissions.

It became abundantly clear that the Dutch, and the Germans, were way ahead of us in the States in addressing climate change then—and to this day.

Postscript

Within days after the attacks of 9/11, Christine Todd Whitman, then head of the EPA, went to Ground Zero, still burning hot and spewing toxic fumes, and urged the Stock Exchange to reopen and the students to return to Stuyvesant High School. She said it was safe. It wasn't.

WHAT IS YOUR WORST NIGHTMARE?

It was July 10, 1997. The place was COGEMA in La Hague in Normandy, not far from where the Americans came ashore in World War II. The board and key staff of the W. Alton Jones Foundation were visiting the central plant in Europe for extracting plutonium, which is then recycled in MOX fuel (an alternative to low-enriched uranium fuel).

Greenpeace had reported radioactive waste in the water expelled from this plant. "Plutonium 239 is a doomsday material with a half life of 24,000 years," as John Adams said in 1974. Greenpeace claimed the plant dumped one million liters of liquid radioactive waste every day. The French said it is less than a routine dose from the sun's rays.

We were given white coats and Geiger counters for walking around on translucent floors above the encapsulated containers of plutonium shipped there from Japan, Germany, and France itself.

Over lunch I sat opposite the man in charge of this operation, who had scrabbled for uranium in Saskatchewan for years. I asked him, "Sir, what is your worst nightmare?"

He replied at once, "Oh, if my wife left me!"

As we were leaving the building, I was walking with a bright, well-spoken gentleman who was the primary liaison with Japan, Germany, and the French government on this nuclear business. I posed to him, a quintessential diplomat, the same question, "What is your worst nightmare vis-à-vis this operation?"

He said, "Human error. We all have erasers on our pencils—human error."

SMALL CARS

In 1956, I bought a beige Volkswagen in Berlin to allow ready travel about the three western sectors of the city—the French, the British, and the American. This purchase was made possible through a generous loan from my father, who forgave the loan upon the occasion of Hella's and my marriage on August 9, 1958.

For another seven years, Hella and I drove that beloved vehicle in Berlin and in this country right up to the time I had pieced together $1,500 to buy a new Volkswagen in 1963.

Then I spied an ad in our local weekly, *Town Topics*, which listed a "mint-condition" Mercedes with red leather seat covers for the same sum. We bought it, and when I rolled into our local gas station, three guys were all over it, polishing the windows, the headlamps, even the side mirrors—things I had previously done myself.

Fast forward. Here in Princeton is a physicist, Robert H. Williams (BS in physics at Yale, 1962, PhD in theoretical plasma physics, Berkeley, 1967), who is an authority on various forms of energy. He has written and cowritten books and papers on many facets of the energy field and has been a consultant to China since 1991. In 1993, he received a MacArthur Fellowship, often referred to as a "genius" award.

James Ferland, for many years CEO, president, and chairman of PSEG (1986–2004), was knowledgeable about all applied aspects of energy. He said he would like to meet Williams, perhaps over dinner since he was constantly being interrupted at work.

I arranged a dinner in Morristown in the mid-1990s and was the proverbial fly-on-the-wall when the two of them interacted for more than two hours, touching on every aspect of the field from coal to oil to natural gas, from wind to sun to geothermal to nuclear.

Some time later, P. Roy Vagelos, then CEO and chairman of Merck and author of 100 scientific papers, said he'd like to talk to Williams. Vagelos said energy was wholly outside his field, but he had heard from Ferland that he had enjoyed meeting with Williams.

I arranged for a meeting at Merck's headquarters in Rahway (before the move to Elysian Fields in Whitehouse Station). Bob and I traveled from Princeton to Rahway in his Honda Civic, which got sixty miles to a gallon of gas.

When we arrived at the gate, I cranked down the window. The security guard asked what we wanted.

"Where might we park the car?" I asked.

He replied, "Go to the end of this lot and then proceed to the back of the second lot, and you will find a third lot. Park at the back of the third lot."

We hoofed it back to the gate. The guard said, "What do you want now?"

"Could you please advise us where Mr. Vagelos's office is?" He blanched and pointed the way.

Moral: In our society we tend to judge somebody by the size and status of his car.

IS IT TRUE THAT WATER IS RUNNING OUT IN THE SOUTHWEST?

In the early days after the creation of the Partnership for New Jersey, composed of leading CEOs of companies based there, meetings were held periodically on topics of interest to the members, typically related to making New Jersey a better place to live and to work.

One day in the early 1980s, a gathering occurred at Drew University to hear from Trammell Crow (1914–2009), the lead developer* in the country who was based in Dallas, Texas, but had offices nationwide.

He gave a charming presentation with graphs and charts. Upon concluding, he asked if there were any questions. I raised my hand. My first question was aimed at verifying what I had heard—namely, that in the southwestern United States, water was being used at seven times the rate it was percolating into the aquifer. My related question: "Why are you pitching us here in New Jersey?"

Mr. Crow replied that my information was correct, which meant that water would run out in the Southwest in the near term when one ran the lines on a chart of water use versus water availability. Regarding the second question, he said that was why he was in the Garden State, where we seemed to have plenty of water. In the intervening thirty years, Mr. Crow's reading of the early signs of climate change was prophetic.

In 2012, Michael Oppenheimer, a friend and lead physicist on global warming and part of the panel that won the Nobel Prize, witnessed the effects of Superstorm Sandy on Lower Manhattan, when the ocean rose and swamped the subways.

Dr. Oppenheimer said, "Climate as we have known it is a thing of the past." Weather will not be the same again. Consider the rapid melting of

Greenland's ice, the disappearance of glaciers, huge Antarctic ice shelves cracking and breaking off, plus the raging wild fires in the American West, the tornadoes in the heartland, and the flooding of rivers everywhere.

Michael Oppenheimer of the Environmental Defense Fund speaking to a group of Earthwatch teachers about climate in 1991.

Trammell Crow was light-years ahead of the politicians, pundits, and doubters about the severity of climate change. On the eve of a gathering of United Nations negotiators in Lima, Peru, December 1, 2014, "scientists warn ... without a deal, the world could become uninhabitable to humans," according to a front page article in the *New York Times*. This is the most direct comment to date I have seen on the implications of climate change.

*With more than $50 billion to date in real estate development, Trammell Crow Company tops William Zeckerdorf and Donald Trump.

WITH DUE RESPECT, SIR

During the time when Russell Train was president of the World Wildlife Fund (US), a little tension existed with international headquarters in Gland, Switzerland, where Charles de Haes, a bit of a control freak, was director general. Train, ever a consummate diplomat, resisted efforts to change the name of our US affiliate to the World Wide Fund for Nature as de Haes (who formerly worked for Anton Rupert) was urging. De Haes was backed up by HRH Prince Philip, who was the international chair.

In the 1980s, with the backing of both boards, Train brought the WWF together with the Conservation Foundation, led by Bill Reilly. Train became chair and Reilly president. Reilly, also a fairly adroit player, was getting along quite well with Gland. Then, a couple of years into his presidency, he negotiated a major land reserve in an African country, and there was a lot of press wherein Reilly was identified as president of the World Wildlife Fund.

When Reilly next met Prince Philip, he encountered an enraged consort. Philip fumed, "Reilly, goddamn it, I am the president of the World Wildlife Fund—not you!"

Reilly rejoined, "With due respect, sir, you are the president of the World Wide Fund for Nature."

Once Hella and I were at a WWF dinner at the British Embassy in Washington in the 1980s seated at Prince Philip's table. In advance, we had been given a list of a dozen topics one was *verboten* to bring up, personal questions such as, why are you still a hunter, or why do you still shoot live birds?

Among many anecdotes from the field is one where a couple of biologists were at work in a remote field site in Africa. When they heard that His Royal Highness was coming for a visit in two weeks, they abandoned their research to build a porch onto the humble shack where they lived in anticipation of the royal visit. When Philip arrived, he harrumphed, "What a godforsaken place this is," turned heel, and left.

Hella with Prince Philip in San Francisco.

On the occasion of Prince Philip's ninetieth birthday on June 10, 2011, the *New York Times* published an article titled "A Diplomat, He Isn't: Prince Philip's Tongue Remains Sharp as Ever." It was studded with egregious examples of this behavior. I note but three, verbatim:

To a museum curator in the Cayman Islands: "Aren't most of you descended from cannibals?"

Perhaps his most famous remark, to a British student in China: "If you stay here much longer, you will go home with slitty eyes."

To the president of Nigeria, in traditional dress: "You look like you're ready for bed."

They got it right: a diplomat, he isn't.

Confucius

When the Master entered the Grand
Temple, he asked questions about
everything there. Someone said, "How can
it be claimed that the son of Shu Lang–he
knows the rites? Every time he is present
he asks about everything!" When this was
reported to the Master he remarked, "This
is precisely the rite.

— From a collection of confucius's Sayings,
Qi Lu Press, 1988, Ji Nan

TEN THOUSAND TO ONE

Ink drawing Cliff on the River Li *by Tom George, who was the first American visual artist invited to China after the thaw, from collection of Mr. and Mrs. Robert Geddes.*

It began with a note from Fritz Mote, who wrote it might be a good time to approach Ta-Tuan Ch'en, who taught Chinese at Princeton and was on sabbatical. For a quarter century, T.T.'s course in Chinese 101 and 102 had been ranked by students among the top four courses at the university. Professor Ch'en also directed the summer program in Mandarin at Middlebury that set the bar for the country. Professor Frederick Mote, ever a twinkle in his eye, was the renowned scholar of the Yuan and Ming dynasties—the golden eras of Chinese art, history, and literature—and a vital force among lead universities in building East Asian studies nationally.

Professor Ch'en's response to my interest in creating an initiative to teach Chinese in high schools nationwide was immediate and encouraging.

I arranged a meeting in fall of 1982 for members of our board at the Dodge Foundation to explore whether we might undertake an initiative to teach less commonly taught languages at the high school level such as Japanese, promising since its economy was beginning to be cited as a model by business schools; Russian, since the Soviet Union was the object of the Cold War; or Chinese, the sleepiest of sleeping giants at that time. Eleanor Jordan, the lead exponent of Japanese language instruction and author of a four-volume set of teaching materials (Yale University Press), and Fred Starr, president of Oberlin College and an advocate of Russian language studies, were invited to make their cases as well. Stacking the deck slightly, Professor Ch'en brought Perry Link, a protégé and brilliant Chinese linguist, and Tim Light, who headed Ohio State's East Asian Studies program.

Our trustees decided on a modest investment in a Chinese language

In 1980, the Dodge Foundation made a grant to St. Ann's Episcopal School in Brooklyn, which became a trigger three years later for a nationwide initiative to teach Mandarin well in high schools. Here Mrs. Bailing Yang is teaching an eager class.

initiative. I secured a purloined list of the top 900 high schools, coast to coast, in the belief that as difficult and challenging as Chinese is to learn, it could be more readily potted in the soil of an otherwise rich curriculum. I wrote the 900 principals by name, inviting them to reply to eight questions to draw out the depth and nature of their commitment. Ads in educational journals invited other schools to apply, too.

The questions were crafted, but the key one was how would the principal support a lonely Chinese teacher when the French, German, and Latin teachers were, maybe, undermining her in attracting the better students? Also, to get the second half of the grant two years in, required Chinese be properly taught—getting the four tones right. In Mandarin they are: high level (first tone), rising (second tone), falling rising (third), and falling (fourth).

As Professor Ch'en stressed—with a broad grin—in the gathering of the first cohort of teachers at Middlebury, "Get the four tones right or it's eternal perdition."

Perry Link, Chinese linguist and scholar, and Wei-ling Wu,
prominent Chinese language teacher and author of 16 Chinese textbooks
at our 50th wedding anniversary at Prospect, August 9, 2008.

The parents of the kids studying Chinese "got it" regarding the imperative of this undertaking more than the principals, who were sometimes smug about how well their schools were humming along.

A team of professors from universities across the country were invited to review the proposals on site, accompanied by a Dodge program officer. Eventually, twenty schools were chosen for funding in 1983. Another twenty were carefully vetted and supported in 1984. A third cohort was supported in 1987.

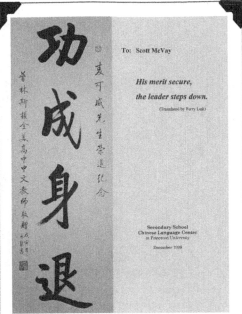

The four characters on the hanging scroll (Gongcheng shentui) come from writings attributed to the ancient Chinese philosopher Lao-Tzu. The calligraphy was done by Qin Yonglong, a famous artist and professor of calligraphy at Beijing Normal University.

The teachers gathered every summer, first at Middlebury, then Ohio State, and then China for a month at the Beijing Language University arranged and organized by Professor Light. When Professor Ch'en showed up and worked with the teachers in Beijng, the faculty there exclaimed that no one in China taught as well, as forcefully and effectively.

Early on, Perry Link made the seemingly outrageous claim that for every student in the United States studying Chinese, there were 10,000 students in China studying English. The assertion was accurate and as troubling as the fact that after September 11, 2001, we woke up to the fact that in the United States we had only 5,000 Arabic linguists. How shockingly insular and isolationist of us!

*Professors Tim Light of Ohio State University and Ta-Tuan Ch'en
of Princeton provided critical leadership in the early years of the Dodge
nationwide initiative to have Mandarin taught well in high schools, 1984.*

Two independent studies of our Chinese language initiative were reassuring. The first was conducted by Dr. Rose Hayden, president of the National Council on Foreign Language and International Studies. She also wrote an article for *Foundation News* (November/December, 1987). The second study, a 139-page document titled "Introducing Chinese into High Schools: The Dodge Initiative" was completed in 1992 after the foundation had invested $2.7 million. Written by Sarah Jane Moore with Ronald Walton and Richard Lambert for the National Foreign Language Center, it offers many ideas for other foundations wanting to promote successful language studies.

A crucial element was bringing the high school teachers together every year for the conference for college Chinese language teachers. This happened through the good offices of Professor C. P. Chou, another Ch'en protégé, and a professor at Princeton who became T.T.'s successor in directing the Middlebury summer Chinese language program. He was ably assisted by Dr. Wei-ling Wu, a master teacher in the West Windsor, New Jersey, schools and creator of sixteen textbooks for learning Chinese in a conversational way, from kindergarten to grade 12.

Today over 2,000 US schools offer Chinese. The group in the vanguard is the Asia Society, where regular newsletters have valuable updates on curricular strategies, educational exchanges, and conferences. It is estimated that 100,000 primary, secondary, and college students are studying Mandarin today in the United States.

Years ago I asked Ralph Nader why he had studied Chinese in college, learning 3,500 characters. He replied, "I'm good at arithmetic—China is one-fourth of the planet."

STIRRING IT UP

Meg Cadoux prepares the good earth for an organic farm at Stony Brook-Millstone Watershed Association in Pennington, New Jersey, 1984.

At the Dodge Foundation in 1984, we made a grant of $32,000 to the Stony Brook-Millstone Watershed Association to assist in the start-up costs of Honey Brook Organic Farm, which is today the oldest and largest certified fruit, herb, vegetable, and flower CSA (community supported agriculture) farm in not only the Garden State but in America.

The first organic farmer at the Watershed was Meg Cadoux, who cultivated four acres. We had a terrific photograph of Meg high up on a tractor that we used as a two-page centerfold in our 1984 annual report.

No sooner was the report off the press than Meg had moved to New Hampshire, where she married Gary Hirshberg, whom she had met at a Northeast Organic Farming Association (NOFA) conference. Gary was engaged in the initial phases of building an organic yogurt company known today for its superb yogurt, Stonyfield Yogurt.

A few years ago Gary was in Princeton promoting his book, *Stirring It Up: How to Make Money and Save the World* (2008). He gave a passionate talk, and I spoke with him afterwards as he was signing books. I showed him the photograph of Meg atop a tractor from our report and said we had been saddened by her departure. He then spoke of their three kids, two sons in college and a daughter in high school, who are but one benefit of his happy marriage.

On Sunday evening, October 22, 2012, at Duke Farms, the annual gathering for NOFA New Jersey featured not only splendid and varied food from several sources, but also two stirring talks by Meg Cadoux Hirshberg and Gary Hirshberg.

Meg had a new book out, in addition to her blogs, called *For Better or For Work: A Survival Guide for Entrepreneurs and Their Families.*

Gary is now chairman of the board of Stonyfield Yogurt, which grosses $400 million per year. They receive milk from 20 percent of the cows in Maine and 17 percent of the cows in New Hampshire—quite a trajectory from starting with seventeen cows and then selling them to obtain milk from other dairy farmers.

But the big news is that Gary has formed a not-for-profit called Just Label It, which has 1.3 million members. Noting that 12 percent of all fruit and vegetable produce in the US is now organic, he points out that we must accelerate the trend. The issue is chemical companies—Dow, DuPont, Monsanto—who are driving the genetically modified growing, which is having a devastating effect on all life and human health. The toxins built into the seeds persist and accumulate in plants and animals, causing in humans cancer, neurological problems, and reduced mental capacity. His reasoning is quick, tight, and unassailable. The prior Friday evening, Gary was the opening interview on Bill Maher's show on HBO.

The contents of much of our food are not labeled—the same issue Theo Colborn is addressing at TEDX—The Endocrine Disruption Exchange in Paonia, Colorado. It turns out that Gary called on Theo, when she was a senior scientist at the World Wildlife Fund, long before creating his not-for-profit.

After his remarks, Gary told me privately he had met with President Obama one on one five or six times in 2012. President Obama told Gary that if he was re-elected he would push the issue.

In May 2014, we saw Gary and Meg and their family at the Middlebury graduation when their daughter and our grandson Philip graduated. Gary said he has received no help from the president but that Just Label It has gathered further steam and clout.

MABEL, COME HERE!

In 1981, early in Tom Kean's first term as governor of New Jersey, I invited him to meet with our trustees at the Geraldine R. Dodge Foundation over lunch to discuss opportunities for philanthropy in New Jersey.

Knowing the governor would be a little late, I invited Nanine Bilski-Dowling of the America the Beautiful Fund to talk with the board about her continuing efforts to engage New Jersey communities in celebrating the bicentennial. Nanine is president of the America the Beautiful fund (based in Washington), which annually distributes six million free packets of vegetable seeds to community gardens across America. She taped up a big map of the Garden State, and she went quickly, brightly, from one town to another to cite defining characteristics, the known and the less known.

When she met with the leadership of one South Jersey town and asked what was distinctive or singular about the place, the response was "nothing." Following her gentle, encouraging inquiries, they began to see the community's farming history went way back. After her departure, they created a little museum containing old farming implements and equipment, neatly labeled, laced with local lore.

Thanks to Nanine and work throughout the state, we came to know Cape May Point, perhaps the dream spot on the entire East Coast of America, at the southernmost tip of the state.

An entirely residential place, except for a grocery and restaurant, Cape May Point is on the southern flyway for hawks—160,000 –180,000 of them—every fall as they wing their way over the Cape May Lighthouse where every one of the sixteen species is identified and tallied by volunteers from the Cape May Bird Observatory of the New Jersey Audubon Society.

The swimming couldn't be better, the height of the waves and the temperature of the water being optimal. Our grandkids just love it.

A number of varieties of sandpipers and sanderlings scurry swiftly on the wet sand nearby, picking quickly at nubbins in the backwash of the waves.

A school of thirty to forty bottlenose dolphins ply the fish-rich waters, traveling around the Point in the morning and back in the afternoon.

Displaying impressive results of long net seine fishing
on Higbee Beach at Cape May Point, ca. 2000,
with Bruce Dowling (left) and Nanine Bilski-Dowling (right).

A number of the houses date back 150 years and more, suggesting countless hours of family enchantment. Our favorite, called Terning Point and located on Knox Avenue, is owned by Bob and Esta Cassaway, an architect and a painter/writer from Philadelphia.

Their next door neighbor, Genevieve Van Bever, a Belgian heroine of World War II, began the Point's annual garden contest. The contest, which takes place during the summer, has led to the encompassing overall joy of this singular place by the sea. The gardens, scores of them, are planted and nurtured by the owners themselves.

At an annual expenditure now of $54 for eighteen ribbons (blue, red, and yellow) in six categories, Nanine and her volunteer scouts have, for a quarter century, selected and announced the prize-winning gardens during an August Taxpayers' Association meeting that is held above the firehouse on a Saturday evening.

The six categories of gardens are: perennial flowers, annuals, flowers and vegetables, bird and butterfly garden, seashore garden, and historic house garden. Each of the gardens must be planted by the homeowner, not some landscaper.

Another notable aspect is the impeccably worded citation Nanine writes for each garden, fully worthy of the handcrafted attention given to honorary degrees at universities.

Perhaps half of the winners receive the award at the public meeting. The balance Nanine delivers that week.

I remember that once when she tapped on the door of one home, a tough hard-bitten Philadelphia lawyer cracked the door and said, "Whaddaya want?"

Nanine smiled and said that he and his wife had won third place for their bird and butterfly garden.

"Mabel, come here!" he called. The door swung open; tears were streaming down his cheeks.

In addition to the eighteen ribbon awards and citations, a silver bowl is presented annually for the top garden on the Point. The Silver Bowl award carries such clout that, as you bike around, your attention is drawn to former Silver Bowl gardens—oh yes, 1994, and that one is 2002.

WHO WAS THAT AGAIN?

For a year a monk had toiled at restoring afresh a Tibetan Buddhist altar at the Newark Museum, which already had a substantial collection of Tibetan art and artifacts. The time came for His Holiness the Dalai Lama to dedicate the altar and give it his blessing on a Sunday afternoon, September 23, 1990.

That morning I was riding my bike after a heavy rain. I usually stowed it high above the Stony Brook beside a double tree, and then jogged down across an old bridge. But this day, for reasons obscure to me yet, I rode the bike down the steep, pebble-strewn road toward the broken slatted bridge. The bike skidded out from under me, and I crashed on my right hand. After putting the bike to one side, I did my regular jog on the other side of the stream.

The Dalai Lama at the consecration ceremony of the Newark Museum's new Tibetan Buddhist altar, greeted by (from left) Desmond M. Tutu, Anglican Archbishop of Cape Town, South Africa; Theodore E. McCarrick, Roman Catholic Archbishop of Newark; and Valrae Reynolds, Curator of Asian Collections, September 1990.

Behind the museum is an impressive sculpture garden. The first work one sees when coming in from the parking lot is the George Segal figure of Sam Miller, the director, hand extended in an old toll-taker's booth. Sam Miller mentioned once that during the making of *The Toll Taker*, he inhaled and held his chest out. One moment he relaxed, and then "his paunch was caught for all eternity." That sun-drenched day, the Dalai Lama spoke from the back steps with grace on the meaning of the rededication of the Tibetan altar.

At the reception my right hand was so sore that I proffered my left hand when folks thrust forth a hand in greeting, something that can be a trifle annoying.

When it came to greeting the Fourteenth Dalai Lama, flanked by Reverend Desmond Tutu, the apostle of reconciliation, I felt I had to put out my right hand out of respect. As I did, I said, "I bring greetings from a mutual friend, Daniel Taylor."

His Holiness beamed as he crushed my right hand in his two hands. *Crrrunch.* He said, "Who was that again?"

I stammered, smiling wanly, "Daniel Taylor." Crackling *crunch* again.

I limped away, passing up the chance to say hello to the Most Reverend Desmond Tutu, my right hand hanging aching, useless. The hand may or may not have been broken, but it hurt for a long time.

Someone asked what had happened. "My hand ... the Dalai Lama."

"Well, it will be okay if you were touched by His Holiness."

In May 2010, after four days of fundraising in New York City, the Dalai Lama was scheduled to speak at the Cathedral of Saint John the Divine. The pews were packed, since folks had waited patiently on line for hours to see and hear him.

Paul Winter had kindly invited us to sit down near the pulpit with the Tibetan monks who chanted, as Paul played his soprano saxophone, before the Dalai Lama's arrival. The Dalai Lama was delayed half an hour, and

Paul played for a full hour until His Holiness walked in, exhausted by unflagging exertion. After an introduction by the dean of the chapel, the Dalai Lama walked up the spiral stairs of the cathedral's central podium. What he said early in his remarks is snagged in a little poem below.

His Holiness

with scarlet cap
shielding his eyes
from the glare,
the Dalai Lama
said that once,
a couple years ago
when he was at Fatima
in the presence of
a small statue of Mary,
the Mother of Jesus,
Mary smiled …
was he jet-lagged?
or just an old man yearning,
did his eyes
trick him?
no, he saw
Mary smile.
why not?

He looked again.
She smiled again.

May 23, 2010

On October 28, 2014, in the Jadwin Gym at Princeton, the Dalai Lama spoke to a throng of 5,000. He was as charming, beguiling, wise, chortling, and joyful as ever. During the introduction by Alison Boden, the dean of religious life, he was grinning and waving at the audience and then faced her, standing right in front of her. She presented him with an orange and black Princeton cap, which he wore and doffed from time to time. His talk was titled "Develop the Heart."

The Dalai Lama spoke from the tall pulpit at the Cathedral of St. John the Divine to a crowd that filled every seat in every pew.

In a wise and witty interchange he said, "One who receives maximum affection as a child has a sense of security. My mother was so kind. I could easily bully her. I sat on her back. My two hands held my mother's two ears. I steer her left and right. If our mothers don't care for us, we die. Women are greater as regards sensitivity."

His theme was "the oneness of humanity. Read more books for different views."

One student asked, "What about investment banking?"

His Holiness said, smiling, "I don't know. Let me spend a year in banking ... at a high salary."

I AM A GAMBLER

*Poster for the Geraldine R. Dodge Poetry
Festival in 1996 features a treasured closed
vessel by Toshiko Takaezu.*

It has occurred to me of late that we know each other not at all. In an accelerated succession of memorial services to celebrate lives of people we thought we knew and liked, crucial facts about their upbringing and their lives come to light.

On the occasion of Toshiko Takaezu's death at eighty-eight

in March 2011 after a stunningly creative life as a potter without peer, 400-plus folks turned up at the Hunterdon Art Museum in Clinton, New Jersey. Five were noted in the program as speakers, and others were encouraged to take the microphone. We learned that every year when the morels emerged at a secret spot in the Midwest, Toshiko flew out there for the foraging and the feasting. Also, a colleague from her days as a student at Cranbrook Academy of Art (1951–54), said she made 50,000 pots when there.

Martha Russo, a sculptor and teacher in Boulder, Colorado, spoke freely with her whole body like all good speakers. Martha said that when she was a student at Princeton University (Class of 1985), where Toshiko taught ceramics for a quarter century and received an honorary degree, she enrolled in her course as a junior. She went to the first class and enjoyed it. The second class she missed since she was called to California for training for the Olympic Games in field hockey. The same thing happened the next week.

When Martha turned up for class the fourth week, Toshiko, a diminutive, determined fireplug, stood in the hall, hands on her hips. "Where do you think you are going?"

"To class."

"No, you are not. There is a long waitlist for this class for students who really want to be here. Also, art has a longer and more enduring life than sports."

When the next year Martha signed up again, Toshiko explained she had had her chance. Martha begged her for a second chance, and Toshiko reluctantly yielded, saying that she could come for two classes on a provisional basis. Martha explained that typically Toshiko walked about the studio looking at clay pieces ready for the kiln and dropped them on the floor if they were not worthy of being fired. Martha produced a large number of pots in the first two sessions and was allowed to continue.

Martha Russo said that later she was accepted as a rare female intern for Toshiko. One night near midnight, they had both kilns fully fired with work that needed more time. It was a full moon. Toshiko asked Martha, "What sport was it that you played?"

"Field hockey."

Toshiko asked, "Do you still have some equipment?"

Martha ran and got her stuff, and before you knew it both were clad with padding on the legs and fully suited out. They were swatting the ball about, and Toshiko exclaimed, "Hey, this is fun!"

After the moving service and supper at Toshiko's place, we drove home and looked up Martha Russo, who at that moment had a spectacular work on view at the Denver Art Museum that had won first prize in a major competition. She taught then in Colorado and elsewhere, and had garnered acclaim as an artist.

Every year for decades Toshiko took on a student as an apprentice who lived with her in Quakertown, New Jersey, and helped not only with the firing of work in two large kilns but also with the gardening of eggplant, purple potatoes, peonies, and Japanese anemones. Nearly all of Toshiko's interns were male. Once I was describing the desirable traits of an intern and how he was chosen, and she added, with a twinkle, "And good looking."

In the fall, Toshiko opened her home for her intern to display his work and sell it to provide a little boost as he went on his way. She was ever a regal presence, radiant in a long dress.

When Tom Kean neared the end of his eight years as governor, he had given a huge lift to the arts by increasing the annual arts programming budget from $2 million to $23 million and creating three major institutions: Liberty Science Center, Adventure Aquarium in Camden, and the New Jersey Performing Arts Center. I was asked by Elizabeth Christopherson, the chair of the New Jersey State Council on the Arts,

"How can we thank the governor?"

I suggested, "A pot by Toshiko."

A few weeks later on December 5, 1989, the entire contingent of artists and arts leaders in the Garden State gathered in the Billy Johnson Auditorium at the Newark Museum. The place was packed and crackled with excitement and gratitude. I introduced Toshiko, and she presented a small pot, *Aurora*, with closed top to the governor. When we think about our origins and our destiny, a clay pot seemed right. As Toshiko had said, "Often the clay has much to say."

In 1994, the second year of our Dodge Foundation initiative to honor and support visual artists who teach, we gathered at George Segal's studio in East Brunswick, a chicken coop with nine rooms for making his iconic work. After a tour of this shrine, pictures were taken of each artist-teacher sitting on a chair with Toshiko and George standing behind them. George was of course reluctant and ever upset when he was kept from making his art, but he put up with it. Toshiko put her hand on each teacher's shoulder. As one after another posed, proud and smiling, George got the hang of it and actually put his hand on the teacher's other shoulder and smiled.

After the tragedy of 9/11, Toshiko was invited to create a work for the Princeton campus in honor of thirteen Princetonians killed that day. A cast bronze bell called *Remembrance* was created, and it resides next to Chancellor Green near the east end of Nassau Hall. Every year during her presidency, Shirley Tilghman led a gentle ceremony at this apotheosis of anguished recollection.

I invited Toshiko to come to Chautauqua in 2003 when we had a week devoted to the visual arts. Her first response was, "Just show the film." (The film, *Portrait of an Artist,* had been made by Susan Walner for television at NJN, and I thought it one of the best ever produced in our home state.)

My reply was, "You can show any five minutes from the film, but you should speak freely about your craft and how you work." That happened with a sweet thrill rippling through our 5,000-seat amphitheater, where some of her friends came from a distance to hear her.

It was July 4 in 1999, and we were driving Toshiko from her home in Quakertown to Montclair for the annual Independence Day celebration. We planned to watch the town parade with Yass and Renate Hakashima and have a potluck picnic afterward. En route, Toshiko tossed out, "I am, you know, a gambler."

"Oh? You mean you go to Atlantic City"?

"Yes!"

"How often? A couple of times a year?"

"Yes!"

"You put a cap on what you bet?"

"Yes!"

Toshiko Takaezu among her larger pots.

"A hundred dollars?"

"Yes!"

"Dear Toshiko, you are not a gambler—unless it is in new forms and shapes and wonderments in ceramics."

Let us return to Toshiko's life work:

"In my life I see no difference between making pots, cooking and growing vegetables. They are all so related. However, there is a need for me to work with clay. It is so gratifying, and I get so much joy from it, and it gives me many answers for my life.

"One of the best things about clay is that I can be completely free and honest with it. And clay responds to me. The clay is alive and responsive to every touch and feeling. When I make it into form, it is alive, and even when it is dry, it is still breathing! I can feel the response in my hands, and I don't have to force the clay. The whole process is an interplay between the clay and myself, and often the clay has much to say."

TAKE OUR DAUGHTERS TO WORK DAY

It was 1994, and we were in the grand ballroom of the Waldorf Astoria celebrating the sixtieth birthday of Gloria Steinem with thousands of others.

It was a tightly scripted, carefully organized evening in which a number of women were recognized. Partway along, a substantial young woman, Nell Merlino, took the microphone. The klieg lights were on her, as she was to describe the progress of the "Take Our Daughters to Work Day" campaign, which she led for the Ms. Foundation.

She blurted out that she had only three minutes, but that she could not stand there without acknowledging, "Mrs. McVay, without your support I would not be standing here today. I was not a great math student, but she encouraged me. She kindly wrote a letter on my behalf as part of the college application process, which I knew would be fair. Mrs. McVay, please stand and be recognized!" Hella slowly stood up, shielding her face from the klieg lights that turned on her.

I wrote this in 2011, when our daughter, Cynthia McVay, director of innovation for the Peace Corps in its celebratory fiftieth year, was in West Africa, specifically in The Gambia and Senegal, with her daughter, Tess, who was then seventeen. An email spelled out what an extraordinary bonding experience this had been as they had worked through various challenges together, from missing the connection to Cameroon due to a five-hour flight delay out of Washington to the perils of traveling over water between the two countries as they met with the in-country leaders and Peace Corps volunteers in a variety of situations.

This was also written on the eve of the airing of an HBO special, *Gloria: In Her Own Words* (August 15, 2011), on the life of Gloria

Steinem, then seventy-seven years old. It began with Ms. Steinem as a young journalist from Toledo, Ohio, who wore a bunny suit for an early exposé on the harsh working conditions at a Playboy Club. She came to feminism in New York in her thirties and helped found *Ms.* magazine, emerging as one of the idols of the women's movement.

Ms. Steinem was not enthusiastic about a project with a focus that was only on her. She insisted that the fight for equal rights for women "has been a collective effort."

When a woman is recognized, the first thing she says is, "This gives me a chance to acknowledge the whole team!" So, too, with Gloria Steinem.

Emily Mann, artistic director of McCarter Theatre, mentioned to me that she is writing a play about Gloria Steinem, who has just turned eighty. How exciting!

At the time of the United Nations's consideration of the gravity of climate change and what we can do about it, just after a huge rally in New York which drew over 300,000, the *New York Times* devoted its entire Science Section on September 23, 2014, to the issue. Claudia Dreyfus asked two questions of two dozen scientists, authors, and world and national figures: What is your greatest worry about climate change? What gives you hope?

My favorite response was by Gloria Steinem: "Thinking about climate change used to give me images of the sun burning down and icebergs melting—horrific, but also impersonal and far away. Now I have intimate fears of storms and floods that drive us off this island of Manhattan and fires that send thousands fleeing—in other words just an acceleration of what we're already seeing....

"I'm willing to lower my standard of living to help create a turning point. We are waiting for a practical, coordinated, understandable set of instructions that counters the Kochs, the deniers, the profiteers. Meanwhile, we try to do whatever we can.

"Somehow, I find comfort in the idea that the earth is a living organism with a will of its own. The global women's movement gives me hope because women are trying to take control of their own bodies and reproduction.... Everything we know says that when women can decide whether and when to have children, growth slows down to a little over replacement level. And that would be the single biggest long-term relief for the environment."

On May 9, 2014, Nell Merlino, now sixty-one, was the featured speaker at the Friends of the New Jersey State Museum's festive annual luncheon. She was pure dynamite on home turf. On women's leadership and empowerment, her remarks were trained on her beloved mother, Molly Merlino, an accomplished artist ever in a smock, a mother of five, and a president of the Friends. She was married to Joe Merlino, the ranking Democrat in the state legislature whose political mannerisms were reminiscent of LBJ's. Molly Merlino would say, "With women it's all about flowers. Women are always caregivers, but, increasingly, breadwinners." Nell said, "At my father's retirement dinner, I created 'Take Our Daughters to Work Day.' My mother insisted that the fight for equal rights for women has been a collective effort."

By now, some 20 million girls and boys have participated in what is now called Take Our Daughters and Sons to Work Day.

KEEP THE CHIEF IN THE LOOP

It was near the end of S. Dillon Ripley's service as secretary of the Smithsonian (1964–1984), and the board was having lunch at the National Museum of Natural History. Upon his death at eighty-seven in 2001, the obituary in the *Washington Post* said that Ripley, the esteemed ornithologist and cultural leader, had transformed the Smithsonian from a bastion of science and culture for the sober and serious-minded into a bright, lively center for education, amusement, and entertainment.

The *New York Times*'s obituary revealed a tidbit from Ripley's early life in the final paragraph: Tom Lovejoy, a biologist himself and assistant secretary of the Smithsonian, recounted a story from when Dillon was in the OSS in World War II in Sri Lanka. He was taking a shower when he saw a bird he'd been trying to collect through the cracks. He wrapped himself in a towel, got a shotgun, and nailed the bird. Just then Lord Mountbatten, with assorted officers and ladies, came around the corner, and the towel fell off. But he didn't lose the bird.

My relationship with Ripley dated from our service on the board of the World Wildlife Fund, when I was one of two who served on his committee to select the next leader of the fund. We chose Russell Train, and WWF's star began to rise. It was Ripley who invited me to serve on the Smithsonian's national board. Hella and I attended two of his and Mary's daughters' weddings.

At the lunch, something was up. An excitement crackled the air. S. Dillon Ripley, whose vision, grace, and spirit had carried the Smithsonian Institution to new heights by shaping the big brush trajectory of the place—creating eight new museums and starting a magazine with eight million readers—as well as the small details, was taken aback.

For three years, something had been going on of which he was wholly unaware. The marine biologists wanted to surprise him and make him happy with their ingenuity.

Quietly, they had been bringing back, bucket by bucket, chunks of a coral reef from the Caribbean for reassembly in the museum as a living organism.

This first-of-its-kind undertaking was not easy. Indeed, the whole living entity had collapsed one night, leaving fish flopping about on the floor, only to be picked up and put back together in a tank with wave action that mimicked the ocean.

Even with good intentions, the successful re-creation of an oceanic reef in the heart of nation's capitol left Dillon upset. You heard this in his voice, and you saw it in his face. The lesson here, as with Lester Brown at a surprise party to mark his sixtieth birthday at the Cosmos Club, is don't try to surprise the chief. He or she likes to know about everything, down to the smallest microorganism.

As I learned from one of my trustees at Dodge, "Scott, I like to be in on the takeoff, not just the crash landing."

Now, this was not a crash landing, nor to the best of memory, did we have any in my years at Dodge.

WHAM! THERE I AM ON ANOTHER COMMITTEE

Upon entering the foundation field in 1972, I was blessed by the character and grace of my superiors. At the Robert Sterling Clark Foundation, my boss was Eugene W. Goodwillie, who was so beloved and trusted that he was named as a principal in more than eighty trusts. At Cornell he earned a Rhodes scholarship (Class of 1927). He was a gentle, wise man. After his death, another trustee, Miner Crary, said, commenting on a little challenge, "That's one we would have liked to ask Gene about."

When I accepted the invitation of the trustees of the newly formed Geraldine R. Dodge Foundation to serve as the first executive director, William Rockefeller was president and chairman of a board of nine. A partner at Shearman and Sterling and president, later chair, of the board of the Metropolitan Opera, he was fair, unassuming, and selfless in relation to the foundation's formation and evolution.

At least once a month in the early years, I met with Mr. Rockefeller in his office in Manhattan to review mail he had received and to raise any questions I had. Invariably and without exception, he gave me the mail and said, "Let the chips fall where they may." In not a single instance did he advance any of his interests, saying even that we should not support the Metropolitan Opera since that would be a conflict of interest.

In the 1980s, however, we did support bringing the Met to New Jersey in the summer for public performances at four locations so that opera lovers, whether they could afford to go to Lincoln Center or not, could enjoy hearing the finest singers from the Met in outdoor presentations.

My duties at Dodge began on January 1, 1976. My first substantial hire was John Robinson, just retired at sixty as a partner with Arthur

Andersen in Chicago, New York, and London. He was a star of the first magnitude in keeping our books and making sure our assets were fully invested with a minimum balance in our checking account. He also had a terrific sense of humor.

While our investments were placed with five or six different managers, each with a different point of view, our cash accounts were with Fidelity Union Trust in Newark, where the president and chairman of the bank there was C. Malcolm Davis, who also served on the Dodge board.

After a year or less, Mr. Davis invited me to lunch at the Newark Club. No sooner had I taken the first bite of the meal than he said I had to get rid of John Robinson within two weeks or my job was on the line. This was a terrifying threat as we were just gaining traction as a philanthropy after developing our priorities and publishing them widely in the first six months.

What was the problem? Mr. Davis said that Robinson was a pain in the neck, forever bothering the Trust's back office with questions and requests.

Governor Tom Kean is greeted by William Rockefeller, president and chairman of the Dodge Foundation—both opera buffs—at the first Dodge Poetry Festival, 1986.

After the lunch, I jumped on the train to New York and called on Mr. Rockefeller to get his advice on what to do. He said do nothing, and don't worry about this.

John Robinson went on to serve for years as our chief financial officer with élan and precision.

William Rockefeller died in 1990 at the age of seventy-one. Bill's zest for life was revealed in little things. For example, as one who served on countless boards and committees of institutions large and local, he once iterated a law of life in these matters:

> When to meetings I go
> with the greatest of skill
> I always contrive
> to keep perfectly still
> for if I show interest
> or seem a bit witty
> wham! there I am
> on another committee.

Bill Rockefeller was involved in the genesis of many of the foundation's initiatives, such as increased minority enrollments at independent schools, our nationwide Chinese language initiative, our endeavors for the welfare of animals, and our hopes for poetry and better writing in the schools.

The trustees and staff remember his steadfast faithful leadership, his compassion, and his unswerving integrity. He participated in all discussions that led to the creation of the five categories of giving—the welfare of animals, the arts, education, public issues, and local projects—and their evolution.

WHO? WHO? WHO? WHO? WHO?

Poster for the Geraldine R. Dodge Poetry Festival in 1990 features a work by Georgia O'Keefe, a friend of David Hunter McAlpin.

Who accompanied Georgia O'Keefe
to Lake George after the war
to take the ashes of Alfred
Stieglitz to their resting place,
the restless man who celebrated
the face, the form, the hands,
the neck, the grace, the little
annoyance at one more photograph,
thereby almost seizing the soul

of O'Keefe, at the very least
nudging it to a destiny
joined to the country's,
the rapture of the city,
the opening of an orchid,
the beckoning of the West
at the brilliant blue noon
with worn white clean steer skull
aloft like some banner
of what's been
and to come?
Who accompanied Georgia O'Keefe? Who?

Who saw genius in
the young Ansel Adams,
years, decades, before
he became one with our image
of a majestic place,
like Moonrise over Sonoma,
or a quiet place
lit with white birches,
or a beauteous spot
capturing the oneness of
one tree and we,
or quite simply the artist
who taught us about the
solitude and splendor
of the West,
the way Frederic Church
did with paint a century earlier?
Who saw genius? Who?

Who noted the keen eye
of Eliot Porter,
who went on to rank
with Adams as the other
master of the camera
for Nature, giving impetus
to preserve
what is being despoiled
before our wet eyes?

Who helped, too,
Edward Weston, who
caught himself in a
youthful pose high upon
a Manhattan building
seeking to say,
thank you, as Adams did
In that magical boat shot?

Who helped to launch
the Watershed Association,
the Conservation Foundation,
and even assist
the New York Zoological
Society in its expanding
job of showing fauna,
discovering their habits,
and working in far places?
Who? Who? Who?

Who takes immense pride in family and in Princeton
with loyalty tracked
in thirty-nine members of his family,
father, son, grandsons and daughters,
great grand, grand great … ?
We know, David, that one day
you will succeed Judge Medina,
Aught Nine, at the
head of the P-Rade!

Who is the unchallenged
patron of photography?
and patron saint?
Who brought it to MOMA
and gave it a boost earlier
at the Metropolitan?
Who led me across field of snow
at a brisk pace when my French car faltered?
Who takes joy in roses
and rhododendrons in full bloom?
Who knows and values
a good dog?

Who—above all—had the
perspicacity to marry
Sally Sage
his life companion?
He fell in love with
her laughter—
sunbursts of laughter.

Who? Who? Who? Who? Who?

The one and only, truly beloved,
David Hunter McAlpin

We salute you, sir,
on reaching and striding right past
your ninetieth birthday!

December 17, 1986
(for his birthday on May 20, 1987)

Photograph of David Hunter McAlpin,
patron saint of photography, by Edward Weston.

Postscript

David Hunter McAlpin was a charter trustee of the Dodge Foundation and a member of the Rockefeller family, whom I drove to every board meeting in Morristown. He was a gentle yet unwavering patron and advocate for photography.

The Art of Leadership

In his memoir, *At Ease*, Eisenhower offered
the following advice:

"Always try to associate yourself with and
learn as much as you can from those who
know more than you do, who do better
than you, who see more clearly than you."

Ike slowly masters the art of leadership by
becoming a super apprentice.

— David Brooks, "The Follower Problem,"
the *New York Times*, June 12, 2012

WHAT'S OUR BIGGEST PROBLEM?

Cartoon of Ronald Reagan, museum in Havana, Cuba, 2002.

When Leipzig and Dresden were firebombed in 1945, as many as 135,000 people, unconnected with the war effort, were killed. Kurt Vonnegut caught the anguish and stupidity of that action in *Slaughterhouse-Five*.

The Germans were used to going under buildings when these intense bombings took place. So, too, Werner Fornos, nine years old, went with his mother and siblings into the basement of their apartment building in Leipzig one fateful evening in December 1942. Afterward, Werner looked around and found no one from his family. He was alone. He beat on a pipe with a wrench. After three days, he was heard and rescued.

In the summer of 1944, continued Allied bombing opened the opportunity for young Werner to flee westward on foot and in freight trains. He survived by stealing vegetables from fields and going door to door to do odd jobs in return for food.

Working his way across Europe, he arrived in Normandy while the Allied invasion forces were fighting their way across northern France after D-Day. During the battle of Rouen, Werner was knocked unconscious by a rock hurled by a grenade explosion. He awoke in an American first-aid tent, surrounded by soldiers speaking a language he could not understand. It was not long before the eleven-year-old boy was "adopted" by members of the 29th Infantry Division of the United States Army, who fed, clothed, and took care of their new "mascot."

Werner stayed with the infantry division as they fought their way into Germany. They taught him how to play baseball and how to speak English. In turn, he served as a German-language interpreter, helped them find food, and crossed the front lines to locate German positions as the Americans advanced into enemy territory.

From 1945 to 1950, Werner tried to escape to America four times by boat, but he was returned to Germany every time

The fifth time he was successful—hiding in the bomb compartment of a plane bound for America via Reykjavík, Iceland. He was unbelievably cold and hungry. When the plane stopped for refueling, he scampered into a PX (post exchange), with which he had become familiar, and got a hamburger.

At the Westover Air Force Base in Massachusetts, the immigration authorities caught him again. But his luck had finally changed. Elizabeth Fornos, an immigrant herself, and her husband heard the boy's extraordinary story and arranged for him to live with them while they petitioned to have him declared a legal immigrant.

In 1954, he enlisted in the US Army and was assigned to Germany. He distinguished himself in Berlin, and in 1958, a write-up appeared in the German papers. It turned out that his own Mother was still alive, and she read the article in amazement, noting "those are the eyes of my little Werner." She contacted him, and they saw each other on the day he rotated back to America. They were in touch the rest of her life.

Werner was grateful for his good fortune. He loved America and was interested in tackling a big issue. Following studies and graduation from the University of Maryland, and serving in the Maryland House of Delegates (1966–70), Fornos founded the Population Institute in 1982 and located it right behind the nation's capitol at 107 2nd Street, NE, for the maximum leverage on Congress. He believed that population was the most pressing issue facing humanity.

The Population Institute provided excellent intern opportunities for college students, six per year. Fornos also organized annual trips to encourage family planning efforts abroad and to recognize journalists, cartoonists, and others for creative efforts on behalf of family planning.

In my years with the Dodge Foundation, a half dozen or more grants were made to organizations working on the burgeoning population issue and women's reproductive rights. Near the end of my tenure, we made a modest grant to the Population Institute.

Hella with Population Institute bus in Mexico City in 2005.

We were lucky to pay to travel with Werner to India in 1999 when a group from Kerala traveled to Delhi to be honored at a banquet arranged through Rotary International. Other trips we participated in were to Cuba (2002), Sri Lanka (2003), Morocco (2004), and Mexico (2005). In every case, journalists came along who had written something of note on the population issue.

An extraordinary trip occurred in 2004 to China when six of us "reviewed" family planning there after being briefed at length by Zhao Baige, director of the National Population and Family Planning Commission. She obtained a PhD in biology from Cambridge University, a five-year program, and then worked in New York City for five years. She had been running the program for the People's Republic of China for nine years at that point.

The one child per family policy begun in 1979 was still very much in place. Dr. Baige and others, however, were keenly aware of the extreme stress caused by the preference for the male child in China, as in India. It had caused the ratio of men to women in China to climb to 117 to 100. In the rural regions, that ratio soared to 154 to 100. Baige and her colleagues were working on financial incentives to encourage more female births. We met two educated, adroit young women, one in Beijing and one in Shanghai, who expressed being thrilled with having a girl. The latter said, smiling, "Unfortunately she looks like my husband."

Our journey across China to several locations and sites was illuminating even though it was wholly orchestrated by the regime. Mothers of minority nationalities were allowed give birth to three children or more. In Tibet, there were no birth limitations at all.

Regarding contraception for family planning, the government respected people's right to choose the means. Of the then 240 million women of childbearing age, 83 percent used some form of contraceptive: intrauterine devices (48 percent), tubal ligation (36 percent), with the rest taking oral contraceptives or having their partners use condoms. The induced abortion rate in China was 28 percent, in contrast to 25 percent in the United States.

Midway in our journey on July 16, 2004, when we were in Chengdu, President George W. Bush vetoed the $34 million that Congress had appropriated for the United Nations Population Fund. The will of the American people expressed through their elected representatives was again ignored, thwarted, and denied for the third year in a row.

The aging population in China presents challenges there as here. We were impressed by the laughter in a model home for the elderly in Shanghai, where women in their nineties were painting with zest and imagination.

In 2003, Werner Fornos received the highest accolade the United Nations can give an individual, an analog to a Nobel laureate. Hella and I flew to New York from Chautauqua for the ceremony. Werner delivered a brilliant speech in acceptance even though he was in pain from gallstones and was operated on shortly thereafter.

This vignette is a salute to a purposeful life dedicated to fighting the rampant rise in our numbers, which puts crushing pressure on finite biological resources and human infrastructures.

Postscript

Within the foundation field, the Green Revolution initiative of the Rockefeller Foundation to grow more crops worldwide is often touted as brilliant and strategic, since it increased yields of crops to feed a rapidly growing human population. One of our program officers at the Dodge Foundation was Robert Perry, whose father directed that program, hiring agronomist Norman Borlaug (1914–2009), who received the Nobel Peace Prize in 1970. One day the elder Mr. Perry, Jesse Parker Perry, Jr., came to our office to share with staff his experience over a brown bag lunch. It was fascinating, but the capper was his final comment: "You know, I think I was working on the wrong problem. I should have been working on population."

Werner Fornos, president of the Population Institute, in Cuba in 2002 applauding the presentation of an award for family planning by Sally G. Epstein.

I WOULD LIKE TO MEET THEM!

Scott with Senators John Heinz and Al Gore,
Tom Lovejoy, and Senator Tim Wirth.

In 1989, Hella and I were in Dubrovnik at a conference organized by the Aspen Institute on foreign policy with a focus on Eastern Europe for senators and congressmen, funded by the Carnegie Corporation and the W. Alton Jones Foundation.

I mentioned to then-Senator Tim Wirth (Democrat, Colorado) that I had asked the leaders of ten environmental groups—among them the World Wildlife Fund, Natural Resources Defense Council, and Environmental Defense Fund—to name a young person who was making an outsized contribution of a singular sort.

Thanks to the kindness of Henry Harter, president and CEO of Chubb & Son, we pulled these ten leaders together on August 11, 1989, for a day at Chubb's new headquarters in Warren, New Jersey, to tell their stories and suggest paths for environmental focus down the road. I also expected a strong rub-off among these accomplished young folks in firing up one another. We filmed the day's proceedings since this gathering produced such a dynamic interchange.

In regards to those accomplished young people, Tim Wirth said, "I would like to meet them!"

I suggested that his colleague and friend from the other side of the aisle, Senator John Heinz (Republican, Pennsylvania), be part of the conversation.

So, at the Capitol on February 28, 1990, we reassembled the bright young activists for an extended luncheon conversation of over two hours that included not only Wirth and Heinz but also Senator Al Gore (Democrat, Tennessee, and author of *Earth in the Balance*), Theresa Heinz, and biologist Tom Lovejoy.

None of the senators took a phone call. Each was 100 percent present and deeply concerned about the onslaught of multiple scourges of human origin on the Earth and what we can do about it. It was a conversation of peers—unaffected, fast moving, and relevant.

As a foundation person, one has convening powers. From the participants here I have heard that this gathering with motivated peers and three attuned United States Senators spurred them on down the years. The youngest participant, Michele Byers, is today the executive director of the New Jersey Conservation Foundation and the leading voice for conservation in the Garden State. Dozens of other assemblages of teachers in the visual arts, theater, poetry, Earthwatch Expeditions, star teachers from the Alternate Route program, and principals as lead learners also carried joyful energy and mutual camaraderie.

Senator Wirth thanked the young activists for breaking stride to meet with them.

Postscript

From 1998 to 2013, Tim Wirth served as president of the United Nations Foundation, founded and chaired by Ted Turner. Tragically, John Heinz was killed on April 4, 1991, when a Bell 412 helicopter and a Piper Aerostar with Heinz aboard collided. Al Gore became vice president of the United States under President Bill Clinton, authored a book, *An Inconvenient Truth*, and received the Nobel Peace Prize in 2007 with the Intergovernmental Panel on Climate Change.

A TREND IS NOT DESTINY

– Jaime Lerner

*Leaders from Newark with Governor
and Mrs. Jaime Lerner of Brazil before
Thomas Jefferson's Rotunda at the
University of Virginia, April 13, 1997.*

In 1989, ecologist Bill McKibben published *The End of Nature*, suggesting that human numbers and behavior would damage the planet beyond repair and resilience. All arrows on the charts of life on Earth pointed down and out.

David Brower, "the Archdruid of Conservation" and leader of the Sierra Club and Friends of the Earth, told McKibben that he should focus on what is working. Six years later, McKibben published

Hope, Human and Wild (1995), describing eloquently and precisely how two very different societies offered models of sustainability: Curitiba, Brazil, and Kerala, India, where the literacy rate for 30 million people was an astonishing 97 percent and folks got by then on $2 or $3 a day.

Thanks to the leadership of Jaime Lerner, who was elected mayor of Curitiba in 1971, the city has no poverty, a superb bus system that has been copied worldwide, a fine health and medical program, an exemplary school system, forty-three libraries, and a beautiful opera house. When BMW wanted to locate a plant in Brazil, the choice of Curitiba was easy.

"Jaime has a saying," explained Lerner's director of training, Ester Proveller, to McKibben. "Don't wait until all your pumpkins are in the truck to start your journey to market. They'll accumulate along the way."

For this reason, she added, many of Curitiba's most important officials are women.

"Jaime says that if women get two good cards, they'll start to play. Men sit and wait for a whole hand. We're not as afraid of failure—in that way we're braver."

Mayor Lerner became known as "the Gandhi of urban planning." He once told some planners from other cities, "You have to have fun. All my work, all my life, we have fun. We're laughing all the time. We're working on things that make us happy."

In April 1997, Bill McDonough, dean of the School of Architecture at the University of Virginia, chose Jaime Lerner, then governor of Paraná, for the Jefferson Medal, given in honor of achievements in architecture, law, and citizen leadership. I then invited ten people from Newark to travel to Charlottesville to meet with Lerner and his wife in the downtime between events in the Rotunda and at Monticello on Saturday and Sunday.

Five of the Newark participants were in their twenties, and the intergenerational trip was intended to root new possibilities for the future of Newark.

We had a total of seven and a half hours with Lerner, during which he sketched his ideas on a large pad of white paper: "Ecology—Equity—Economics." Our group included Robert Curvin (author and expert on urban politics and social policy), Clement Price (Rutgers professor and Newark historian), Rebecca Doggett (professor of child and adolescent psychiatry), William Crawley (former executive director of the Newark Downtown Core Redevelopment Corporation), and the then-unsmiling Cory Booker, an aspiring politician who in time became mayor of Newark and who visited Curitiba twice. Booker was elected in 2013 as a United States senator from New Jersey, another indirect ripple of Lerner's urban leadership.

I HAVE SPENT MY ENTIRE LIFE
LEARNING TO WRITE

Few environmentalists do I admire more than George Woodwell. Not only was he a founding trustee of both the Environmental Defense Fund and the Natural Resources Defense Council, and a chair of the board of the World Wildlife Fund (where we were colleagues and friends), but he also founded the Woods Hole Research Center in 1985 and led it for years. The center has provided an incalculable scientific base for documenting the facts of climate change planetwide and the gravity of the threat. With his colleagues he has communicated new information on the decline of forests worldwide with oomph and grace. He was also the first scientist I heard make the case for global warming in 1985 at an NRDC event at Lincoln Center.

Not all that long after graduating from Dartmouth in 1950 and earning a PhD in biology from Duke, where his dissertation examined forests in the coastal plain, George was engaged in a major experiment defining the ecological effects of ionizing radiation at the Brookhaven National Laboratory on Long Island.

George was planning a conference with other scientists and thought it would be interesting to invite John Steinbeck (1902–1968)—author of twenty-seven books, including *The Grapes of Wrath*, *East of Eden*, and *Of Mice and Men*—to speak to the group after dinner.

A line in Steinbeck's acceptance speech for the Nobel Prize in Literature in 1962 read, "Man himself has become our greatest hazard and our only hope." That might well be a motif in George Woodwell's life.

Woodwell is an accomplished wordsmith and quite persuasive in person and on paper regarding his aims, which are propelled by a spirit of conviction. So he penned a good letter inviting the esteemed writer, then living on Long Island.

The reply came back like a boomerang. Across the face of George's clean one-page letter of appeal, Steinbeck wrote, in a broad-nib black-felt pen, the following in block letters: "Woodwell—I have spent my entire life learning to write and now you want me to speak. No thanks! Steinbeck."

THE DRIVE FOR PERFECTION
AND THE NATURE OF OBSESSION

Merlin Tuttle, founder of Bat Conservation International,
with bat and Charlie Rose, January 13, 1993.

For several years we had known and admired Merlin Tuttle, founder and president of Bat Conservation International based in Austin, Texas. He had dazzled our Dodge Earthwatch teachers at our retreats in Blairstown with revelations about bats, whose more than 1,331 species comprise a fourth of the mammalian kingdom. Bats are critical pollinators and disbursers of seeds, and consume every night huge numbers of insects, many deleterious to crops and to us.

In 1991, I joined the board of Bat Conservation International (BCI), and shortly thereafter, in 1992, the board traveled to Belize to an appealing lodge, Chan Chich, situated at a former Mayan village, where the bellbird bongs. Mist nets were hung the first evening, with Merlin noting that after the board meeting, he would go to a yet more remote site to find a bat he hadn't seen in twenty years.

When the first bat hit the net and was carefully extracted, it turned out to be that very species, an adult male wrinkle-faced bat. It is the *only ugly bat* (though one of Merlin's favorites) of the hundreds we netted with him in subsequent years, mainly in Venezuela in 1995 and 1999, a mega-diversity country with 160 bat species.

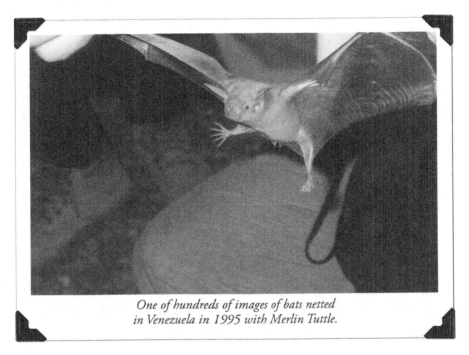

One of hundreds of images of bats netted in Venezuela in 1995 with Merlin Tuttle.

Many bats were caught that evening, examined, touched, photographed, and released.

At midnight, we turned in, but Merlin stayed up all night photographing this bizarre-looking bat, so strange that it has a flap of furry skin it can raise to cover its corrugated face during courtship, so that only the eyes look out.

When we came to breakfast, Merlin was glowing with the results of the night's photography (he later sent us two photographs of this little guy, flap down and flap up).

Merlin then suggested we walk with David Bamberger along the river on the right. He said to look under the trunks of trees leaning out over the river for what "looks like loose bark."

Hey, what's that? Looks like loose bark. In a nanosecond Merlin was in the river, waist deep, coming in from the other side with a camera draped around his neck.

Every step he took closer to the bats, they shook as if about to take off. Merlin just paused, talked to them in gentle tones that seemed to calm them down, and continued his approach.

Then he sighed. Why? No longer could he catch all the bats in a single frame with his telephoto lens—they were a group of nine below and thirteen above. He had to shoot each patch separately as he closed in. To our amazement, the bats had allowed him to approach so close he needed a close-up lens.

For three hours Merlin photographed those bats. No wonder that thousands of his images of bats are on the BCI website. As the foremost bat scientist and preeminent photographer of bats, it is unlikely that anyone will reach or exceed his accomplishments planetwide.

For my eightieth birthday on June 1, 2013, Merlin and his wife Paula surprised us with an elegantly wrapped package holding a spectacular photograph of an orange and black adult male painted bat (*Kerivoula picta*) in flight. This species is widely distributed in tropical areas of Southeast Asia but is rarely seen by humans. It lives in dead or dying leaves, especially those of banana plants, normally as a pair with their single pup. When flushed from hiding in the daytime, these bats have a characteristic, butterfly-like flight and thus are sometimes called butterfly bats. The image was taken by Merlin on August 23, 2012, in Pa Po Village, Thailand, in an enclosed studio set up in a shelter for chickens and ducks beneath a local home.

In October 2015, Tuttle will publish a major book on bats with Houghton Mifflin Harcourt called *The Secret Lives of Bats*, which is eagerly awaited.

WOULD YOU LIKE TO SEE THE SHACK?

The place was Wisconsin, forty-five minutes north of Madison. The date was August 9, 1996, and we were celebrating our anniversary. The next day, Merlin Tuttle, pioneer bat biologist, was getting married to a Dr. Love, a veterinarian who specialized in exotic animals.

But that day was centered on George Archibald, the lead authority on cranes worldwide. George went to Dalhousie University in Halifax, Nova Scotia, and earned his doctorate in biology at Cornell in 1975. He had cofounded with Ron Sauey the International Crane Foundation (ICF) in 1973 in Baraboo, Wisconsin. From the beginning George showed diligence in seeking to preserve the habitats of the fifteen species of cranes on Earth and engaging people who live nearby in this heroic effort—in such places as Australia, Afghanistan, Cuba, Cambodia, China, Ethiopia, India, Russia, and the Korean Demilitarized Zone (first visited in 1974), as well as North Korea.

The ICF headquarters in Baraboo treads lightly on the land with a subdued, elegant design by a protégé of Frank Lloyd Wright. All fifteen species were present as we toured the circular facility, even the whooping crane, the species that had been reduced to just fifteen then in the wild. In fact, we saw Gee Whiz—the result of a mating dance in 1982 between George and Tex. George was dressed as and acting as a male crane—walking, calling, dancing—to lure Tex into reproductive mode. Through George's perseverance and the use of artificial insemination, Tex eventually laid a fertile egg. When the resultant chick burst forth from the egg, George squealed, "Gee Whiz," and that stuck.

George organized a conference in Africa in 1993 to protect the principal habitats of six species of cranes—two migratory and four found in Sub-Saharan Africa. They are the oldest in the crane family and some have the habit of squatting low in the grass so that their tufted tops are less conspicuous. At the conference held in Maun, Botswana, where representatives of twenty-four countries came together (including those from Senegal, Mali, Nigeria, Ethiopia, Uganda, Kenya, Tanzania, Malawi, Tunisia, and South Africa), George arranged for musicians, singers, and dancers to celebrate these cranes. Reports praised the imaginative choreography of the gathering, uniting the arts and conservation in such a glorious way. Today the art of children is an integral part of conservation at key habitats everywhere.

Although George does not speak other languages, his emotional intelligence makes folks think he does. At the International Crane Foundation, George and his colleague Jim Harris saw to it that native grasses were planted to the west of the site and that "Crane City" was built across a shallow valley. His efforts earned him a MacArthur genius award early on in 1984.

It is worth recalling what George Archibald said on the *Charlie Rose* show on September 28, 1993:

"Cranes are enormous creatures. Some of them stand almost six feet tall. In captivity they live as long as a man. We've had them live into their eighties. They are monogamous. They have an elaborate communication system with sixteen different calls. It's not what you say but how you say it, and males and females have different voices for different calls. They travel thousands of miles between the area in which they breed and where they winter, and they become social and have much communication between their flock. They get along together."

After a visit of three or four hours, where Hella and I felt lucky to be at the epicenter of crane research and conservation worldwide, George asked if we would like to see the shack where Aldo Leopold (1887–1948) wrote the essays on a land ethic for which he is renowned and which were gathered in a book, *The Sand County Almanac* (1949) that his children published after his death. It contains this stunning thought: "A thing is right when it tends to preserve the integrity, stability, and beauty of the biotic community."

George Archibald, International Crane Foundation,
Charlie Rose *show, September 28, 1993.*

After a drive of perhaps forty minutes, we arrived at the shack, the only such edifice granted National Historic Landmark status. I kneeled down and kissed the ground while a swarm of hungry mosquitoes attacked me.

Then George asked, "Would you like to meet one of Dr. Leopold's daughters, Nina?" Sure. George said she, then seventy-eight years, lived just down the road in a house that she and her husband (then eighty-one) had built themselves. He wasn't sure if she was home. George tapped on the door. It swung open and Nina embraced him with a whoop of delight. She uncorked a bottle of chilled white wine, and I noticed a small bat flitting about above—doubtless a sign of Merlin's marriage on the morrow.

Nina rolled out a long piece of paper, whereon she had notated carefully the date of the first appearance of every biological phenomenon in the area. She had twenty years of data, including the date when a given bird or plant was last seen. She had information on some seventy species that extended her father's fifty years of observation.

"Everything was arriving two weeks earlier and staying two weeks longer, presumably due to climate change," she said. "Should I publish this?"

Our suggestion was to put it out on the internet to inspire others elsewhere to track local biological events.

This was our thirty-eighth anniversary, and we looked forward to the wedding of Merlin Tuttle the next day.

HOW ARE YOU SO PRODUCTIVE AND PROLIFIC AT EIGHTY?

In early 2008, I invited Edward Albee, who had just turned eighty, to speak to the Old Guard of Princeton, a group of lifelong learners between the ages of sixty-five and eighty-five who gather for a lecture every Wednesday morning. He said he had an agent and that would require him to charge us. I said the Old Guard has a policy of not paying speakers.

"However," Albee continued, "if we had a conversation, there would be no fee."

We opted for the conversation.

On the appointed day in May, we gathered in a larger than usual space, since members wanted to bring guests. I introduced him, noting that six of his plays were running in the New York area, including two new ones. At only one time previously, I explained, had the Old Guard had a conversation instead of a talk followed by Q and A.

"That was in 1944 with Albert Einstein." Albee smiled. He liked the company.

"How are you so productive and prolific at this stage of your life?" was my first question. He answered with verve that he exercised regularly and was still fascinated by life's lumpy questions, tangled relationships, and ethical concerns. The entire session clicked for him and for his grateful audience.

We had lunch at Prospect afterwards. I was interested to ask him about Easter Island (Rapa Nui), which he had written about in the *New York Times* three years earlier, since we were slated to go there shortly. He said he was planning to return to the remote island and was contemplating writing a play called *Silence*.

Our experience there turned out to be anything but silence since the winds howled steadily and the Rapa Nui "cowboys" galloped through town on horseback or roared up a long hill in town on a motorcycle. But the mute Moai's full story has not yet been deciphered. How were these massive figures transported from the quarry to the shores of the island and erected as guardian spirits? Our experience was an awakening but not silent, whether we were viewing music and dance performances, sitting close to the kitchen in a restaurant, or exploring every corner of the island. We saw where glyphs were carved in stone, which is near where annual swimming contests take place. Participants swim through shark-infested waters to capture the first bird hatched on a nearby island. The winds were ceaseless during out entire visit.

Albee handwrote a note after his conversation with the Old Guard, which began:

"Thank you for your kindness the other day in shepherding me and feeding me with such good conversation."

In preparation for the exchange with Albee, I had read on a trip in India the book *Stretching My Mind*, containing forty-two pieces by or about him, who is often considered our nation's leading playwright. It prompted the following poem, "for Edward Albee."

FOR EDWARD ALBEE

You can't do a dramatic act about a well-adjusted couple sitting
around being happy. There is absolutely no dramatic conflict.
You can't do it. And you examine the ladies in literature …
Is Clytemnestra fun? Were Lear's daughters nice to have around?
Wasn't Hedda Gabler a rather awful person?
— Edward Albee

I underlined the 42 pieces
in *Stretching My Mind*
so what questions could I yet have?
You have clarified the murky,
distilled the ambiguous, into tighter ambiguity
challenged the indolent,
skewered the wacky sometimes nutty
        human plight,
rattled the conditions of being alive,
provoked the sleepy,
nailed ideas against the church door
        of possibility,
cajoled our conceit,
laughed at our ludicrousness,
smiled at vanity,
twitted at twists of intention,
plumbed depths of desire,
agonized over trapped innocents,
wondered at the miracle of life,

blanched bravado,
loved the antics of gestures
    creating a new way of seeing,
blinked at violence,
chastened chastity,
upheld fidelity,
tweaked the pious,
plagued the Pharisees,
jolted the jealous,
sunk the sycophants,
wrestled the righteous,
foiled the fakes,
tilted at the bloated,
tried the unjust,
tempted the jury,
finagled at faithlessness,
flirted with the outlandish,
dangled the participles,
dropped the drawers,
quartered the cumquat,
loaded the loquat,
stiffened the wimpy,
sorted the sectarians,
chased the cults
qualified the terms
doubted the faithful
questioned the non-believer
shot from the outside
fathomed inner desire
quelled the quaking

seared the soul
snagged the snakes
writhed in pain.
Explain.

May 2008

From Whales Sing and Other Exuberances

PROBING HOW A WORK OF ART MAY CAPTURE A NATIONAL AGONY OR A GREAT PRESIDENT

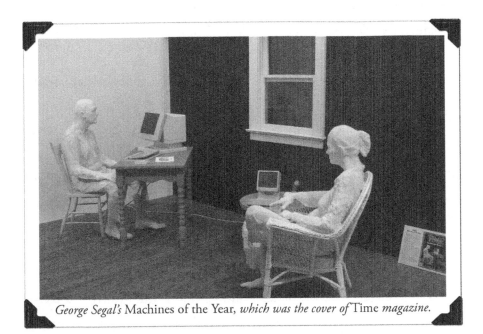

George Segal's Machines of the Year, *which was the cover of* Time *magazine.*

George Segal (1924–2000) was invited by Peter Putnam in 1978 to undertake a work of art for Kent State University to remember the killing of four history graduate students—Allison Krause, Sandy Schreuer, Jeffrey Miller, William Schroeder—who were shot by the Ohio National Guard on May 4, 1970, shortly after Nixon escalated the war in Vietnam by going into Cambodia.

Segal created *Abraham and Isaac*, which was initially approved by Kent State and later rejected. The exchange of communications suggests that the university was propelled by a desire to please a diverse public but did not want to deal with an event that helped to propel a nation's anguished questions about what we were fighting for in Vietnam.

Segal's correspondence and statements reflect a man wrestling with the dilemma and an ethicist of the first rank. On May 31, 1978, in connection with submitting the drawings for *Abraham and Isaac*, George Segal wrote the following to Kent State University's president, Bradge Golding:

"The students struck me as genuinely idealistic in their demonstrations against the spreading of the war into Cambodia, yet so single minded they disregarded law, democratic process, and wittingly or unwittingly, fanned the fears of those in charge."

Segal saw the events of May 4, 1970, through a generational, rather than political prism:

"The older people had … equated patriotism with obedience, were convinced of a Communist or Anarchist threat to our political structure, and a sexual threat to our religious morality. The fevered encounter between the students and the National Guard reminded me strongly of Abraham's willingness to sacrifice his only son … because God had ordered him to, i.e., he believed in an invisible, difficult abstraction."*

The sculpture depicts Abraham, with his sword held high, facing his son Isaac, kneeling with his hands bound behind him. Today the piece rests quietly between the University Chapel and Firestone Library at Princeton University, with a plaque on the wall with the passage from the Bible. I have stood flat against Abraham's back and then knelt behind Isaac. Abraham is on the verge of killing his son, believing that action is God's will. This piece joins the Putnam Collection of Sculpture on campus, which contains works by Henry Moore, Jacques Lipchitz, and Pablo Picasso. That collection is one of a kind for universities in North America.

We knew George and Helen Segal. When we drove them to Newark for a panel on how an artist's perception may differ from that commonly held or nationally proclaimed, Helen said, "You know, we would never leave home if it were not for you two."

Segal kindly opened his nine-chambered studio, transformed from a chicken coop, one special Saturday for the second Dodge Foundation cohort of twenty-five teachers who were visual artists.

In 2009, Helen and daughter Rena directed all of Segal's papers, totaling 8,800 of them, sixty-eight linear feet, to Princeton University, including a massive collection of photographs from the periphery of everyday life.

George and Helen Segal came to the celebration of our fortieth wedding anniversary at Prospect on August 9, 1998. Two months later, on October 4, 1998, George Segal and I received ZAMMI appreciation awards from Rutgers University's Zimmerli Art Museum. For that occasion I wrote something to acknowledge Segal's works.

His sculptures—*The Breadline* and *The Fireside Chat*—are in the second of four open-air rooms that make up the Franklin Delano Roosevelt Memorial along the Potomac River, where each room represents the ideas of each of FDR's four presidential terms.

From the Nassau Weekly, *May 26, 2010*

The Breadline *by George Segal, 1991, FDR Memorial, Washington, DC.*

THE MEMORY OF THE MAN

The FDR Memorial
walks along the Potomac
the four-term
New Deal President's
ideas are seized in stone
at each turn

The larger than life man is seen in 3D
the wife Eleanor
(alone)—full height—
in a kind of separate stand-alone
say it and speak to it (tomb)

Water splashes here and there, not only
in the coursing river,
the depression & war
receding years fly by
in a past
larger deeper
than the future

Near the close,
knowing the earlier
low years of the mid '30s
in the Depression Bread Line,
the work that defines the memorial
what the crippled leader
sought to overcome
and did

It's a somber hatted line of
five men, distilled from
George's boyhood
so it was a little jolt
in June to see five Presidential Scholars
clowning & posing
interleaved in between
bright as they are
but not knowing
not knowing
what it's like to be
without bread

what it's taken to get
the frail democracy to
where we are
"click," snap
"snap," maybe click
and they're gone,
the bread line stands
as a sober chrysalis
one of a 1,000 markers
defining who we are
where we're heading

Your eyes are held
held by the gravity
of the men standing there
but eventually the eye
travels to the right
where a man is bent over
his radio
catching every word

of a fireside chat
and on the left
the Appalachian couple
    (from Berkeley Heights
    Billy Kluver and his wife)
standing, emerging

and the whole, the three works
are the soul, the conscience,
the memory of the man
his years as leader
encompassing the attack on Pearl Harbor
& the galvanizing response

the words are Franklin Delano's
the images George Segal's
the memory indelible
the source a chicken coop
with wings
Helen close by.

October 4, 1998
From Whales Sing and Other Exuberances

Anything That's Precious

It's mighty hard right now to think
of anything that's precious that isn't
endangered. There are no sacred and
unsacred places; there are only sacred and
desecrated places. My belief is that the
world and our life in it are conditional
gifts. We have the world to live in on the
condition that we will take good care of
it. And to take good care of it, we have to
know it. And to know it and to be willing
to take care of it, we have to love it.

— Wendell Berry on *Moyers & Company*
October 6, 2013

HAVE YOU SEEN ANY?

Pete Dunne, author of 16 books on birding,
after leading a Monday morning walk in
Cape May Point in 2013.

On October 7, 1985, some grant recipients and staff took a hike along the Appalachian Trail to mark the tenth anniversary of the first two grants by the Geraldine R. Dodge Foundation. Beginning at Peters Valley, New Jersey, with twenty-five leaders in the not-for-profit world (including Olympia Dukakis of the Whole Theatre Company), we were blessed with a blue-sky day.

We began with a trust circle led by Phil Costello of Project USE (Urban Suburban Environments). After a couple of hours on the trail, we stopped for a picnic lunch on Rattlesnake Mountain. Each person was invited to talk about their hopes and dreams for the next five to seven years, which we tape-recorded. Pete Dunne of New Jersey Audubon Society said, "Our own backyards have become critical habitats." To date, Pete has written eighteen books on birds and wildlife, and he founded the World Series of Birding, a bird-counting competition.

Each leader was alerted, however, that if Pete spotted a "new" species of hawks on its southern migration over the lighthouse at Cape May Point and southward to Latin America, he would interrupt and sing out the identification. For at least a dozen different species, Pete pointed and said the hawk's name.

At that time, Pete Dunne had already written a hawk watch guide for high schoolers, especially in Northern New Jersey, that made identification easy and definitive.

On October 4, 1977, Pete had his best day spotting hawks from the platform at Cape May Point just north of the iconic lighthouse, counting 21,800 hawks. The airspace over Cape May was simply awash in birds—primarily sharp-shinned and broad-winged hawks.

On the beach nearby, a woman had been relaxing for the better part of the day. At about five o'clock, she asked Pete, "What are you doing?"

He replied, "Counting hawks."

"Have you seen any?" she asked.

The moral of the story: We inhabit different worlds. You have to look up.

HE KNEW THE CALLS OF 4,000 SPECIES OF BIRDS

Tom Lovejoy's Camp 41, two hours by truck north of Manaus, Brazil, was the portal through which over time twenty-six senators became acquainted with a tropical rain forest. It was the hub of a critical size experiment to test the relationship between species diversity and the size of a tract of land, whether it is 10,000 acres, 1,000 acres, or 100 acres. Visitors slept in hammocks, and the idea was to fall asleep ahead of the snorers.

On one of three occasions, in January, 1993, when Hella and I visited, we had the privilege of meeting and walking with Ted Parker (Theodore A. Parker III), an ornithologist without peer who knew the vocal repertoire of 4,000 species of birds. The next most attuned bird man knew about 1,000 calls.

"No one knows anything about how birds live. We just invent these little formulas and pretend we understand something," Ted observed in *A Parrot Without a Name: The Search for the Last Unknown Birds on Earth* by Don Stap.

As we walked with Parker, he recorded the call of a given bird, played it back, and the bird came in out of curiosity and walked on the ground beside and before us. Within twenty minutes, we had a dozen different bird species, including a pair of hefty Amazon vultures, waddling along with us. It felt as if we were accompanying Saint Francis of Assisi*—for these were sacred moments of communion with another part of creation.

On August 3, 1993, Ted Parker, forty, and Al Gentry (Alwyn Gentry), forty-four—his counterpart in the world of plants—crashed into a mountainside in Ecuador and perished. They were engaged by

Conservation International to make rapid assessments of biodiversity of species in uncharted rain forests in an effort to enhance their preservation. E. O. Wilson said, "We have lost 40 percent of what we know about the living world."

The W. Alton Jones Foundation, the sponsor of our board trip early that year, made a grant of $100,000 to Cornell's Laboratory of Ornithology to transcribe Ted Parker's notebooks and journals and to catalog his recordings for the benefit of others. Charlie Wolcott, director of the laboratory, said that they had 10,000 of Ted's recordings, representing something close to 1,000 bird species.

On August 7 and 8, 2012, we visited the lab, courtesy of Greg Budney, and saw forty-three of Parker's bound journals. We understand that his recordings are now fully digitized, a worthy tribute to his accomplishments.

* Saint Francis of Assisi (born in 1181 or 1182 and died in 1226), founder of the Franciscan Order, believed nature itself was mirror of God and called all creatures brothers and sisters. See his "Praise of the Creatures," in which he describes "preaching to my sisters the birds."

THAT'S NUMBER 3,500!

Scott and Hella among the emperor penguins deep in the Ross Sea,
December 2000.

In December 2000, I was invited to accompany William Sladen, MD, PhD, to the Antarctic for the month of December. Bill was turning eighty and had studied the Adélie penguin and other phenomena in the Antarctic over a span of fifty years. The assignment for me was to give four whale lectures as I had done for Lindblad in the Galápagos in 1999.

We were encouraged to invite others. I invited Jim Macaleer, a classmate from college (where he was an outstanding wrestler), who went on to found and lead, as CEO, the Shared Medical Systems Corporation in eastern Pennsylvania until he sold the company in 1993. Jim also created the William and Edna Macaleer Professorship of Engineering and Applied Science at Princeton in honor of his parents, ably occupied by James C. Sturm.

Jim and his wife, Jean, took a suite on the Russian icebreaker *Kapitan Khlepnikov*, owned by Quark, which departed from Hobart in Tasmania.

We had rough passage through the latitudes of the Roaring 40s and Ferocious 50s, with the ship swinging through arcs of 90 degrees. Eventually, we entered gentler waters and the Ross Sea, observing at close quarters along the way a variety of penguins, including the Adélie and finally the emperors. The latter were never seen by Roger Tory Peterson, who did see the king penguin.

One evening Jim invited us to his suite for a drink. He popped open his computer, showing a Cape petrel aloft that he had photographed that day. "That's number 3,500, in seven years!" He had also seen and identified every bird in Tasmania during the fortnight before our departure.

The same drive and spirit, if you will, that led him to found and direct a major corporation had carried over in retirement, where birding became a primary and exhilarating avocation.

Now, years later, Jim has seen and photographed some 4,500 species of birds on all continents.

EXPLORER OF BIRDS AT BOTH POLES
— William J. L. Sladen, MD, PhD

Hella and Bill Sladen, aboard the Kapitan Khlenikov, *Ross Sea. Antarctica, 2000.*

We gather now to honor a man and a day
that occurred a while back
    before we knew of "ecstatic display"
    or for that matter "mutual display"
a fellow named Wilson
came up with the phrase
but it's not that good man
whom we would here praise
another Wilson studied ants, did he ever,
eighty-eight hundred for the big book,
but Bill with his flippered bands bonds
to a single species, Adélie,

took a long deeper look
at Cape Crozier, year after year,
he found Adélies (males), fasting
for forty days and forty nights
where midst that large yik-yakery click-quackery
was the recognition uncanny by parents
of their chicks through calls blasting

Bill knows, too, the leopard seal's open jaws,
he knows the Far North and distant South's bitter maws.
he has a glorious beak that would be
the envy of the great calm emperor
whether upright, dignified, stately
or tobogganing on its belly
oh, note the white chin on the chicks
the black chin on the adults
     click, roll that Bolex, click
now that other Wilson said something
     of socio-biology
even the concept of altruism
his hypothesis the biophilia hypothesis
you know, the innate affiliation with nature,
which Bill exemplifies
be it with the trumpeting swan
     or the whistler
(God forbid, not the invasive mute)
his spirit, his humor, his life
were incomplete, however, without his wife

who embodies and enshrines
    the notion divine
of ecstatic display in her rhyme
    and her sweet motions, quick eyes, dance sublime
so only dear Jocelyn could bring
this wandering hooligan home to Aires
where the swans and their students could flock
    to share their calls, musings, and broodings
in mutual display
but the big birthday's here
eighty on the nose
we're the privileged few
in this southerly lair
who salute you, Bill, your empathy
with what lives, fasts, incubates, huddles in crèches,
what joy, exultation as we laud
Jocelyn and Bill in octaves from basso to trill
the world will turn
    the skies up north grow dark
but here in the Antarctic with you
    we'll know light, bright daylight
    around a stopped clock
        a pounding heart.

Aboard the Kapitan Khlebnikov
December 19, 2000

Postscript

I first met Bill Sladen when we were roommates in the Hotel Rosita near the Kremlin in Moscow in January 1973. We were part of a team of US biologists planning to work with Soviet biologists on nineteen endangered species projects.

In April 1971, I encountered a place south of Point Barrow, Alaska, at Icy Cape where Bill had marked a narrow passage—just fifty meters wide—that delineated the divide between birds migrating from Siberia that flew down the eastern or western flyways, soon to be 3,000 miles apart.

A SPECIES UNKNOWN TO SCIENCE

The ideal scientist thinks like a poet,
stressing the virtues of passion, introversion,
and dedication.

— E. O. Wilson

Pheidole fullerae **new species**
Only known habitat: Kathryn Fuller's WWF office

*T-shirt produced by the World Wildlife Fund to
acknowledge E. O. Wilson's discovery of a new subspecies of ant in WWF's Washington headquarters.*

When I first met E. O. Wilson, who was to become the voice for
biodiversity on Earth, upon joining the advisory council of Princeton's
Department of Biology in the 1970s, I said, "In a university, a great
university, the good ideas rise and the bad ones fall away."

Wilson said, "Are you kidding? When I advanced the idea of

sociobiology, I was attacked, skewered mercilessly, by Stephen Jay Gould and Richard Lewontin. They thought, what can an ant guy tell us about human behavior? It was so painful I could hardly breathe for weeks."

Years later, in 1990, long after Wilson joined the board of the World Wildlife Fund, the very day he got the first copy of his opus *The Ants*, written with German entomologist Bert Hölldobler, he said to me, "I can die now. The book has one-page descriptions of 8,000 species of ants beautifully illustrated, showing front, top, and side views of every one."

I asked, "You mean, that's it? That's all there are?"

"No," he sighed, "but I had to draw a line in the sand."

Wilson has since, with his colleague, described many additional species of ants and published *The Superorganism: The Beauty, Elegance and Strangeness of Insect Societies* (Norton, 2008).

Later, when Wilson chaired the program committee of the WWF, he once began his remarks after lunch by saying: "I hope my fellow directors will forgive me for a brief diversion from our topic. Yesterday, in the fifth story of this very building on M Street in downtown Washington, I was meeting with Kathryn Fuller, our president, regarding the report of the program committee. I noticed a procession of ants moving along the floorboard that ascended the spiral cord of her telephone into the drawer of her desk. It is a species unknown to science. I do not know whether it should be known as *kathrynae* or *fullerae*."

At this point one of the directors suggested *"Kathrynae."* Wilson retorted, "Best left to science."

Later yet, it was named *Pheidole fullerae*, sketched on a T-shirt, noting that the only known habitat was Kathryn Fuller's WWF office. It turns out that it is a subspecies of a known species.

Of late, as a culture we are noticing what eminent artists or scientists do in their last years, whether Oliver Sacks on the human condition or Matisse with his bold, bright cut-outs, or the ever incisively quotable

Gloria Steinem. In Wilson's new book, modestly titled *The Meaning of Human Existence*, he writes, "Earth relates to the universe as the second segment of the left antenna of an aphid sitting on a flower petal in a garden in Teaneck, NJ, for a few hours this afternoon."

At eighty-five years, he is uncompromising in saying, "The great religions are sources of ceaseless and unnecessary suffering. They are impediments to the grasp of reality needed to solve most social problems in the real world."

Postcript

In 1993, Island Press published a book, *The Biophilia Hypothesis*, edited by Wilson and Stephen R. Kellert, which came out of a meeting of twenty scientists at Woods Hole who were examining Wilson's proposition in his book *Biophilia* (1982) that our species has an innate affiliation with the natural world. The participants included Richard Nelson, Gary Paul Nabhan, Jared Diamond, Elizabeth Atwood Lawrence, Lynn Margulis, Holmes Rolston, and David Orr.

My essay, "A Siamese Connexion with a Plurality of Other Mortals," opens *The Biophilia Hypothesis*. In it I sought to show how individual explorers of the natural world, from whales and elephants to microscopic organisms, allow us to see anew the diversity and behavior of many fellow mammals and other creatures of this blue-green orb. In fact, my essay carries several ideas about how pioneers blaze the way for our evolving perceptions about the beauty and intricacy of the Earth, for which our understanding is still woefully primitive. This piece reveals a core thread of my life.

HOW CAN WE SAVE THE AMAZON RAIN FOREST?

On July 12, 1988, in Ghillean T. Prance's last weeks at the New York Botanical Garden—before he took on leadership of the Royal Botanic Gardens, Kew, in England and was later knighted—a few of us from the W. Alton Jones Foundation called on him as we sought direction in our quest to support biological diversity at the Foundation.

The W. Alton Jones Foundation had the twin mission of striving to sustain the biodiversity on Earth (60 percent) and reducing the nuclear threat (40 percent).

Prance was vice president for research, and he had led expeditions annually for twenty-five years to the Amazon to bring back four samples of every plant, one for the New York Botanical Garden, one for the Royal Botanic Gardens, one for the Smithsonian or Missouri Botanical Garden, and one for a small museum in Manaus. He had then published seven books and edited a further six and written 130 scientific papers.

I asked him if he planned to just keep on collecting specimens or if he had any idea what could be done to stop the wholesale depletion of the largest rain forest on Earth through cutting, burning, and mineral extraction.

A lightbulb appeared over his head. He suggested a conference of many days be held in Manaus, Brazil, with biologists from Europe, the United States, and the nine countries in South America who have a piece of the Amazon.

The biologists, Prance suggested, could offer ideas about certain areas, seemingly rich in the biota of their specialty, even though data may still be skimpy and woefully inadequate. Then, a map could be made with an overlay of, say, primates, fish (2,000 species had been described and catalogued by Michael Gould), trees, plants, insects, and so on.

That idea was actively pursued and implemented through a conference in 1989 of biologists in Manaus. The coordinators included Prance, Tom Lovejoy, and others. The lead staffer was Carlos Miller. The detailed proposal was funded in full by the Jones Foundation with promising results. A second conference was held a few years later. We learned later yet in a meeting in Manaus that two of the larger exploiters of Amazonia in Brazil apparently began to heed the emerging map of singular biological phenomena as they continued to wrench out resources. The vast Amazon is of immense importance in and of itself and as "the lungs of the Earth."

The caliber of Prance's work, with his colleagues Balée, Boom, and Carneiro, can be understood through a path-breaking paper published in *Conservation Biology*, December 1987, called "Quantative Ethnobotany and the Case for Conservation in Amazonia." Why path breaking? This landmark paper reveals how four indigenous Amazonian groups, the Ka'apor and Tembe in Brazil, the Panare in Venezuela, and the Chacobo in Bolivia use products of trees in their immediate vicinity. The tree species in one hectare with a diameter of at least ten centimeters fell into various categories of use: edible (fruits and seeds), construction (post and beam, canoes, bridges, and leaves for roofing thatch), technology (lashing material, glue, pottery temper, dye, soap, pipe stem, arrow point), remedy (for sinusitis, congestion, diarrhea, headache, vomiting, fever, unwanted pregnancy, bleeding wounds, snakebite, canker sores, insect repellent), commerce (boat caulking, rubber, souvenirs), and other (magic, toys, dog fatteners, fermentation aids, and perfume). This study is a persuasive confirmation that the rain forests of Amazonia contain an exceptionally large number of useful species, the lead being the palm family. The implications for conservation policy are inescapable: many reserves are needed throughout Amazonia.

In an October 1, 2012, cover article in *Time* by Bill Clinton, "The Case for Optimism," which details five ways in which the world is changing for the better, the final section, "The Fight for the Future is Now," affirms that our efforts may have had a longer ripple and impact:

"In places once synonymous with conflict, like the Balkans and Rwanda, former antagonists are now working together to solve problems. In 2011 I attended a global-sustainability conference in Manaus, Brazil, at the edge of the rain forest. Remarkably, utility companies and all the oil companies were represented. The native Brazilian tribes that live in the rain forest, which are protected by law and will be hurt if there's further development, were represented. The woman who ran for President on the Green Party ticket and spoke out against all this development was there. Small businesses and environmental groups were represented. The delegates sat around small tables, speaking to one another with great respect, believing that if they worked together, they could find an answer. They all understood that if this were a simple issue, someone would have already solved the problem."

THAT WAS *NOT* IN THE SCRIPT

It was their individuality combined with
the shyness of their behavior that remained
the most captivating impression of this first
encounter with the greatest of the great apes.
— Dian Fossey, primatologist

In the late 1980s, I was seated next to Sigourney Weaver at a Natural
Resources Defense Council dinner in Manhattan. She had roomed with
Frances Beinecke at the Ethel Walker school. After college at Stanford,
Weaver pursued an MFA at Yale University School of Drama and roomed
again with Beinecke. We had traveled with Frances along the southeast
coast of Alaska in 1979 on the first NRDC excursion with Michael and
Winsome McIntosh of the Boat Company. Our group had included
Louis and Adele Auchincloss. Frances later became executive director
and then president of NRDC.

I commented to Sigourney on the spectacular scene in Gorillas
in the Mist: The Story of Dian Fossey (1988) when an old silverback
mountain gorilla chased Sigourney down the mountain. She crouched
down and covered her head with her hands, as she had been taught, in
full submission to his supremacy.

That sequence, I said, seemed dangerous. She said, "That was *not* in
the script." They had been working with a habituated group of gorillas for
the film and had somehow gotten into the territory of an unhabituated
group. It all happened so fast, she said.

When the chase occurred, it was pure happenstance that a cameraman
caught it, since no filming was taking place at the time.

This unexpected vignette meant all the more to me since I had met Dian Fossey at a World Wildlife Fund board meeting and had arranged for her to visit Emma Willard School in Troy, New York, for a few days. Dian talked about her singular experience in studying mountain gorillas with the young women enrolled there.

In an interview on National Public Radio, Fossey explained that she was more comfortable in the company of the mountain gorillas than in human company. She said she could imitate the behavior and grunts of the gorilla and was never more at ease than in their circle. And Weaver played the lead role in what turned out to be a tragic story of the lead defender of our relative the mountain gorilla. Fossey was brutally murdered in her cabin in Rwanda in December 1985. Money was not the motive since her passport and plenty of cash were left untouched. The murder followed months of intense harassment.

As Dian put it, "The more you learn about the dignity of the gorillas, the more you want to avoid people."

WHY ARE TWO MAMMALIAN SPECIES—WITH BRAINS THREE TIMES BIGGER THAN OURS— MATRIARCHIES?

Cynthia Moss and Paul Spong at Liberty Science Center on October 15, 1997. Having met that day, they gave back-to-back lectures on elephants in the Amboseli of southern Kenya and a "resident" pod of orcas near Spong's home and laboratory on Hanson Island, each accompanied by strong visual and sonic images.

On our thirtieth wedding anniversary (August 9, 1988), Hella and I visited Paul Spong and his wife, Linda, on Hanson Island north of British Columbia. Paul had long since made the study of *Orcinus orca* (the killer whale, so called) his life's work and had created OrcaLab on Hanson in 1972. To catch a little of his fervor, you need only read his splendid narration in *Mind in the Waters* (Charles Scribner's Sons, 1974). Paul took his flute out in his canoe one morning at dawn, and for hours, he was accompanied by four orcas on the port side and four on the starboard side.

It turns out that the close-knit resident pods along the North Pacific Coast are caring matriarchies who eat fish, and that the sons often hang out with their mums into their thirties. Each pod has its own distinct dialect of seventeen to twenty-one phonations.

Some time after a welcoming supper, Paul escorted us to his tidy laboratory down by the water, which contained an ample double bed and two large speakers for continuous monitoring of the sonic activity of the orca in Johnson Strait. The lilt of their yelps, sonic click trains of inquiry, and aesthetic peals of shifting frequency rocked us quite wondrously to sleep.

The next morning Paul gave us tapes of the sounds produced during the night of our anniversary. Topping that, he also gave us an audiotape of the whales' sonic emissions from a night in 1982 when the sky was stunningly illuminated by an aurora borealis surpassing any night Paul and his family had witnessed in their years there.

Later, I used that singular 1982 audiotape—combined with a film of the aurora obtained from the University of Alaska Fairbanks—for a talk in Jefferson's Rotunda at the University of Virginia on the biophilia hypothesis, or an affinity to the natural world.

I arranged for Paul Spong to address the Whales Alive Conference in Maui in the 1990s, when he showed the filmed sequence of the female orca Corky in captivity at SeaWorld in San Diego, when Corky first heard the vocalizations of her home pod. In a nanosecond, she responded convulsively in immediate recognition after a quarter century of isolation in captivity. Paul was arguing for her release and retirement to her home pod. It didn't happen.

In 1998, I invited Cynthia Moss, whom we had met in Kenya in 1986, and Paul Spong to speak at Liberty Science Center in New Jersey before an audience of leading educators. Cynthia had studied elephants in the Amboseli. Her book, *Elephant Memories*, from years of close study of a large population, recorded, among many things, the joyful greeting of elephants at a reunion after a long separation. Three BBC documentaries enlarge and enrich the understanding.

As of 2011, after nearly four decades' study, Moss and her associates have identified and recorded more than 1,400 elephants belonging to fifty families in an immense 400 square miles.

Our species has a three-pound brain, the largest on land except for the elephant, who possesses a nine-pound brain, similar in size and configuration to orcas in their a weightless environment.

Moss and Spong had not met previously. On this occasion, they became vividly aware of each other's work and the complementary nature of their endeavors.

In describing the behavior of these two mammalian societies, one on land and the other marine, they gave slideshow lectures with striking similarities—the most notable feature being that both species are caring nurturing matriarchies, operating almost without rancor or violence.

We have much to learn from both societies.

DON'T WORRY ABOUT SNAKES

Brian Rosborough had hounded me to take an Earthwatch expedition for some time. Nearly 100 opportunities to work with scientists in the field worldwide were offered in 1978, and I asked him for a recommendation. He said Dan Janzen, a madcap biologist of the first order, would be his choice. Formerly with the University of Michigan, then and now at the University of Pennsylvania, he was hardwired to understand the life history of the dry forest of Guanacaste in Costa Rica.

Hella and I went for a couple of weeks with Janzen to the Corcovado Osa Peninsula, where we flew in from San José. We spent the night at the airstrip field station, where the remains of a small plane sat at the end of the grassy strip, and saw vampire bats quietly sipping blood from horses and sleeping chickens the next morning.

Janzen had briefed our small team in San José about snakes.

"Where we will be are only two poisonous snakes: the fer-de-lance and the bushmaster. If we are bitten by either of them, we would die within four hours.

"I have an antidote, however, which, properly injected in the thigh, would fight the deadly venom of the snake, and one would survive. A cautionary note, though: If the snake was misidentified, and if it was nonpoisonous, the antidote would kill you."

That's all I recall of the briefing.

We forded two rivers that poured into the Pacific as we walked north with provisions—rice, beans, garlic, sugar—on a mule and packhorse to our idyllic campsite. It was marked by a hundred-foot waterfall, where we showered, and by lovely stone formations that spilled into the sea. The beach before the waterfall was ankle deep in shells of many species that one was forbidden to collect. Hella spotted a new one according to Janzen, number 145. This large shell was later placed in the small museum where the plane dropped us off.

Our daily mission was to gather insects with a butterfly net as well as seedpods along a trail. We did that all day long and sorted the bugs into groups and subgroups of insects.

At night by a fire, with a black light on a nearby screen where moths were attracted, Dan talked about the coevolution of plants and pollinating insects with passion and know-how. Dan would talk with animation for four or even five hours about this stuff. I couldn't believe how eloquent he was. Later, Hella pointed out that Winnie Hallwachs, a student, was in our group. The two began a courtship, which led to a lifelong partnership.

In our group was the already-accomplished lepidopterist Philip DeVries, who had been with the Peace Corps in Costa Rica and had stayed on with his savings to photograph, catch, identify, and describe nearly every species of butterfly in the country. How many so far? I asked. He said more than one thousand. Where was he getting the last few? High in the mountains, which climb to over 3,800 meters, road kill. Today, a third of a century later, DeVries has written over ninety papers, won many awards including a MacArthur, and published books with the Princeton University Press.

At the suggestion of Tom Lovejoy, I met with the president of Costa Rica, Rodrigo Carazo Odio, a father of five daughters, who knew nothing of the biology or biodiversity of this studied one percent of Latin America. The country was getting nearly fifty cents of the US conservation dollar since it was varied terrain, containing many altitudinal transects and it was convenient and pleasant to work there or travel through. Every year thirty-five top US graduate students of biology spent the summer there as a group, doing independent projects and creating deep grooves for future research.

Janzen agreed to come along for the meeting with the president but sat yawning in the corner. Only in 1985, when his beloved Guanacaste was under threat, did he undergo a conversion experience. Later yet, he had four candidates for the presidency of Costa Rica on a high school stage, grilling them about their commitment to conservation.

On October 29, 1987, Dan wrote me, "Costa Rica—bless her heart—has come to her own realization that their only chance in the world at large is to come up with a serious national plan and strategy for sustained use of her natural resources."

Near the end of our stay, Gary Hartshorn came through our camp early on a Sunday morning and invited us to walk with him three hours further north to see a rare and majestic tree, a Humberadendron, with massive buttresses, one carrying a colony of bats. I asked Dan if we might go. He harrumphed and said okay. Upon our return, Gary and Dan argued whether Costa Rica had two or three specimens of this formidable tree.

Stories of Dan Janzen, later a recipient of the Blue Planet Prize, a MacArthur in 1989, and the Kyoto Prize, abound.

One more yarn from me. After we returned to the capitol over supper the last night, I asked Dan, "What would you have done if one of us had an appendicitis attack?"

He eschewed taking along a radio, and there was enough dirt under his fingernails to grow potatoes. Without hesitation, Dan said, "I would operate!"

"Anesthesia?"

"I would use the bottle of rum we brought with us."

But we drank it the third day when our little machete-wielding, jockey-short-wearing guide had a birthday. Dan said he would operate anyway and carry out the patient. In any event, we didn't need to worry about the snakes.

This adventure led the Dodge Foundation to fund eighteen biology teachers for an Earthwatch at STRI (Smithsonian Tropical Research Institute) in Panama in 1985, and, over time some 200-plus New Jersey teachers of every discipline and educational level.

THE ULTIMATE CHECK-OUT

In April 1999, I thought Sven-Olof Lindblad's invitation to serve as a naturalist on the *MS Polaris* in the Galápagos was, if you will, a dream gig in retirement.

I was given T-shirts and a jacket with the Lindblad staff logo and a modest salary to give four talks on whales.

Hella and I were thrilled to be going finally to the fabled islands. They had impressed Charles Darwin on the voyage of the *Beagle* (1835), of which he wrote, "The Natural History of these islands is eminently curious and well deserves attention. Most of the organic productions are aboriginal creations (endemic species) found nowhere else." In his iconic journal he sketched the beaks of four species of finch, which in our day Peter and Rosemary Grant have demonstrated undergo very rapid changes in beak and body size in response to changes in the food supply, an evolution driven by natural selection.

Beyond swimming above circling hammerhead sharks and at a little distance from elephant seals and encountering them underwater, I was moved by the older couples aboard, some married forty-eight to fifty-three years, who were so attentive and attuned to one another. Here we are, now married fifty-seven-plus years and doubtless older than most of them at that time.

After speaking quietly with several of the passengers about a book that had changed their lives, I gave a talk on books, inspired in part by the marvelous 1995 Books of the Century exhibition and book created by the New York Public Library, as well as by the comments of fellow passengers.

Among the highlights of the voyage—right there with the giant tortoises—was a visit to Española, "the island of seabirds," on April 11, a time when the waved albatross (with a magnificent eight-foot wingspan) gather for courtship, grooming, and mating. Viewing such intense courtships was a privilege that appeared to affect the albatrosses' behavior not at all.

In a couple of stanzas from a long poem written at the journey's end, I tried to register the singular magic of the creatures we encountered:

> What better way to convey the wonder
> of the albatross on its nesting ground
> the flightless cormorant, the courting blue-footed
> booby, penguins to the equator bound
>
> the marine iguana stately waiting,
> the spotted eagle ray below skating,
> the seals beach-strewn or sea sporting,
> finches hopping, giant tortoise slowly mating

The standout encounter of those days occurred after lunch on April 13, when Hella spotted a large congregation of bottlenose dolphins, *Tursiops truncatus*, numbering perhaps 200. We jumped into three or four Zodiac boats and zipped out to them, noticing that they seemed to have sentinels leaping straight up into the air at points 12 o'clock, three o'clock, six o'clock, and nine o'clock keeping vigil.

The week before this trip, Hella and I had been down on Tavernier, Florida, with Roland Barth, cofounder of the Principals' Center at the Harvard School of Education. Off of one of his sailboats, I had swum with a couple of dolphin families numbering eight or ten each. In each case the alpha male dolphin had nuzzled me in a friendly way, I thought.

But this day when we approached the edge of the congregation and I slipped over the side of the Zodiac wearing my newly acquired prescription goggles, I faced a surprise.

Four dolphins were swimming below me, upside down, with right eyes cocked upward. I was being sprayed with sonic clicks. (One needs to recall that, for example, a mother will scan her infant sonically to "see" where a bubble of air may be, and then, ever so precisely, "burp" the infant with a poke of the rostrum seeking to expel the gas through the rectum or the mouth.) One should also remember that a dolphin may scan another dolphin or a person to note from the lungs the mental state along a spectrum from relaxed to anxious.

After the first four dolphins came another four in a similar formation. Then another four. Four more. On and on in rapid succession, all checking me out by spraying me with high frequency clicks as my dial swept from totally relaxed and full of curiosity to highly anxious and really frightened. What was their intent? Their sheer numbers and exacting military formation gave me pause. They are masters in the water. We are intruders, helpless and vulnerable.

I scrambled back into the Zodiac and suggested no one should enter the water. We returned to our mother ship.

A stanza near the end of my poem reads:

> For me the high point, no surprise,
> was the vast school of dolphins Hella espied
> off the stern, and the chance to swim
> amid their cracklin' din, noting squadrons
> of four after four after four after four
> scanning, ogling, pinging, from below.

CETACEANS IN CAPTIVITY?

Hella, nose to nose, with a female captive orca, SeaWorld, San Diego.
Summer 1968.

In September 1997, Mitchell Fox of PAWS (Progressive Animal
Welfare Society) of Seattle organized an effort to release Lolita, a female
orca in captivity for twenty-seven years in the Miami Seaquarium, to her
home waters in Puget Sound. The undertaking was backed by governors
and members of the House and Senate.

In my essay making the case in the Autumn 1997 issue of *PAWS*, I
wrote, "the gathering evidence suggests that at least the larger creatures,
like orca, are not appropriate for confinement, and that their days in
captivity must be lonely and boring in contrast to the life they have
known as animate members of a pod, probably a 'residential' pod."

Through the indefatigable and practical leadership of Dave Phillips,
an orca called Keiko had been removed from desperate conditions in
Mexico City where he was the inspiration for and star of the *Free Willy*

movie. Keiko was transported to a halfway facility in Oregon and nursed back to brimming good health before he was returned to the waters off southern Iceland where he was netted years earlier. The exercise led to mixed results, since Keiko was not able to reintegrate in the home pod.

Worth emphasizing are the unflagging efforts of Paul Spong and hundreds of thousands of concerned citizens to release Corky from SeaWorld in San Diego. In 1993, Corky, who had been in captivity for twenty-eight years and had become lethargic in her small tank, was played a recent recording of the sounds from her original pod (A5) near British Columbia, which she had not heard in a quarter century.

An immense shudder rocked her body as she recognized her family's voices. I have seen the film shot of this painful cognitive event.

As one reflects on the predicament of Lolita in the Miami Seaquarium, one conjures up that moment in time when Lolita actually returns to her large resident group of pods in Puget Sound (pods commonly referred to as J, K, and L based on early work by the late Michael Bigg and pursued by Ken Balcomb and others).

The first thing to remember about cetaceans is that they are profoundly acoustic animals. I once participated with John Lilly in the capture of a bottlenose dolphin in Biscayne Bay in 1964. We placed the seemingly relaxed dolphin in a sling in a box with water so that the internal body organs would be less depressed by gravity. Even so, during the first hour, the dolphin seemed to go through its entire sonic repertoire, trying to solve the problem of captivity acoustically. The bottlenose dolphin's acoustic nerve is eight times larger than ours.

Dolphins live in an acoustic world. They use sound to travel, navigate, and find food, and with companions plumb the depths by sound. Putting a dolphin in a small tank is, as the late William Schevill would say, like putting a human in a telephone booth who gets all wrong numbers.

These reflections bring to mind Easter evening 1966, when I spent the night beside the tiny pool containing a fifteen-foot female orca at the New York Aquarium on Coney Island. The concrete pool was only nine feet at its deepest spot. That meant she could never rest at the surface, since her flukes would touch the bottom, a position intolerable to her. She had to keep stroking continuously to keep her tail up. No awning was provided. The top of her head was blistered from the sun. A Pacific white-sided dolphin swam figure eights beneath her. I had recording gear and a sleeping bag, but she made few utterances through the night, and I didn't sleep. At dawn I whistled once, and she replied with two whistles. I answered with three whistles, and she with four. I tried five, and she was silent.

Imagine for a moment the reunion that will occur for Lolita in Puget Sound with her extended family, especially if we manage to make those waters safe and secure and an adequate flow of salmon can sustain their appetites. Imagine, if you will, that very first hour when Lolita is placed in some sort of temporary pen in her home waters when possibly some siblings or nieces or nephews or cousins turn up and she first hears the sounds that were the stuff of her childhood.

Imagine for a moment eavesdropping unobtrusively on the sonic exchange, the immediate bursts of whistles and clicks and squawks and bleats that will etch the euphoria of this reunion after such an immense chasm of time. That first hour will be revelatory because these resident pods typically make seventeen different kinds of sound. The variety of sounds they produce are more than sufficient to convey information about their world and their responses to being in it. How rarely we are granted a Rosetta stone moment to begin the decipherment of these exchanges.

In 1968, I put the last sound spectrogram in place after thousands that I made over many months. I understood for the first time that the humpback whale makes a song that repeats like a bird song, only for much longer—say from twelve minutes to half an hour. I was depressed. The song, which unfolds over six octaves, is hauntingly beautiful, and it became the anthem for whale conservation, selling over 500,000 records. We learned later that the song is produced by the male, perhaps to register his presence and availability (what else is new?). But I was depressed. Why? Because I was hoping for some give and take, some real conversation. I was looking for something more.

The yearning or longing for another sentient form of life on this watery orb may, conceivably, begin to be answered in that first hour when Lolita enters her home waters for a long-awaited reunion that will be carefully prepared step by step in the most humane manner we can envision. Therefore, let us do it carefully and well, and then be open to the lessons we will learn once we understand better the ways and wiles and wonders of the orca—societies apparently based on long-standing relationships. Mature, thirty-foot males still prefer not to take a breath apart from their mothers (who are up to a "mere" fifteen feet).

That campaign did not succeed. Lolita was not released—she was too much of a moneymaker.

Postscript

In the Spring 2014 issue of the *AWI Quarterly*, is a somewhat hopeful article, "Parole Possible for Oldest Captive Orca." Lolita, now almost fifty years old, was a member of the Southern Resident distinct population segment of orcas when she was captured off Whidbey Island, Washington. Under the Animal Welfare Act, she had been held and displayed in an enclosure long believed to be noncompliant. Comments submitted to the Fisheries Service by the Animal Welfare Institute could lead to her retirement to a sea pen in her native waters where she would once again feel the ocean currents, be well cared for, and not be made to perform or be exposed to loud, artificial music and noise. Here she would finally find peace.

What is at stake here is nothing short of whether we are able to assume the stewardship of life on Earth now that we have, quite unwittingly, found ourselves in that odd and difficult situation. What we may learn from this experience could well affect how we live and how we think of ourselves in relationship to other forms of life in the watery and natural landscape.

A MEMORABLE MEAL

Biologist Tom Lovejoy, Madagascar, 1986.

We were down to our last four hours of an astonishing visit to Madagascar, where 70 percent of the animals, plants, and insects are endemic—found only on that island off the east coast of Africa.

A high point was seeing Alison Jolly's ring-tailed lemurs, the focus of a lifelong, revelatory study.

On our last day, we were in the Port of Toamasina (Tamatave), an area devastated by a recent typhoon, and we were hungry, looking for a place to eat. It was three o'clock in late fall 1986. We saw a sign, HOTEL, where the "L" had slipped in the recent cataclysm. We tapped on the door, and a small French woman, about seventy-five, said, "Come back in half an hour."

The meal, served elegantly by a tall spare man with white gloves and a black patch over one eye, was fabulous. Long forgotten is what we ate, but the conversation and ambiance made it memorable.

Our group included Russ Mittermeier, a primatologist who had provided endless encounters with lemurs every night with our head lamps and days filled with sightings of other species, including fruit bats, feisty aquatic tenrecs, sifaks—looking like white lazy pipe cleaners—and one fossa, the largest mammalian predator on the island. At the outset, nine of us embraced, fingertip to fingertip, a mighty mystical baobab tree.

I asked Russ what primates he would most like to see. He named a lemur that had not been seen since 1937. He would look in an area about one hour north of where we sat, and believed he could find it within a fortnight. He also mentioned a primate in China and another in Vietnam that had not been seen in decades that he would like to locate.

Primatologist Russ Mittermeier,
scanning for lemurs, Madagascar, 1986.

Russ thought a new primate species will be identified and described from Central and South America and Africa every year for the foreseeable future. That has turned out to be an accurate anticipation. These are tiny primates, all fluff and bluff, typically weighing in at well under a pound.

The rare aye-aye, a nocturnal lemur* found only on Nosy Mangabe, eluded us in a torrential downpour, but Russ was profoundly intrigued by a chameleon as we landed there. In fact, he shot four rolls of film and then put this little guy in his camera case while his fancy camera hung out in the rain. I asked Russ at that last supper what was more interesting: his then-two-year-old son or one of these odd, rare beasties.

Russ replied, "That would be a hard call."

*The aye-aye finds tree larvae with echolocation and scoops it out with a long, curving fingernail, a creature so singular that it is in its own family.

Postscript

In 1989, Russ Mittermeier was named president of Conservation International. In Tom Friedman's column, "Maybe in America," (*New York Times*, July 29, 2014) after touring Madagascar with Russ Mittermeier, he wrote, "Since 90 percent of Madagascar's forests have been chopped down for slash-and-burn agriculture, timber, firewood, and charcoal over the last century, most hillsides have no trees to hold the soil when it rains." Russ explained, "The more you erode, the more people you have with less soil under their feet to grow things. When I first came here in 1984, the population was nine or 10 million. It is now approaching 23 million."

HOW MANY WORDS IN ENGLISH?

Still from a video by artist/linguist Aimee Morgana of N'Kisi, an African grey parrot.

In April 2008, I met Aimee Morgana at the New York Public Library at the launch of David Rothenberg's eighth book, *Thousand-Mile Song*. Among scientists and musicians who spoke or played that day were Roger Payne and myself, authors of the cover paper in *Science* describing the long, complex six-octave songs of humpback whales.

Morgana invited me to visit her home and laboratory. That did not happen for several months, but when I did visit my initial surprise was that N'Kisi, the African grey parrot she had worked with for fifteen years, was immediately part of the conversation. He occupied a perch above us. When Jane Goodall first visited, N'Kisi asked, "Where is your chimp?"

Morgana maintains meticulous, extensive records of N'Kisi's evolving active use of the English language, plus many videotapes, revealing interactions that can only be considered participatory conversation.

I visited a second time in 2011 with my grandson, Matthew, then fifteen years old, and we stayed for five hours.

Since I worked with a precocious dolphin, Elvar, on a one-on-one basis in Lilly's Communication Research Institute in Coconut Grove, Florida, for two years doing experiments morning and afternoon, six days a week, to "teach" Elvar English, I am aware of the challenges. For well over half a century, I have been fascinated by the voices of whales and dolphins.

It is out of this context that Aimee Morgana's steady yet staggering results with N'Kisi strike me as singular and at the outer reaches of all efforts to date to train a being other than a human to converse. Consider for a moment that the five most successful deliberate efforts with animals (Koko the gorilla, about 1,000 words; Kanzi the bonobo, about 400 words; Washoe the chimp, about 130 words, Nim Chimpsky the chimpanzee, about 125 words; and Alex the parrot, about 100 words) do not all together come to N'Kisi's vocabulary to date (May 2015), namely 1,996 words, plus 165 words of his own making.

As impressive as these results are, the undertaking is extremely frail when one considers that N'Kisi almost died when he was bitten by another parrot a couple of years ago and nearly bled to death, and Aimee herself had a serious life-threatening experience in 2012.

The next step is the writing of a book, the elements of which are in hand from the rich, amazing exchanges that have taken place and are thoroughly documented. The only remotely analogous books that come to mind are *The Double Helix* of fifty years ago by James Watson and *Silent Thunder* by Katy Payne, describing her discovery of low frequency utterances in elephants in a zoo in Portland, Oregon, in 1984 and her later recording of these infrasounds in Africa.

Two frames occur to me in considering the ultimate merit of Aimee and N'Kisi's work and play. This first is the iconic essay written by Loren

Eiseley, "The Long Loneliness," in 1960 in *The American Scholar*. The second is Ms. Morgana's laboratory.

Eiseley wrote that as children we speak to animals. As we grow older and think the animals are not responding verbally, we may stop talking to them. The early work of John C. Lilly, MD, on the bottlenose dolphin, as initially described in *Man and Dolphin*, reported a creature with a formidable brain and elegant, supple neurological wiring. The hypothesis offered was that this marine mammal may have a level of cognition and awareness akin to ours, however alien. This startled our species in a way that Copernicus and Kepler stunned our flat Earth ideas, or the way Darwin and Wallace described a theory of evolution in 1859 when our ideas ran to a hierarchy among the animals that put us a little below the angels, or the way Freud and Jung broached the notion of a powerful unconsciousness in our minds that underlies seemingly conscious lives.

Eisley wrote of the prospect of our ancient longing to communicate with the natural world as something now within the realm of possibility.

The singularity and import of Aimee Morgana's work with N'Kisi will, we trust, influence our treatment of not only African grey parrots but also other life forms that share our Earth.

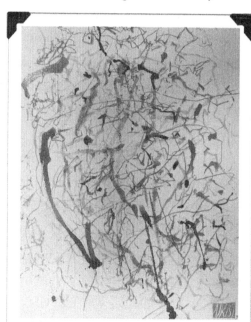

This work by N'Kisi was painted in 2014 with both beak and claw. First-time viewers, not knowing the source, sometimes think it is a Cy Twombly.

AS HAPPY AS AN OTTER

It was the summer of 1986. After reading John Wesley Powell's harrowing account of rafting the Colorado River in 1869, Hella and I walked down the five-mile trail from the South Rim to Phantom Ranch to raft the Colorado for nine days through the Grand Canyon.

The trip was organized by the Environmental Defense Fund (EDF) with Fred Krupp and Jim Tripp in tow and led by OARS (Outdoor Adventure River Specialists). We had four guides for each of four small rafts, three of whom were experienced with over 100 runs, and one, Zeke, who was inexperienced.

The leader, a woman named Liz who was also a splendid photographer, briefed us. She made two points: first, there was only enough toilet paper for the use for which it was intended, not for draping on the one john.

Second, the temperature of the water in the mighty river was 53 degrees Fahrenheit. If we were tossed out of a four-person raft when hurtling down a number-ten cataract, we should bounce off the big rocks with our tennis shoes. Then, below, we would be "fished out" before hypothermia began to set in at the three-to-five-minute mark.

It seemed as clear and persuasive to me as any signal on the first day of school or before a big adventure.

The next day, when we were underway, I noticed that Arlie Schardt, an athlete and a former executive director of EDF, was on his back in the water, seeming to be as content as a sea otter smacking an abalone on a stone on his chest near Monterey.

Five minutes passed. Ten. Fifteen. Twenty. Twenty-five. Thirty. Thirty-five. Forty. Forty-five. Fifty. A big cataract was coming up. Our rafts were hauled out and beached on the right side of the canyon for lunch under a huge overhanging boulder.

Arlie, a cover story writer for *Time* (Mohammed Ali, Martin Luther King, Jr.), staggered out of the water and grinned. He said the temperature in the air in the canyon was 110 degrees. He said he lay at the surface, 53 degrees, which was perhaps a bit warmer than the depths, and a bubble curtain formed quietly around his body.

That afternoon and every day thereafter, I, too, was floating at the surface of the river going down stream. What a pleasure, what a delight—which I owe to Arlie's bravado and athleticism.

The Colorado River has some seventy-five tributaries—the same number, Paul Winter pointed out, as Lake Baikal, Russia's most spectacular physical feature. As a consequence, the force of those inflows creates ever-changing cataracts, of which there are eight or ten. Whenever we were near another one, the three knowledgeable guides ran up a trail beside the river to case out the options, since the picture was ever new like the turning of a kaleidoscope.

Time and again, they agreed that down the left side was the best choice, or down the right side, or down the middle.

When we approached Lava Falls, the steepest and most irregular, I walked quietly behind them and heard, "Not on the right."

"Not on the left."

"Certainly not down the middle."

We were assigned to Zeke's raft, and we were the last. Zeke gestured with his hand. I said, what was that? He heard Native Americans say it was important to make an offering to the river. Again, what was that? Zeke said, "Two M&Ms." I asked, is that a worthy and appropriate offering? He said it was all he had.

Where did you get that name, Zeke? He said he thought it would be a good name for a river guide. He also sang a little song about a double bubble partway down on the left and an Indian maiden, who got trapped in the lower part and drowned.

Zeke said that if the raft swung straight up into the air and he yelled "Hit it," we should throw our weight forward.

Well. One sits four in a row in the front, with the guide in back steering. One holds onto a loose thin rope, more for psychological purposes, it seemed to me, than anything else.

Sure enough, our raft shot straight up and back a bit, and Zeke yelled, "Hit it."

We had no purchase. We just dangled out there. The raft wavered. And eventually, it fell forward, still right side up.

There you have it: Arlie, a friend, and Zeke, a new acquaintance.

ONE WHO PAID ATTENTION

Scott and Hella with a wigman in the Tari Gap, Papua New Guinea, 1993.

The year was 1994. We were lucky to be on a tour of Papua New Guinea, a place of some 800 wholly distinct languages and spectacular biodiversity: birds of paradise, numberless moths in remote places, bowerbirds of architectural and aesthetic prowess. We traveled with the board and spouses of the World Wildlife Fund and were led by Meg Taylor.

As the well-schooled daughter of an adventurous Australian and a woman from the Tari Highlands, Taylor had been ambassador to the United States from Papua New Guinea in the 1980s and a member of the WWF board throughout. She also had run in the Boston and New York marathons.

Among our myriad adventures, I will describe one, a bit of a pickle that one member of our group resolved.

We were at the Karawari Lodge, designed in the style of a *haus tambaran*, or spirit house, in western Papua New Guinea on a hilltop overlooking the Sepik River. Rodney and Sukey Wagner had celebrated their thirty-sixth anniversary the prior evening, August 1. Rodney was vice chair of J. P. Morgan, an internationalist, and treasurer of the WWF board. According to local custom, Rodney had worn a penis gourd during a festive ceremony after dinner, with his customary good humor. We thought to surprise our sons-in-law by bringing back a penis gourd for each, but without them having had our experience, they did not know quite what to make of them.

Later, we heard a shriek in the middle of the night from our immediate neighbor, the typically calm and relaxed Adrienne Mars. We all slept under mosquito netting to reduce the possibility of a lethal local insect biting us. We ran over to Adrienne and found one of these creatures—long, skinny, and ethereal—on her pillow. I put it under a glass, and in the morning we learned that it was indeed the one to avoid at all cost.

We were told that the next morning we would travel up river by boat for an hour to a village to meet a naturalist of local renown. The vessel to propel us was a flatbed boat with white plastic chairs—a dollar a pop—nailed to the floor. We set forth up river, and as we passed villages high on the bank, we waved, and folks waved back, village after village.

After thirty-five minutes, the motor conked out. What about a backup motor? There was none. What about oars? No oars.

We began to drift down the mighty Sepik River, and the boat banged against the bank repeatedly.

Almost everyone was giddy. Folks giggled and laughed. As we slid past the villages where we had exchanged smiles and waves earlier with the inhabitants, those above on the bank put their hands politely to their mouths in embarrassment for us.

We were adrift on a big river headed toward the Bismarck Sea off north Papua New Guinea.

Only one of us, Rodney Wagner, was bent over a gnarled bit of string. It was not a rope. It wasn't even a cord. It was a gnarly, knotted bit of string.

Rodney sought to untie every knot, unsnarl every snarl. As we drifted downstream, he worked for fifteen or twenty minutes almost unnoticed. Then he took the end of the string and made a small lasso.

The last of the branches from bushes on the bank was coming up. I quietly alerted Rodney. He tossed the flimsy thing and snagged the protruding branch. At last we were secure. We were, by then, opposite the lodge. I whistled loudly. A little boat came over and pulled us across the river.

Another motor was affixed to the stern. We were on our way for what turned out to be another revelatory day led by a naturalist in that upstream village.

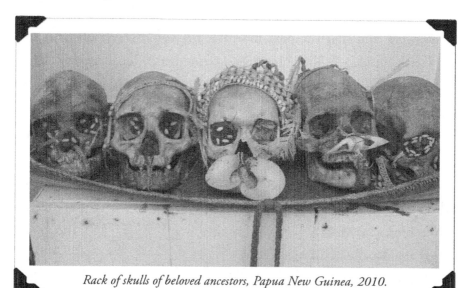

Rack of skulls of beloved ancestors, Papua New Guinea, 2010.

Aesop's Fables

Aesop's Fables are a collection of fables credited to Aesop, a slave and storyteller supposed to have lived in ancient Greece between 620 and 560 BC. Apollonius of Tyana, a first century philosopher, is recorded as having said about Aesop:

Like those who dine well off the plainest dishes, he made use of humble incidents to teach great truths, and after serving up a story he adds to it the advice to do a thing or not to do it. Then, too, he was really more attached to truth than the poets are; for the latter do violence to their own stories in order to make them probable; but he by announcing a story which everyone knows not to be true, told the truth by the very fact that he did not claim to be relating real events.

TWO QUESTIONS

*Cake prepared for Scott's 70th birthday, depicting humpback whale's song.
June 1, 2003, at Chautauqua.*

Before I turned left in Manhattan and drove some 420
miles to the Chautauqua Institution in the southwest
corner of New York State, I asked a worldly and cultured
New York City friend what she knew about the place.
"I'ts in Westchester," she advised me, "but I think it's
pronounced Chappaqua."

— Opening paragraph of an article, "An Edification
Vacation," by Lisa Schwarzbaum, Travel Section of the
New York Times, July 20, 2014

In "retirement," I thought I already had the ultimate gig, namely
serving as a naturalist with Lindblad Special Expeditions.

Therefore, in July 2000, when I was approached by a headhunter working with the search committee at the Chautauqua Institution—a nonprofit adult education center and summer resort—to find their sixteenth president, I initially declined interest.

"Will you meet with me?" she asked.

"Yes," I finally agreed.

She came to Princeton, and we met in the gardens at Prospect on campus for an hour, when she peppered me with questions and scribbled pages of notes.

Later, when I was invited to Chautauqua, still uninterested and never having been there, I accepted the invitation to meet with the search committee of ten. I arrived one afternoon in July when the summer program was in full swing and went for a swim in Chautauqua Lake, something I would do every morning, June to September, for three years. That evening I went to a concert in the welcoming amphitheatre designed and built by the first president, Lewis Miller. A gentleman spoke to me. Upon learning this was my first visit, he scooted over to the Colonnade and gathered a passel of materials to give me the larger picture and an idea of the staggering range and diversity of the nine-week summer program.

The next day, a Saturday, I walked the grounds and engaged several persons about the place, which has been a learning, cultural, religious, and recreational hub since its founding by Lewis Miller and John Vincent in 1874.

At one o'clock, I met with the search committee, and Joe Musser, a professor of English at Ohio Wesleyan University, explained that the committee had been at work for two years. They had a number of questions for me that were part of their protocol if that was okay. Certainly, and then I would have two questions for each of them. When one is not seeking a job, one is more relaxed.

Their questions ended.

My questions were: Why do you care so much about this place? What are your highest and best hopes for the future?

Their replies were charged with the binding fact that Chautauqua knits together the generations with their offerings in education, the arts, religion, and recreation, appealing to many interests, inclinations, and ages.

I closed with a poem saluting what I had learned in less than a day on the grounds. An invitation followed to become the next president, even though the fifteen prior presidents were all ordained ministers. The closing pitch, made on the phone by Marty Coyle, a leader on the board, seemed appealing. Marty loved the place and thought I would be a good leader. Hella was reluctant, since we had finally slowed down a bit and loved the freedom of our lives at that juncture.

She and I went up to Chautauqua, and she thought, well, maybe. It was a wrench for her since she would have to let go of her leadership roles at the Whole Earth Center, and at the D&R Greenway Land Trust where she was vice chair. I must say, however, I cannot imagine a First Lady of Chautauqua who gave so generously of herself in the endless entertaining (1,278 dinner guests on the president's porch in 2003), keeping up the president's garden, and being ever a source of sage advice.

We had spoken of the possibility in retirement of joining the Peace Corps and going somewhere remote for three years, where she would teach mathematics and I English literature. Not to put down Chautauqua but that was our private thought: service.

The appeal of Chautauqua to me was that many of the elements of its mission fit within my experience in education, the arts, critical issues, and working with leaders across a span of fields. I had a substantial Rolodex, which would be drawn upon in choosing and recruiting riveting speakers.

Chautauqua has nine themed weeks every summer, from late June to late August, which draw 6,000 to 8,000 persons every day. Some 1,200 homes are on the grounds, as well as fifteen inns and an old hotel, the Athenaeum. Some 2,100 events are packed into those nine weeks for toddlers to seniors, which require planning and integration. The arts flourish with two symphonies in residence, an opera company, a theater troupe, a dance company, and visual arts. At least sixteen religions are present. Sailing, kayaking, and water sports await Chautauquans on the lake.

It is the dream place to bring a family and keep it together. Chautauqua's rich history is propelled by the original vision in 1874 of John Heyl Vincent, a Methodist minister, and the equally persuasive and eloquent Lewis Miller. It has attracted leading lights: Teddy Roosevelt, Susan B. Anthony, William Jennings Bryan, Thomas Edison, Booker T. Washington, John Philip Sousa, George Gershwin, Franklin and Eleanor Roosevelt, Margaret Mead, Thurgood Marshall, Kurt Vonnegut, Jane Goodall, Mark Russell. Although people may have heard about Chautauqua, it cannot be understood nor appreciated without being in residence for a couple of weeks in season. Participation is mainly from Midwesterners, who are lifelong learners. The only lecture that captured the history and spirit of the place was given by renowned historian David McCullough, after spending two or three weeks in the archives. Dozens of independent Chautauquas have been created elsewhere, the most prominent today being in Boulder, Colorado.

Upon my arrival in the fall of 2000, when I was to be introduced to the full board, I was told to be on deck at nine o'clock. I was not called in until 9:45. I said, I thought you may have changed your minds and was told no, each member of the search committee had looked into different parts of my life and wanted to give separate reports.

Since I was the first non-ordained minister, in the early days, I was often pressed regarding my religious convictions. I replied by remarking on the wonders of the natural world, from the dung beetle to the whale, suggesting that a divine hand might well be behind these marvels, which I would then begin to enumerate.

A good record of my years serving as the sixteenth president is found in *The Daily Chautauquan* of that period and three detailed, exciting annual reports. No regrets. A real challenge, gratefully embraced.

WHAT A JOY ...

In late December 2000, after returning from our voyage deep into the Ross Sea of the Antarctic, we tried to pack in thirty-six hours and move our belongings to Chautauqua for New Year's Eve.

We also had four buckets of mail to plow through. One note caught my eye. It was from Mary Frances Bestor Cram, the daughter of Arthur Bestor, president of the Chautauqua Institution from 1915 to 1944, when he died on the job.

Mary Frances had written a book, *Chautauqua Salute: A Memoir of the Bestor Years* (1990), which I had read closely in the Antarctic. I had noted several points for discussion inside the back cover. She had written that her father regarded the mission of Chautauqua as built upon "the fundamental assumption that education is the only solution to the problems of society."

She also cited a pivotal quote from Bishop John H. Vincent, the cofounder of Chautauqua with Lewis Miller (who was the first president): "Chautauqua is an idea embracing the 'all things' of life, art, science, society, religion, patriotism, education—whatever tends to enlarge, refine, and ennoble the individual, to develop domestic charm, and influence, to make the nation stronger and wiser, and to make Time and Eternity seem to be what they are—part of one noble and everlasting whole. Chautauqua is a force, developing the realities of life in the consenting personality; applying to the individual the energies to make for character, wisdom, vision, vast horizons, ever-brightening ideals, strength of resolve, serenity of soul, rest in God, and the multiplied ministries that enable the individual to serve society."

Not knowing we were away, Mary Frances had invited us to visit her at her daughter Louise's home near Lambertville, noting the phone number.

I called her and reviewed my questions for an exhilarating forty minutes, starting with how things had changed and evolved from the early leaders to her father's long run to the present day. Her replies were illuminating and inspiring.

Before I was officially on the job, in November 2000, I wrote to the leaders of the two orchestras, the theater, the opera, the ballet, the piano program, and the visual arts to invite them to describe their vision for their discipline at Chautauqua twenty-five years hence (beyond the current players), indicating ways they could work together. Their responses were electrifying, including a push naturally for more scholarship support, which I honored. I pulled them all together at our home for a joyous lunch early in the season.

I also inscribed, in fall 2000, *The Books of the Century* from the New York Public Library for every member of the board of trustees, since Chautauqua has the oldest book club in the United States, the Chautauqua Literary and Scientific Circle, which is still vigorous and demanding of summer-long participants.

At the first meeting of the senior staff in January 2001, I had invited each person to convey what he or she felt to be "the soul of Chautauqua," which I was searching for as Diogenes with his lamp looked for "an honest man." I thought my colleagues might quote from ample material written by the founders, Lewis Miller and John H. Vincent, who were both eloquent and precise about the institution's mission. No, each offered a bit of doggerel—actually pretty good doggerel.

Within the first few months, I traveled with Hella to North Carolina to brief Chautauquans there about the forthcoming nine-week summer program. Hella and I sat with Mary Frances Bestor Cram, a local resident, over lunch and felt her warmth, welcoming, and sensibilities about Chautauqua. After my remarks, she inscribed my well-thumbed book with: "What a joy to, at last, meet you and Hella—I am filled with deep confidence in the future of my beloved Chautauqua, now."

At the end of my duties there, I concluded that the soul of Chautauqua resided in three older women, who were mentors throughout my stewardship: Helen O'Boyle, whose life was dedicated to creating peace and justice with a flair and a sense of humor; Florence Norton, a year-round resident and superb bowler with red shoes, who often sported a button reading "Dissent Is Patriotic"; and Mary Frances Bestor Cram, a guide and guru from before day one.

As Mary Frances wrote once:

> My pulse is wildly raging
> As I see the stars above
> My heart, of course is aging
> But not my love.

CHANGE?!

As some of us considered year-round Chautauqua resident Florence Norton's approaching ninetieth birthday, we thought a balloon ride at dawn would be just about perfect. Why? With her piercing wit and trenchant quips, she lifted the winter community at Chautauqua like no other.

I arranged for my classmate, George Denniston, MD, to send his book on ballooning, quite the best ever written and illustrated. It carried a fitting inscription to this rare, remarkable woman.

Our first winter at Chautauqua, Florence invited Hella and me to join the Friday afternoon bowling group. It carried, as I recall, the word "temperance" in its moniker. We marveled at her red shoes and red ball and even more at her exquisite proficiency. She walked up to the line holding the ball in both hands, then released it. It rolled slowly down the alley, moving implausibly toward the pins. She watched it closely and then gestured deftly with her right hand. The ball hit the pins. They flew, and she had another strike!

I recall, too, being in her basement standing on a ping-pong table and changing a lightbulb. She asked me, "How many Chautauquans does it take to change a lightbulb?" I had no idea. She replied, "CHANGE?!"

A leader at Chautauqua in the visual arts and opera, as well as one truly troubled about the health and vitality of the lake, Florence was active, too, in the League of Women Voters in western New York State. She often wore a big button that read "Dissent Is Patriotic."

Florence was among the international citizens within our community, thanks in part to her active and continuing involvement with the American Field Service (AFS), an international exchange program. Young people from diverse countries, including Indonesia and France, often showed up and stayed at her lovely home perched above the lake. Her travels, too, led to an understanding and celebration of other cultures and also, unerringly, seeing ways we here could be more open-minded, fairer, and more inclusive.

Florence Norton, whose presence and lively, surprising ways ever enchanted and raised our spirits, left a deep glow of gratitude with us that we were able to spend many hours in her friendship.

OH, I'VE ALWAYS WANTED TO OBSERVE THE CREATION!

Sketch of Stanley Kunitz by teacher-artist Sharon Brady, 1986, "I dance for the joy of survival at the edge of the road."

In my first year at Chautauqua, the summer of 2001, the biggest hit of the forty-five morning lecture speakers was Stanley Kunitz, then at ninety-six years US Poet Laureate for the second time. Bill Moyers had asked me in spring 1994, when he was contemplating a second PBS series on poetry, "Can I go for half an hour with Stanley Kunitz?"

I replied, "You could go the rest of your days with Stanley." He, with Galway Kinnell, was a guide in creating the Dodge Poetry Festival.

Stanley had seven events that day, beginning with the customary radio interview at the edge of Bestor Plaza. The interviewer did this every morning during the season, for decades. Folks gathered round, coffee mugs in hand.

The old radio guy asked, "Mr. Kunitz, if you could visit any three points in history or in time, what would they be?"

Stanley lit up and replied in a nanosecond, "Oh, I've always wanted to observe the Creation! I would be in a bunker taking a really good look!"

The radio duffer, instead of dropping to his knees and saying: "Hosanna! In all my years in radio, I've never had such a response!" blurted formulaically, "AND the other two points in time?"

Stanley said simply, quickly, "Tomorrow and tomorrow."

Stanley's lecture with poetry held the audience in the 5,000-seat amphitheater spellbound. He said, "Man will perish unless he learns that the web of creation is continuous tissue. Touch it, disturb it at any point, and the whole web trembles. The arts, like that web, comprise a far-flung network, a psychic membrane along whose filaments communication is almost instantaneous. All arts, all artists, are somehow connected."

Stanley Kunitz at the 1998 Dodge Poetry Festival

He sold and inscribed more books than any other speaker that summer.

Similarly, at the revered Hall of Philosophy, Chautauquans flocked to hear more of whatever Stanley chose to say.

That evening at the President's House, a joyous

dinner celebrated what we had heard and felt that day. Knowing Stanley's preference, but checking still, I prepared a dry martini along the lines of my father's regard for Bernard DeVoto's approach, as recorded in *The Hour*. Over dinner I noted that drinking dry martinis does not lead to great poetry, but at day's end ...

As Stanley hoped, his life has become a legend.

LOOK, LOOK!

Margaret Geller, astrophysicist, Charlie Rose *show.*
February 9, 1993.

It was Monday, July 14, the first day of a week devoted to "Exploration: Land, Sea, Air, Space" at Chautauqua in the summer of 2003.

The speaker was Margaret Geller, an astrophysicist with the Smithsonian Astrophysical Observatory in Cambridge, Massachusetts, who was the first person to map a swatch of the universe.

She had tied two helium-filled balloons to the podium in the inviting amphitheater.

After a couple of minutes, Geller snipped the strings, and the balloons climbed rapidly to the klieg lights and burst.

Geller said, "Nearly all the helium in the universe is 14 billion years old. It was made within the first three minutes of the Big Bang."

"Wow," thought I, "that we know this with only three pounds of putty upstairs."

The lecture was a spellbinding sparkler. Just a stanza from her interview on Charlie Rose's show on February 9, 1993, will suggest a tingle of the whole:

"We collect the light, and this light has been traveling through the universe for tens of millions, hundreds of millions, maybe billions of years. Here are these ancient photons, they haven't hit anything, and they plop into our telescope. That's the end of life for them, but they bring us information about the universe that we can interpret."

Chautauqua trustee Ted Wolfe had put up a mind-stretching exhibit of twenty-one deep-space images in the Hultquist Center in anticipation of this week on exploration that stayed up, fortunately, for the balance of the season.

As a bonus to her morning lecture, Margaret Geller, with her husband Scott Kenyon, a fellow astronomer, spoke at nine o'clock that evening to a crowd spilling on to the Hultquist porch about the structure of the expanding universe she had been mapping for twenty-two years.

She spoke about the status of each galaxy, whose light we were seeing some billions of years later. Two cameras were following her every move, gesture, and word. She danced adroitly from one galaxy to the next, describing their individual and idiosyncratic features. Geller was grateful to have this video later.

I remembered meeting Geller years earlier at the retreat Edwin Schlossberg and I organized for ten young high achievers to consider the question, "Why push for excellence when adequacy will do?" On that occasion, I recall Margaret having a book of images of galaxies on her lap, and when she spoke for the first time to the group, she got goosebumps as she looked at each image and talked about them.

When Geller concluded her spontaneous remarks, she said she would be happy to try to answer questions. A woman asked her, "What about the Bible?"

Margaret replied, "That is a good book, but what we are talking about here are empirical observations that we alter as we get better data."

Then, for those who were interested, about 150 of us trooped down to the lake to view the clear night sky, where Scott Kenyon pointed out salient features.

En route at one point Margaret pointed to the sky with delight. "Look! Look!" she said.

"What is it?" we asked.

"The Big Dipper!" said she—just as if she were seeing it for the first time.

FIVE AMERICAN POETS
WHO HAPPEN TO BE WOMEN

*Jane Hirshfield, poet and essayist,
speaking at the 1998 Poetry Festival.*

In summer 2002 at Chautauqua, we had an early week devoted to the poetry of five women who speak in gloriously distinct voices about their takes on the human predicament.

The first four I called responded with élan, and I felt that any or all of them could quite readily, in time, become Poet Laureate of the United States: Lucille Clifton, Jane Hirshfield, Naomi Shihab Nye, and Pattiann Rogers.

I was challenged in finding a fifth in their league and received a letter from Joan Murray, who had written a poem after the attack on the World Trade Center called "Survivors—Found." She read that poem on National Public Radio's *Morning Edition* four days later. The response was so vibrant that she edited a little book called *Poems to Live By in Uncertain Times* containing sixty poems, nine of whose authors are found on our Poetry Trail in Princeton.

Joan Murray explained: "Difficult events—whether personal or historic—have a way of overwhelming us; they can leave us weeping, raging, or numb. All the words of politicians, experts, and reporters only add to the muddle and our sense of powerlessness. But poems can cut through confusion to speak knowingly and intimately to us and stir us from within."

She had also written an epic poem, *Queen of the Mist* (1999), a book of 110 pages that tells the story of Annie Taylor, a destitute sixty-three-year-old schoolteacher who shot over Horseshoe Falls at Niagara, plummeting downward 165 feet, on October 24, 1901—and survived. She entered the barrel one and a half miles above the falls. She had thirty-two pounds of air in the barrel and 100 pounds of weights. She was rescued 600 yards below Niagara Falls on the Canadian shore.

Joan Murray opened that glorious week on Monday, July 2, by reading that poem in the welcoming amphitheater. It is a powerful, lucid, and moving poem that she read with her whole body. I sat behind her and to the left and saw that the audience was denied my view of how her entire body sang with the song of this heroic, perhaps foolhardy, and desperate feat. I felt like moving her away from the podium so that everyone could see the way Joan Murray spoke of the anguished effort by Annie Taylor to right her fortunes. Annie Taylor survived the plunge over Niagara, but, sadly, her fortunes did not improve. She traveled a bit, but not to acclaim.

That performance gave the week a rousing start. Naomi Shihab Nye read on Tuesday, saying at the outset, "This is the place I feel I've been looking for all my life." Lucille Clifton, originally from nearby Buffalo, came with her family on Wednesday and participated in the Fourth of July festivities with the children after her thoroughly engaging reading. Pattiann Rogers gave a sterling reading on Thursday. The women read from their beloved poems and some new ones.

When Naomi was on the escalator at the airport in Buffalo to catch her plane on Thursday, after kayaking with her son Madison on the lake, she hooted over to Jane Hirshfield, who was on the other-way escalator, "You will have a great time!"

Four of these five women are on the Poetry Trail in Greenway Meadows in Princeton: Lucille Clifton, Jane Hirshfield, Naomi Shihab Nye, and Pattiann Rogers.

Naomi Shihab Nye at the 1990 Dodge Poetry Festival.

Poet Pattiann Rogers at the 1996 Poetry Festival; years later she would design an imaginative poetry trail in the Milwaukee County Zoo.

GENTLE ARCHITECTURE

Having read *The Fountainhead* by Ayn Rand as a kid, I thought maybe I would like to be an architect. After college, I worked for an architect in Denver, Jim Sudler (Class of 1941), as a gofer, before entering the service in the fall. Sudler was the top architect in the Mile-High City then and later designed the noteworthy Denver Library after seeing Le Corbusier's Ronchamp Chapel on a trip to France.

My interest in design persisted in my and Hella's choice of Arzberg china, Gral glass, and Wagenfeld's WF flatware, as well as a brace of furniture by Hans Wegner in Copenhagen. But I couldn't draw the way Hella or Cynthia do and lacked other skills.

After our home burned to the ground in February 1981, I had lunch with architect Bob Hillier to see whom he recommended as an architect for us to rebuild on the site. He suggested Cyril Beveridge. Hillier also told us also of Malcolm Wells, an "underground" architect based in Cherry Hill, New Jersey, who was a seer of the first rank. We sought him out and relished his company and fresh approaches to putting buildings into the southern side of hills so that they would, summer or winter, be at 55 degrees Fahrenheit, the temperature of the Earth. Mac always made sure that plenty of natural light filled the rooms, same as in above-ground buildings.

In the Wellses' home were the thoughts of Emerson and Thoreau neatly incised into the wood stairs and in other places. There was a metal ring one inch in diameter on a string that one could sail across the room to land, maybe, if the release was precise, on a hook.

Mac Wells had been the architect for RCA for years after designing the RCA pavilion at the 1964 New York World's Fair. Years later, at

Herb Mills's behest, he designed his last above-ground building—the beautiful Wetlands Institute in Stone Harbor, New Jersey, a place that is flourishing today.

Mac and Shirley moved to Cape Cod in the late 1970s, where Mac designed a new home with four feet of turf on top where wild grasses grew (completed in 1979). In front was a pole where Mac tracked the sweeping movement of the sun throughout the year. When we entered the house, I lay down, here and there (which I have never done before nor since in any abode), and said that wherever I am, here I feel I am in the right place. Usually, in a room there seem to be perhaps one or two inviting spots where one might feel all right, but here one was comfortable everywhere.

Mac Wells's hallmark was little books, crisply drawn, beautifully hand-lettered, that etched his critique of how we build and live on this precious Earth. Among them were: *Gentle Architecture* (1981), *InfraStructures* (1994), and *Recovering America* (1999). These books, sold on the cheap, were snapped up by architecture students who often made pilgrimages to the Underground Gallery at 673 Satucket Road in Brewster, Massachusetts, to meet with this rare, insightful bearded man who felt a profound responsibility to the planet, which he hoped to save and restore through informed design that worked and inspired.

After 9/11, Mac designed a memorial for Ground Zero that was the best in our view, by far, of anything we had seen proposed.

When I was at Chautauqua and before we conducted a national search for a new master planner (Hugh Hardy was chosen from twelve who responded to our invitation), I invited Mac Wells to tour the grounds on April 1, 2001 (including the thirty-six-hole golf course above the grounds), to meet with senior staff, and to give a talk to elevate sensibilities and prospects. It was a thrilling visit that did lift our sights. An excerpt from a long note beforehand suggests his frugal, shy ways:

"US Airways will deliver me to Jamestown via LaGuardia and Pittsburgh. After the usual frustrating fare negotiations, it came down to $970 after getting my old-age discount, or $392.25 if I stayed over a Saturday night. I chose the latter and now have my tickets. Arrival: late Saturday, March 31, at which time I will go to my Jamestown motel (already booked) and not awaken until the following month. Knowing that you and Hella would say, 'Oh no no; stay that extra night with us,' I will go to that unnamed hostelry wearing a disguise, so a pick-up (if you're still willing, say, after lunch on Sunday) would be nice."

From a fat file of correspondence down the years, I have reveled in reading thirty letters, six books (of more than twenty), and nine postcards from Mac, which contain a sweetness, wit, gratefulness, topicality, and immense humanity. Owing to their variety, it is hard to snatch a typical example, but here's one from 1992.

"Thinking about the downhill slide of just about everything on Earth gets a little heavy at times, doesn't it? I guess that's why we were given the arts, music, etc. and the ability to appreciate the wonders of nature."

In early 2000, I sent *Recovering America* to a half dozen architects, among them Robert Hillier, who found it "a pure delight," noting, "I am not only going to hold onto the book myself as opposed to giving it away to a young architect as you suggested, I am going to buy some more copies for those young architects and a couple of clients I have who are considering building turf-covered houses."

In his book, *InfraStructures* (1994), a hardcover beautifully illustrated work, with washes as well as sketches and photographs, Mac Wells's dedication suggests his spirit and regard for other forms of life here:

"I wish this book was worthy of being dedicated to all the non-human creatures of the world but since it's not, I'll have to settle for the wish alone."

A CAPE AND A BOW TIE

In 1995, Hella and I were in a sleeping compartment of a train from Shanghai to Qufu, where Confucius (551–479 BC) lived and worked. Our bunkmates were Bob Williams, an energy expert, and Bill McDonough, a green architect who was then dean of the School of Architecture at the University of Virginia (1994–99).

Beyond the lively conversation, Bill quietly modified our small space in (count 'em) forty-one ways to make it more hospitable. First, he pushed the curtains back all the way for a full view of the countryside. Second, he cleaned the inside window. Third, at the next stop of the train, he hopped out and cleaned the window outside. Fourth, he rearranged our luggage to make sitting, and later sleeping, more commodious—and so on. That trip to China was for the board of the W. Alton Jones Foundation, and it was focused entirely on energy, since 60 percent of our grants were for the maintenance of biological diversity, and the balance to reduce the nuclear threat. Bob Williams, a MacArthur Fellow, was, then as now, an advisor to China on all spokes of the wheel of energy for human use: coal, oil, natural gas, nuclear, solar, and wind. On that trip, thanks to Bob, we even visited a "new" reactor, based on a twenty-five-year-old French model with a tiny staff.

The next pop-up in my mind was when we, again with the W. Alton Jones Foundation (WAJF), visited Curitiba, Brazil (June and July 1996), which Bill McKibben described in *Hope, Human and Wild: True Stories of Living Lightly on the Earth* (1995) as one of two sustainable places on Earth thanks to the visionary leadership of Jaime Lerner (see "A Trend Is Not Destiny"). Bill McDonough had flagged Lerner and Curitiba for WAJF as exemplary. The other sustainable place was Kerala, India, then numbering 30 million souls with a literacy rate of 97 percent and earnings of only $3 a day.

When Bill got married, he asked if I might try to secure Paul Winter to play at his wedding at the Cathedral of St. John the Divine in New York. I did, and Paul played beautifully. A memorable moment occurred over dinner when conservationist and businessman Paul Hawken offered a toast in the Cathedral Carriage House saying, one, he wasted a couple of hours that afternoon trying to tie a bowtie (looking at Bill and me); two, he was glad that Michelle was not dressed in leaves, leaving us to worry that they would fall off; and finally, that he thought Bill might be among his best friends—no, he was his best friend.

Bill invited me to come to the University of Virginia in Charlottesville to give a talk in the renowned Rotunda at the head of The Green. I had brought images of the aurora borealis for a rippling vivid display in the great circle while playing vocalizations of orcas recorded by Paul Spong. He had made the recording in 1982 during a spectacular aurora that inspired different vocalizations from typical nocturnal peals and squeals.

They seemed to mirror or sonically choreograph the colored wavering images in the night sky in their staggering vocal range. That talk on "A Siamese Connexion with a Plurality of Other Mortals," evolved into the first chapter of *The Biophilia Hypothesis* (1993).

In 2003, I brought McDonough to Chatauqua after he had published *Cradle to Cradle: Remaking the Way We Make Things* with German chemist Dr. Michael Braungart. He gave a spellbinding talk.

Bill's first commission as an architect was the 1984 Environmental Defense Fund's headquarters in New York. An early and major project was the twenty-year $2 billion environmental re-engineering of the Ford Motor Company's legendary River Rouge plant in Dearborn,

Michigan, with a living roof, covered in vegetation, of 1.1 million square feet. In 1996, McDonough became the first and only individual recipient of the *Presidential Award for Sustainable Development.*

A story in the Business Day section of the *New York Times*, March 25, 2013, begins with Bill meeting Buckminster Fuller (see vignette "What a Gift!") when Bill was a student at Dartmouth. That lecture, followed by a long walk and talk, was a decisive moment for Bill. His meetings are now being filmed and his telephone conversations recorded for the living and are immediately accessible archives at Stanford, where, it so happens, Bucky's papers are housed.

LIVING HISTORY

*Hella and Scott accompany Senator Hillary Rodham Clinton
to the Hall of Philosophy at Chautauqua, August 2003.*

In May 2003, a conference on health and health care was held at Chautauqua, and Senator Hillary Rodham Clinton (Democrat, New York) asked me if she could return to Chautauqua in August when her fourth book, *Living History*, was to be published.

I said we would be delighted to try to arrange for a reading, book sale, and signing as part of her national book tour, but that our 2,100-event nine-week schedule was already set.

Within an hour of that conversation, her scheduler asked me in an email about possible dates. It took me ninety minutes to come up with six dates and times, awkwardly over meals, and I relayed those dates to her. She shot back asking what about August 26? I replied, wide open, but the season was then over and the grounds lightly populated. I suggested she look again at the dates and times offered.

A date was agreed upon to take place at dinnertime at the Hall of

Philosophy, one of the cherished places on the grounds. Hella and I were with her for half an hour before the event, and others were pushing to have her sign the book for them. We did not, but the senator inscribed a book, "To Hella with best wishes—Hillary Rodham Clinton."

I had the honor of introducing Senator Clinton. We had understood she would read from the book for about twenty minutes, but she actually read from four sections of the book, including a priceless account of when she and Bill took Chelsea to Stanford. Hillary lined the chest of drawers with paper as her mother had done for her at Wellesley. President Clinton, a little jumpy, looked out the window.

The crowd numbered about 1,500, and most of them bought books. It was a spectacularly smooth operation. The queue was long, maybe an hour and a half for the last in line. Each person was welcomed by Huma Abedin, Clinton's longtime personal aide. After the purchase of a book, the senator looked the buyer in the eye as she wrote "Hillary Rodham Clinton" neatly in round black letters.

Were you to ask each person how much time she had with the senator, she might have said maybe a minute, since face time with a celebrity may be exaggerated in one's mind.

In fact, by my watch, ten books were signed and handed over every single minute. That is one book every six seconds.

Our granddaughter Tess, then nine, stood close by, watching intently, just as she had done while watching musicians play up close.

Five years earlier, Hella and I were fortunate to be among 150 poets joining the Librarian of Congress, James Billington, on April 22, 1998, at the White House, when Hillary Rodham Clinton and President Clinton hosted the Third Millennium Evening with Poets Laureate Robert Pinsky (1997–2000), Robert Hass (1995–97), and Rita Dove (1993–95). It was an amazing evening. The audience in the East Room had been drinking wine for quite a stretch without food. Then the three poets walked in flanked by the Clintons.

*Rita Dove at the 1992
Dodge Poetry Festival.*

*Robert Hass, Poet Laureate
of the United States, 1995–97.*

The First Lady eloquently opened the festivities, which were broadcast live worldwide. Each poet spoke in turn. Robert Pinsky was awarded $500,000 that day from the Council on the Humanities for his Favorite Poem Project. Robert Hass spoke of the River of Words poetry contest, which captured the imaginations of teachers and students nationwide. Rita Dove's poetry and jazz program reached an engaged audience.

When the president finally had a chance to speak, he cited the words of Octavio Paz, the Mexican Nobel Laureate who had died a few days earlier:

> Between what I see and what I say,
> Between what I say and what I keep silent,
> Between what I keep silent and what I dream
> Between what I dream and what I forget:
> poetry.

Clinton also said that when he was in high school he was required to learn 100 lines from *Macbeth* that cautioned one not to be troubled by blind ambition, which drew a peal of laughter from the audience. Over inviting food at the reception, the poets clustered around the Clintons, standing apart, as if their focal interest was only poetry.

In ten years since Chautauqua, it is astonishing what the junior senator from New York State has done. She ran for the Democratic nomination for the presidency in 2008 and came within an eyelash of beating Barack Obama in a brutal pitched battle for votes in the primary.

Our daughter, Catherine McVay Hughes, a lead player* in the struggle to reclaim and rebuild Lower Manhattan after the tragedy of 9/11, lived with her family on Broadway looking right into the gaping pit where the Twin Towers had stood. Catherine found Hillary Clinton to be the only politician who educated herself about the burning, toxic brew in the pit of the World Trade Center. Clinton called Catherine to testify before Congress. When Clinton ran for the presidency, Catherine was one of forty-three who testified on her website, tears in her eyes, about Clinton's leadership traits.

The rest of the story is in the public consciousness. President Obama wisely invited Clinton to be his secretary of state. She accepted and served the president and the country with vigor, fidelity, and intelligence. As an indefatigable secretary, she logged 956,733 miles on planes to 112 countries.

Her courageous speech in Beijing in 1995 on behalf of women and women's rights was a signal of what was to come in the international arena, as was her meticulous attention, town by town, issue by issue, to the citizens of New York State.

In the *New York Times* of April 7, 2013 ("Can We Get Hillary Without the Foolery?"), Maureen Dowd wrote, "As long as there are no more health scares—the thick glasses are gone—Hillary's age won't stop her. The Clinton scandals and dysfunction are in the rearview mirror at the moment, and the sluggish economy casts a halcyon glow on the Clinton era. Hillary is a symbol and a survivor, running on sainthood. Ronald Reagan, elected at sixty-nine, was seen as an 'ancient king' gliding through life, as an aide put it. Hillary, who would be elected at sixty-nine, would be seen as an ancient queen striding through life."

*See Pulitzer Prize–winning journalist Anthony DePalma's *City of Dust: Illness, Arrogance, and 9/11*, chapter eight, "Life and Dust," pages 145-167.

WHO WAS A HERO?

At Chautauqua, we had a week in the summer of 2003 devoted to heroism. The opening speaker on Monday morning in our singular amphitheater was S. Georgia Nugent. She was a professor of classics at Princeton before taking on the presidency of Kenyon College in Ohio.

Her topic was a discussion of what it took to become a hero in ancient Greece.

Dr. Nugent said four criteria had to be met:

First, the candidate had to be *a man.*

Second, he had *to kill* a lot of people.

Third, he had *to be killed* himself.

Fourth, someone had to *write about it,* preferably Homer.

Since I was under the impression that the Greeks in the fifth century had an exemplary society, this unblinking cryptic assessment was a stunner.

Then, I reflected on four of Shakespeare's great plays: *Hamlet, King Lear, Macbeth,* and *Othello.* They seize the soul of the actors and the audience by casting our attention to a stage where the darkest aspects of human nature play out, leaving hardly any player standing at the close. Most came to an untimely end.

When I returned to Princeton in 2004, I called upon my old boss, Robert F. Goheen, who was himself a classical scholar of note and valedictorian of his Princeton Class of 1940.

I recited the four elements of a Greek hero enumerated by Dr. Nugent. Goheen blinked and nodded in assent.

"She is right," he said, seeming a little surprised at this revelation.

OUR STOLEN FUTURE

*Hella snaps Scott photographing Theo Colborn
at the Black Canyon of the Gunnison, Colorado.*

At the end of the week on heroism at Chautauqua in 2003, I had invited one of my personal heroes, Dr. Theo Colborn, the lead scientist addressing the horrific panoply of health issues caused by endocrine disruption. These issues include autism, cancers, learning disorders, Parkinson's, Alzheimer's, diabetes, and obesity. She was the lead author of *Our Stolen Future* (1996) and is the founder of TEDX, The Endocrine Disruption Exchange in Paonia, Colorado. She gave a stellar talk, which was an update on her path-breaking book of seven years earlier.

In 1988, I called a meeting of folks who cared about the welfare of animals—one of the foci for support at the Dodge Foundation—to help us think through strategic next steps. Even though this was the smallest part of our philanthropy, we were number one nationally in support of humane treatment of animals.

Pete Myers, then senior vice president for science at the National Audubon Society and a Berkeley PhD in biology who wrote his dissertation on the sandpiper, couldn't make it. I met with Myers separately later for two hours. Myers talked almost exclusively about endocrine disruption.

As I walked with him to his car, I mentioned we were looking for a new leader at the W. Alton Jones Foundation in Charlottesville, Virginia. Myers expressed an interest and was hired shortly thereafter. He created a Senior Fellow position and appointed Theo Colborn, a senior scientist with the World Wildlife Fund and a key analyst of the chemical contamination of wildlife in the Great Lakes.

In 1991, Colborn and Myers brought together a group of expert scientists at the Johnson Foundation at Wingspread in Racine, Wisconsin, for a work session on endocrine-disrupting chemicals (EDCs). Their conclusion was: "Many compounds introduced into the environment by human activity are capable of disrupting the endocrine system of animals, including fish, wildlife, and humans."

In 1996, *Our Stolen Future: Are We Threatening Our Fertility, Intelligence, and Survival? A Scientific Detective Story* by Theo Colborn, John Peterson Myers, and Dianne Dumanoski was published by Dutton, with an introduction by Vice President Al Gore who wrote: "Last year I wrote a foreword to the thirtieth anniversary edition of Rachel Carson's classic work, *Silent Spring*. Little did I realize that I would soon be writing a foreword to a book that is in many ways its sequel ..."

Pete inscribed my copy: "For Scott McVay whose gentle leadership in many settings is making this world a better place to live."

In serving on the board of the World Wildlife Fund for twenty years, I thought Theo Colborn was as sharp as any member of the staff and that she was working on a problem of transcendent importance.

In 2000, Theo Colborn received the Blue Planet Prize, which carries an award of $500,000 that gave her the freedom to create her own not-for-profit, TEDX, The Endocrine Disruption Exchange. This is a major acknowledgement of the gravity and impact of the work. Among prior recipients of the award, often considered the Nobel Prize for the environment, are Lester Brown, Maurice Strong, David Brower, and Paul Ehrlich. Those since 2000 include Gus Speth, Amory Lovins, Tom Lovejoy, and Dan Janzen.

In September 2001, NHK, the Japanese analog to Britain's BBC television, made a two-hour documentary (which cost them $2 million to make) on Theo Colborn called *Superteachers: Wisdom for the Future— Dr. Theo Colborn*. NHK also made a one-hour documentary on Jane Goodall, the primatologist. Sadly, even though these were both shot in English, no English version was made of either. The insular nature of Japan, even to this day, is odd, indeed characteristic.

In the winter 2006 issue of *onEarth* journal, published by the Natural Resources Defense Fund, is a blockbuster article, "Bad Chemistry" by Gay Daly, calling attention to the fact that "hundreds of manmade chemicals—in our air, our water and our food—could be damaging the most basic building blocks of human development." The eight-page cover article gave a dramatic update on the health hazards that pile up and accumulate from one generation to the next.

A glaring example from my experience are the dolphins, 850 in Tampa bay who have been studied for forty-two years by Dr. Randall Wells of the Mote Marine Laboratory in Sarasota. The female dolphins die, on average, at age fifty-five years, the males at forty-five years. Why? The chemical toxicity in the water is absorbed by their bodies. Nine out of ten newborn calves die at birth or during the first year. In the process the adult females slough off some the toxins from their system. The males of course do not—hence, the broad discrepancy in ages at death.

The *onEarth* article suggests that the toxic burdens every human child bears in utero are an issue our society must confront and reduce.

Colborn is meticulous about what she publishes. If one goes to the website of TEDX, the inquirer can quickly learn in detail about the prenatal origins of endocrine disruption, including the revealing critical window of development in the human fetus based upon scores of sources, the chemicals used in natural gas operations, and the impact of pesticides on plants and animals everywhere.

Along with TEDX's ongoing intensive work of dissemination of reliable information about endocrine disruptive chemicals from a databank of 40,000 scientific publications is a parallel effort on hydraulic fracturing or fracking. A full-page "Mother's Day Letter to the First Lady of the United States, Michelle Obama," appearing in the *New York Times* on May 12, 2012, was signed by Theo Colborn and scores of other mothers. It was a telling and brilliant screed, underscoring the health threats to our children posed by extreme forms of fossil fuel extraction—in particular the process of drilling oil and natural gas using high-volume hydraulic fracturing, known as fracking. The letter enumerates manifold deleterious affects on health and provides ten scientific references, including one by Theo Colborn.

Her letter to the president of December 2012 urged a revised upgrade of our national priorities to act on what we know about EDCs and push the research agenda.

On October 22, 2013, TEDX's tenth anniversary of getting its 401(c)3 from the IRS, Theo relinquished her leadership to Dr. Carol Kwiatkowski, the executive director for the prior five years. Kudos poured in from around the globe, for Theo Colborn is considered one of Rachel Carson's primary heirs.

How single-minded her focus, determination, and follow-through. That's why I invited Dr. Theo Colborn to be the final speaker in our week on heroism at Chautauqua in 2003.

On December 14, 2014, Theo Colborn died peacefully at home in Paonia, Colorado, age eighty-seven, with family by her side. Praise and plaudits from the scientific community poured in, none more eloquent than that by Richard Liroff, a colleague from the years at the World Wildlife Fund and a vital member of our board at The Endocrine Disruption

Exchange.

Staff at TEDX has pinned to the wall Theo's favorite inspiration, a poem by Goethe, "Until One Is Committed …"

Until one is committed,
there is hesitancy, the chance to draw back,
always ineffectiveness.

Concerning acts of initiative (and creation)
there is one elementary truth
the ignorance of which kills countless ideas
and splendid plans:

That the moment one definitely commits oneself
then Providence moves too.

All sorts of things occur to help one
that would never otherwise have occurred.

A whole stream of events issues from the decision,
raising in one's favor all manner
of unforeseen incidents and meetings
and material assistance
which no man could have dreamt
would come his way.

Whatever you can do, or dream you can, begin it.
Boldness has genius, power and magic in it.

Begin it now.

NOT SINCE HEIFETZ

On August 17, 2012, at Tanglewood, the Boston Symphony Orchestra played three works in the Shed under the baton of guest conductor Bramwell Tovey: *The Suite from Appalachian Spring* by Aaron Copland; The Concerto for Violin and Orchestra, op. 14, by Samuel Barber; and Beethoven's Symphony no. 7. It was the orchestra's seventy-fifth season at Tanglewood, and a torrential downpour in the ninety minutes beforehand did not dampen the spirits or enthusiasm for what nearly 5,100 persons heard, saw, and felt that evening.

We were privileged to hear the three works in rehearsal the prior morning on a sun-dappled day. The wizardry of violin virtuoso Augustin Hadelich playing the solo for the Barber work was a thrill to behold. Hadelich, twenty-eight years, played a 1723 ex-Kiesewetter Stradivarius violin with a flowing sensibility that took the observer to the inner recesses of manifest genius. As a solo encore, he played Paganini's Caprice no. 24 with agility and dexterity.

Why did this mean so much to Hella and me? Ten years earlier, Augustin Hadelich, then eighteen, on the Thursday evening of our week on heroism at Chautauqua, played his first concert in America. Of German parentage (born April 4, 1984), living in Northern Italy, Augustin had then already mastered the European canon for violin and piano and composed sixty to seventy pieces himself. Members of the Chautauqua Symphony Orchestra, made up of musicians from many orchestras, were so bedazzled that the next year Augustin was invited to play with a dozen American orchestras.

Dr. Theo Colborn, who was to speak the next morning, said, "Not since Heifetz."

In the intervening decade, Hadelich has played with eminent orchestras and conductors here and in Europe and Asia, moving to the front rank of the most sought-after musicians.

Among the many subsequent rave reviews was one by Alex Ross in the *New Yorker* of January 4, 2010, under the heading "LIEBER AUGUSTIN":

"If a layer of surface noise were added to Augustin Hadelich's recent solo-violin recording on the Avie label, you might think you were hearing a virtuoso out of the Golden Age. Hadelich, who is twenty-five, has all the fast-fingered brilliance that modern conservatory culture requires; the musicality and the freewheeling fantasy that he brings to bear, though, cannot be taught. With the pianist Rohan De Silva, Hadelich gave a riveting recital at the Frick on Dec. 13. in which he ranged from Beethoven's Sonata in G Major, Op. 30, No. 3, to showpieces by Sarasate and Ysaye, and on to Prokofiev's Second Sonata and Alfred Schnittke's First Sonata, from 1963. The crucial thing was the command of color: luminous sweetness in Beethoven and Prokofiev, a wide, ruddy tone in Sarasate's 'Carmen Fantasy,' and savage sounds from Schnittke, including something like electric-guitar fuzz. Hadelich shows similar versatility on the Avie disk, combining classic and modern fare. Here is a young artist with no evident limitations."

The tragedy of Augustin's young life was being in a house fire at age fifteen that severely burned his face and bow arm. He was not able to resume playing until 2001.

The evening in the Shed in 2012 became all the more amazing when Hadelich came out for a solo encore, and the crowd could hear him unburdened of even a great orchestra.

NUREMBERG? MY FATHER WAS IN NUREMBERG

Joseph J. Ellis, a popular and engaging professor who previously taught at Mount Holyoke College, authored the iconic biography of *Thomas Jefferson American Sphinx: The Character of Thomas Jefferson*, which won the 1998 National Book Award. He went on to win the Pulitzer Prize in History in 2001 for *Founding Brothers: The Revolutionary Generation*.

Yet on June 18, 2001, Walter V. Robinson broke the story "Professor's Past in Doubt" in the *Boston Globe*, revealing that Ellis had falsely claimed duty in Vietnam:

"Ellis's historical focus extends beyond the country's early days. For years now, his course on Vietnam and American Culture has been one of the school's most popular—enriched, say his students, by his sometimes-detailed recollections of his own army service in Vietnam. But Ellis did not serve in Vietnam at all, according to military records obtained by the *Globe* and interviews with his friends from the 1960s. He spent his three years in the army teaching history at the US Military Academy at West Point, New York. Ellis also appears to have exaggerated the extent of the involvement he claims to have had in both the antiwar and civil rights movements."

Ellis admitted lying to his students about serving in Vietnam. Mount Holyoke President Joanne Creighton rebuked him for his lies and suspended him for a year without pay.

Joseph Ellis had been invited to speak at Chautauqua in summer 2002, and he had accepted. We were given the chance to rescind the invitation. It was my call to decide whether or not to hold with the invitation.

I picked up the Jefferson biography and was jolted by his statement that when he looked in the mirror, the cut of the jaw and the red hair made him look a lot like President Jefferson. Examples of plagiarism in his work were also popping up.

I concluded that on the chance that he might be willing to talk about how as a writer of history one can be tempted to exaggerate, puff up, inflate, and embroider one's own life, it might be worth offering him the chance to speak in a morning lecture.

Ellis arrived the evening beforehand at the historic Wensley Guest House for visiting artists and speakers, which then could handle up to nine guests.

Another guest and a Chautauqua favorite was there, too, John Q. Barrett, the meticulous, esteemed biographer of Supreme Court Justice Robert H. Jackson. Justice Jackson was the chief prosecutor at the Nuremberg trials of Nazi war criminals in 1945–46.

When Ellis heard this, he said, "Nuremberg? My father was in Nuremberg."

Barrett, a professor of law at Saint John's University, was familiar with the names of 2,000 persons involved in those trials, and so asked, "In what capacity?"

Ellis paused, seemed to recall being on the carpet as an exaggerator, backed off, and said, "He was just an MP."

The lecture the next morning was not a soul-searcher as I had hoped.

THE DOPPELGÄNGER

When I headed Chautauqua, letters tumbled in. In March 2003, I got a letter from Chagrin Falls, Ohio, from a Scott McVay. M-C-V-A-Y—that spelling is typical only two times out of ten versus three times for M-C-V-E-Y or five times out of ten for M-C-V-E-I-G-H. The most straightforward spelling is the least common.

This was the first time I had heard of someone with the same name, although Hella was sort of surprised by a birth announcement in our hometown newspaper of Princeton of a baby named Scott McVay Ferguson.

The letter from Chagrin Falls was well written—the only unusual thing was the letterhead: Iditarod Sled Dog Race.

It closed with a proposal of lunch—any time, any place, I should name it, he would be there.

I replied, "Fine, April 11, 1:00 p.m., Chagrin Falls," since a Gates Mills couple had invited us to Mozart's *The Magic Flute* that evening in Cleveland.

A little later Scott McVay called to propose lunch near Chautauqua, since he had a place south of the grounds on Chautauqua Lake, a houseboat.

Hella and I met him at 12:30 at the Ironstone on April 4. Scott McVay is a big man—six feet five inches tall—a native of Shaker Heights (where I was born!), and he had a wonderful wife named Jane.

With another chap he wrote the rules in the 1970s for the Iditarod, the long trail sled dog race in Alaska every March—1,122 miles—and he had raced in it a few times himself. The race takes eight to twenty days.

He seemed as proud of helping out a high school radio station beginning in 1985, which had only one watt of power. He put in $50,000 of his own money and managed to get equipment for the school worth $400,000. The station then had 1,000 watts and played "songs with a tune."

Scott and Jane were sweethearts at Shaker Heights High School and went to the senior prom together. He went on to Miami University of Ohio, and she to Ohio Wesleyan. They saw each other for a while in college and then, he thought, mistakenly, she lost interest. Jane explained, "In those days, the initiative was left to the man, and he misread the tea leaves."

She heard, later, that he had married someone else. In time, she married, too. Decades passed. Their spouses died, and someone who had a photograph of them from the night of their senior prom at Shaker Heights High reconnected them. They had married in 2000 on the Isle of Skye in kilts, with their families present.

On the morning of April 11, 2003, the phone rang.

"Scott McVay? It's Scott McVay. Are you going to *The Magic Flute* in Cleveland this evening?"

"Yes, we are."

"Don't forget to tune in to 91.5 FM."

"Starting when?"

"After Ashtabula."

We did just that. Click.

"Ole Buttermilk Sky" followed by "It Had to Be You."

What a sweet story.

We have the same name, were both born in Shaker Heights, both worked in Alaska, are both on the tall side, and are of the same generation, but that's as far as it goes.

BOOKS, IMMORTAL BOOKS!

It is with books as with men: a very small number play a great part, the rest are lost in the multitude.

—Voltaire

What are the books that helped shape and define the last hundred years? That was the question put to the librarians of the New York Public Library, sixty-three of them, as part of the library's hundredth anniversary celebration in 1995.

Elizabeth Diefendorf, a Cornell graduate and curator of the exhibition, asked her colleagues, which books had influenced the course of events for good or ill? Which interpreted new worlds? Or delighted millions of readers? Their answers formed *Books of the Century*, a highly popular exhibit.

The 159 books chosen from more than 1,000 suggestions fell into such categories as: Landmarks of Modern Literature (three in Spanish), Nature's Realm, Protest and Progress, Mind and Spirit, Women Rise, Utopias and Dystopias, War, Holocaust, Totalitarianism, Optimism, Joy, Gentility, and Favorites of Childhood and Youth.

The exhibit was breathtaking in the way each individual book was displayed, whether in mint condition or as a well-thumbed copy from the stacks. Each book was opened to a pivotal passage, with a concise description of the book in two or three paragraphs. Among them are *The Magic Mountain* by Thomas Mann, *A Sand County Almanac* by Aldo Leopold, *Silent Spring* by Rachel Carson, *The Grapes of Wrath* by John Steinbeck, *Coming of Age in Samoa* by Margaret Mead, *The Cat in the Hat* by Dr. Seuss, *My Fight for Birth Control* by Margaret Sanger, and *Pygmalion* by George Bernard Shaw.

At the same time a small book, also called *Books of the Century*, was published by the Library.

In this piece, a departure from our usual format, we reflect on books as the cornerstone of a civilization—or of a life—especially since the invention of a press in Europe by Johannes Gutenberg in 1450. Books became more widely available and contributed to the Renaissance, Reformation, and scientific thinking. Also, in my view, the gift of Andrew Carnegie toward funding for libraries in forty-six states, and the training of librarians, was a splendid contribution to the possibility of a functioning democracy.

After four visits to Chautauqua in 2000 to meet with trustees and senior staff, I mailed to every member of the board a copy of this book at Thanksgiving, as a talisman of thanks for the opportunity to serve as Chautauqua's sixteenth president and to work with each of them to envision the future of Chautauqua.

So, too, I gave *Books of the Century* to key staff, since they would nudge the vision into a strategic plan—and bring the plan into being, building ever on a rooted legacy.

Since Chautauqua is a community of lifelong learners, including many avid readers, I thought the elegant effort of the librarians in New York, under Elizabeth Diefendorf's curatorial and editorial leadership, would strike the right chord.

It is inspiring to see what Chautauqua's founders had to say about books. Lewis Miller wrote in 1883:

"The treasures that lie hidden in books may well awaken our inquiry and admiration! I do not wonder at the hunger there seems to be after the hidden treasures of books, for in them is power, wealth, and pleasure."

Three years later in *The Chautauqua Movement*, John Heyl Vincent declared: "What professors I have, in books! Immortal books of history and science and art, books of poetry, fiction and fact."

Chautauqua boasts the oldest book club in America, the Chautaqua Literary and Scientific Circle, and offers a reading program every summer of nine books, leading to a graduation ceremony in the Hall of Philosophy.

In August 2003, a day of radiant sunshine, I spoke at that ceremony to scores of graduates in white robes—all who had read nine prescribed books and discussed them weekly.

Mir Ali Haravi (died 1550), calligrapher and the most celebrated master of nasta'liq script, wrote:

> There is no friend in the world better than a book,
> in the abode of grief that is this world, there is no consoler
> (better than a book)
> in a corner of loneliness, every moment,
> it provides a hundred comforts, and there are never any vexations.

Cartoonist Ed Harmon depicts the "new Chautauqua
president" deciphering "C.L.S.C." on chart as the
Chautauqua Literary and Scientific Circle,
the oldest book club in America.

The Thing Which Interests You

Twain had decided by early 1904 to dictate his recollections to a stenographer. He had also decided to plunge every day into whichever moment of his life he pleased to consider, with no regard for chronology.

"Talk only about the thing which interests you for the moment" is how he describes his working method. "Drop it the moment its interest threatens to pale, and turn your talk upon the new and more interesting thing that has intruded itself into your mind meantime."

— Richard Lacayo, "A Man In Full,"
Time, November 22, 2010

PHILIP: EXPLORER, FINISHER, FRIEND

*Tess, Philip, and Matthew
at the piano in the early days.*

When we first glimpsed Philip, our firstborn grandchild, shortly after he was born at Mount Sinai Hospital in New York City, he was on his belly, head up looking around. The drive down Fifth Avenue and through the Holland Tunnel into New Jersey en route to our home in Princeton was exciting for me, since I knew I was driving a precious bundle. Tom and Catherine's place on lower Broadway was under renovation, so Philip's first weeks were at our home. As a result, he always feels comfortable here.

The iconic image of Philip, before he was one, is in a canvas bag being carried by his folks to the beach. We had rented a new house in

Cape May Point, where Philip was ever climbing up the stairs, two full flights, with one of us spotting him every step of the way.

We made a little film, "What's Poppin' in the Provinces?" beginning with popcorn spilling out of a hot skillet that is followed by young Philip walking around a playground as he explores and pushes every dimension.

When he was in preschool at Trinity Church in Manhattan, I gave a talk to his classmates on whales. The question in the air was, "Isn't that Philip's grandfather?" A happy connection and sole identity.

As a little kid, Philip was hooked on LEGO, the snap-together plastic bricks from Denmark that one can fashion into planes, skyscrapers, aircraft carriers, and hundreds of other configurations. We marveled when he made something with a thousand pieces in a couple of hours. But he went beyond that. He also knew the names and behaviors of all seventeen species of penguins. His home, to this day, is adorned with several memorable watercolors he did as a boy, notably including a horse.

He was a little older when he learned pi to more than one hundred digits.

Philip is a good athlete. Whenever the family came to us, he shot baskets in the stone-paved plaza before our garage, even in his pajamas, making hoop after hoop, many rimless. When we played "GHOST" he usually won, unless I shot a left-handed hook walking away. He soon caught on.

He was a good student at Packer Collegiate Institute in Brooklyn, two subway stops away from his home, excelling in math, science, and history. He was president of his senior class and cocaptain of the volleyball team that won their division in New York City.

I took him on a college tour to visit Middlebury, Dartmouth, Amherst, George Washington University, and Johns Hopkins, where he had taken six of their CTY (Center for Talented Youth) summer courses. The visit to Middlebury was vividly memorable. He is a big guy with tousled blond hair and tends to sleep late. We were staying at the Middlebury Inn, notable for unexpected shelves of *Reader's Digest* condensed books. His appointment at the admissions office was at eleven, so I roused him at 10:30.

If I recall correctly, Philip was wearing flip-flops as we strode across the campus. Flip. Flop. Flip. Flop. At the office he filled out a form and then met a tall woman, and they spoke for about forty minutes. Other applicants came and went in short intervals. Finally, Philip came out smiling—as did she.

Philip applied to Middlebury for early admission and was accepted. He responded with alacrity. It is noteworthy, however, that he went into senior year taking more Advanced Placement examinations and earning two fives and a four in May.

I gave him my cap and gown from 1992 when I received an honorary degree at Middlebury for initiating a major Chinese language initiative at the Dodge Foundation that took root in dozens of strong high schools nationwide.

He majored in physics at Middlebury and gave as much time to studying Mandarin, even taking an eight-week course between sophomore and junior year (amongst guys from the CIA and FBI who dropped from the course like flies), filling a lined notebook with every new character he learned. The first year was so tough that he did not even ski once, an activity he loves. But the second year he did ski frequently.

A high spot of his college years was working in Beijing for a travel agency for eleven weeks and even slipping off to Mongolia for a weekend while his roommate renewed his Chinese visa. He also visited and relished Taiwan. But the capper was a forty-hour train ride in a crowded car with the locals where he did not have a seat. Philip had brought with him a collapsible chair, which collapsed in the first hour. He sat on the floor between some bicycles and the toilet with his cowboy hat pulled down over his eyes. Eventually, two construction workers offered him a bucket, which he turned upside down. When the first dawn came, Philip said no sunrise had ever been as beautiful or welcome.

The second day some grandmothers took pity on him and offered him their seats, which he accepted for a bit, but they were not designed for this tall drink of water.

When Philip finally reached his destination, Chengdu, Sichuan, where the massive Buddha is carved into the steep hillside beside the river and people seem to move like ants in the hills around it, he felt the pain and anguish of the trip was worth it.

The last day before he left for China, Philip came to our fifty-fifth anniversary party at Prospect House and Gardens on June 9 and offered a sparkling toast. We were honored by his observations and grateful that he delayed his departure.

In July 2014, Philip returned from a cross-America trip in a white 2000 Volvo, given to him upon graduation from Middlebury. His trip led thoughts to well up in my mind of my sojourn out west with Sam Sloan while we were college students.

With a classmate, Philip traveled over 8,500 miles in twenty-three days through twenty-five states. High points of their trip were Glacier— long hikes, spectacular scenery—Ashland, Oregon,

The three caballeros, Philip, Tess, and Matthew, before solar array at Middlebury College at Philip's graduation in 2014.

where they saw *Richard III*; Bryce and Zion; and Ashville, North Carolina, where they had a personal connection. Two sets of parents and one set of grandparents heard some of their stories over a long vibrant dinner at Cape May Point in an old house known as the "Gray Ghost." As I recall, we all hung on every word as Philip and his friend completed each other's sentences. What a wonderful way to cap off his college career and start the next chapter of his life.

Philip offers a toast at celebration of our 55th wedding anniversary at Prospect House and Gardens on Princeton campus, 2013.

TESS: ARTIST, RUNNER, SCRABBLER

Matthew, Tess, her bear—her oft-repaired bear.

"She has brown eyes," Hella squealed with delight. "A glorious mutt with four lines—Russian-Jewish, Mexican, German, and Irish—a beautiful amalgam for the twenty-first century."

The other grandma, with beautiful, big brown eyes, said, "Tess's eyes will soon turn blue."

Among the early clues of Tess's precocity was painting after amazing painting at the ages of two and three—all on display now at Field Farm in Ulster Park, New York.

Her empathy is seen in her feeling for Charlotte, a truly courteous female black Lab. On one occasion five or six years ago, she saw a newly hatched bird squeaking in the bushes and tenderly cradled her in her cupped hands. She built a home for the wee bird with a branch to perch on, water, food, moss, and leaves and spoke to it softly. Later, two other small birds were detected from the clutch, and they made a menagerie. She cared for them a couple of days until they took wing.

In 2010, at the age of sixteen, Tess signed up for a study venture in the South Seas. In waters near Fiji, she was almost fatally afflicted by an infection from the ocean waters. When we were in the same place a few months later, she had written out a crisp note for us to deliver to the chap who saved her life by carrying her to a neighboring island and getting her the medication she urgently needed. Oddly, Hella was also stricken by the same malady. If the naturalist/physician on board our ship had not accurately diagnosed the problem, a tropical bacterial infection, she, too, could have been severely at risk.

Looking back, we note a turning point in her life in 2010, when her mother left New York for Washington, DC, to become director of innovation at the Peace Corps heading into its fiftieth year. Tess had been at Dalton, a place we found short of the mark as a community and a place for learning. In Washington, she enrolled at Georgetown Day School for her last two high school years. Everything seemed to click for her there. She became a runner, and I saw her compete with her team at the Penn Relays, a hallowed event I had heard about from my father. In her senior year, two weeks before graduation, she broke the school record for running the mile by a whopping eight seconds, coming in at 5:22. We gave her a silver necklace with a running-shoe pendant with 5:22 incised thereon.

Cynthia threw a terrific party for Tess's graduation from high school, writing a dazzling poem about the events of her young life, "This is Tess." Here are a few stanzas from seven pages:

This Is Tess

Conceived in Princeton
Grammy figured that out
At their house
Thanksgiving
She pulled out her Planned Parenthood wheel
I hadn't done the math

And then
in pre-born moments
She broke
her water
Then hanging on to breathe
Hung by her own umbilical cord
Twice wrapped
Setting off alarms
At birth
Fortunately or mama would have done it alone
Squirreled away in Lenox Hill

Black hair
Brown eyes
Little head

This is Tess:
On the way to the
Highly competitive
Preschool interview
We are jay walking across
Park Avenue
And she says,
"We are bishops":
I lose her words in the din of traffic

Ask for
Hear them again
Because we're traveling
On an angle

Bishops

This is Tess
finding a small bicycle
stranded in the city street
Red blue yellow
Bat mobile
Small
Perfect sized
Tess-sized
Tess gets on
I let go.
she learns to ride a bike
in an instant
on Park Avenue
gliding over sidewalk cracks

Batmobile

Tess accepted early admission to Washington University in St. Louis, Missouri, where the women's cross-country team were the national champs.

Following the continuing "itch for things remote," Tess traveled in 2011 with her mother on Peace Corps business to Senegal and the Gambians, taking more than 1,500 photographs. In May 2013, after her first year at Washington University, Tess went with an anthropological study group to Greece, organized by a professor.

If I were to pick one example of Tess's quick wit and linguistic dexterity, it would be her prowess at Scrabble—to the dismay of her cousins Philip and Matthew, who are good, too. Tess invariably lays down seven tiles—for a bonus of fifty points—almost every game. In fact, the last game we played with her, she laid down seven tiles for three unusual words while learning new Spanish words on her cell phone.

For her nineteenth birthday, August 21, 2013, we gave Tess a necklace with Scrabble tiles that spelled W-I-N-N-E-R, but she is a winner all around.

Tess in her banana dress in Perth, Australia, where she worked to reintroduce two rare parrots, western rosella and the red-capped parrots from the zoo into a 400-hectare park, April 2015.

IMMIGRANTS: THE PRIDE OF AMERICA

On the morning of the eve of July 4th
at the wharf of the ferry to Cape May
Philip decorated, delighted, and embellished
the faces of 39 of 40 notable immigrants
in Carnegie's full-page ad in the *Times*.

The actress Salma Hayek alone was left untouched
too pretty to defile
while Tess 12 days later noted by her
"I'm with ... Stupid————"
Charles Simonyi, business leader, now "Stupid."

Freeman Dyson, lower left, was "improved"
by both with green glasses, a strengthened nose
Tess redubbed him (physicist and mathematician)
"Plastic Surgeon," and gave him a stethoscope.

The central figure ANDREW CARNEGIE, larger than others
was made more dashing by Philip
odder by Tess with spiders, stitches, and gnats.

Ted Koppel gets an eye patch from Philip,
mustachio and stitches; Tess pens bags
under eyes, calls him "second oldest person alive."

Liz Claiborne, designer, loses teeth at hands of Phil and Tess,
her hat now says for Tess "HE HE,"
she's a cross-eyed "Clown."

Close inspection rewards the inspector every time
the sanctified sublime are not beyond a satirical line
Rupert Murdoch, media tycoon, is now (surprise!)
according to Tess "unemployed."

Closer note yet reveals changes in jobs.
In Tess's lexicon, to such enviable posts as
"sewer cleaner," "trash collector," "toilet urology,"
"pirate," "mess maker," "crazy eyes," "wart remover,"
"bewitcher," "convict," "dali artist," … an expurgated list.

The sacrosanct are not seen so
by youth who have made swift strokes
with devastating authority and speed
the rarified reduced to old weeds.

October 31, 2007

I WOULD LIKE TO THANK ...

Matthew with bottlenose dolphin, at Roatán, Honduras, 2008.

"I would like to thank my mother for making things happen and my father for his love of books." Thus spoke Matthew Hughes, twelve, on the occasion of his parents' twentieth wedding anniversary. The toast occurred on a beach with live music in the middle of a big storm in September 2008, which lifted the tent ceaselessly.

When Matt was three in August 1999, his mother organized a trip out West to a couple of dude ranches. I recall vividly when he first reconnected with his cousin Tess, four—he was so excited he jumped up and down. He was ever coordinated, calm and confident. For example, Matt rode a horse at the last round up at Lone Mountain Ranch carrying an egg on a spoon. Not dropping the egg after a couple of circuits of the corral, the organizers said, "You win." Also on that trip we visited Yellowstone and recall him holding his nose due to the noisome sulfurous stench of the bubbling lava pools.

When school was out in 2008, we traveled with Catherine and Tom and their sons, Philip and Matt, on the Elbe River from Berlin to Prague. On deck was a large chess set where one could push big pieces around. Matthew had won a Brooklyn-wide chess tournament at the age of five, even though he hates competition. He plays well but he was ever into a book.

About a week into the voyage, a woman from California said she had a twelve-year-old grandson who wasn't much of a reader. Could he recommend a few books? A lined piece of paper and a pen were on the table. Matt said sure, and filled the page with the names of books and their authors, noting the kinds of books, such as adventure, history, fantasy, science fiction, biography, and including the number of volumes in a series. He looked up and asked if that would do, and she said thanks, it's more than enough.

In summer 2009, we received two letters, back to back, from Matthew, then thirteen, describing a long, formidable paddle with three of his buddies—Isaac, Ben, and Austin—in a group from Camp Hurontario, north of Toronto. This undertaking was the finale, after three years of outdoor activities, from sailing to swimming to canoeing. This particular paddle began at six in the morning and lasted until one a.m. the next day, with four hours when they pulled ashore for a lightning storm. His staying power was an inspiration to us in late July 2013, when we paddled a kayak through the Pinelands on the Batso River from nine to four.

The summer of 2013 vaulted Matthew to a mature plane of experiences for which he seemed to be prepared. It began with his fourth CTY (Center for Talented Youth program) in advanced mathematics at Princeton University with fifteen others, eight from abroad, four from China. On the second Saturday, I arranged for him to meet with Professor James Sturm at nine o'clock at the Engineering Quad entrance.

We had arranged to meet at 8:30 in the Whitman College courtyard. No Matthew. No response on his cell either. At 8:40, I went to the desk of the leader of nine CTY programs for 175 students, and he said he would fetch him. Matthew, now six foot five, erect, smiling, sailing along beside me, said in a deep voice, "I'm 100 percent, Grampa." His cell phone went down overnight. Hence, no alarm,

Matthew and Tess in the Galapagos.

and no response, when I called. Professor Sturm, who guides twenty Princeton undergrads in entrepreneurial engineering, gave him a full hour one on one saying things that if they had come from a parent or grandparent might be discounted. Matt's summary of the meeting seemed to say he felt his compass well aligned, and he knew what he would be doing.

Before he left for Alaska for five weeks of clearing trails with the Student Conservation Association, which he had done in South Dakota in 2012, Matt said he would write us five letters. Really? He did so with vigor and joy. They were detailed, witty, incisive two-sided missives. We got a sense from the outset of every participant and the growing cohesion and mutual support of the group at Chugach National Forest. They were working on trails up to ten hours a day with twenty-two hours of sun. A natural cook, he one night prepared for the group burritos with guacamole. At the Russian River, they went to sleep listening to the swiftly moving waters. Phil, with the US Forest Service, reflected the hospitality of the big state by sharing both fishing rods and a private stash of homemade smoked salmon. We shivered when Matt reported only a "thin tent fabric between (him) and a bear."

What a summer for a New York kid. Matthew, with his sense of humor, capacity for work, and natural empathy, reminds us of the huge promise of youth.

In his senior year at Packer Collegiate, he was captain of the volleyball and squash teams and continued to play the slide trombone with the band. They went to New Orleans over spring break and played in Preservation Hall. In summer 2014, he was an intern with Ruby Rocket's, a company that makes frozen fruit and vegetable concoctions on a stick. Matt enjoyed promoting the product in Brooklyn and Manhattan.

In August, he entered Colby College in Waterville, Maine, and we learned that he was taking Russian. Russian, we asked in amazement, a tough language: the Cyrillic alphabet, the roiling situation in eastern Ukraine with Vladimir Putin rattling the nuclear saber, and my impression in 1973 that Moscow was the saddest place on Earth in contrast to the biologists we worked with on endangered species. Russian? Then, suddenly, we learned he had switched to German.

Matthew offers a toast at our 55th wedding anniversary.

Hella wrote Matthew as follows:

How did you make this decision, my youngest and tallest grandchild?
Is this because you really know already so many words of that language?

English	German
light	*licht*
knight	*knecht*
night	*nacht*
thank	*danke*
might	*macht*
and	*und*

und so weiter

And of course, when you need a little extra help, you have a free tutor.

I am so flattered that you study math and a little German on the side.

Hugs on tiptoes from your grandmother.

No reply, so Hella resent it to Matthew's new email with the following introduction:

Wie gehts?

I guess I used the wrong email and you did not switch your language oh, *mon dieu* to French or Mandarin *chin chin mao mao tse tse.*
Viel Glueck in and auf Deutsch
(Where are the Umlauts on the computer to be found?)
Grandmama

The next day, September 14, Matthew replied,

Yes, I'm taking German. It's a bit of a weird choice, considering the German-speaking population isn't as prominent as the Chinese or Spanish population, so I'd like to explain my reasoning a little bit. During our freshman orientation, one thing that was stressed time and time again was the importance of a liberal arts education, and how critical it is to keep your brain open and elastic. I had the opportunity to take a Spanish placement exam and basically test out of having to take a language—but that would've been the easy way out. Instead, I get to challenge myself and struggle/wade through a completely new mindset.

Miss you guys,
Matthew

Matthew, Tess, and Philip on the Poetry Trail on the day of the dedication.
October 2012.

WHAT QUESTION ARE YOU WAITING FOR?

At Franklin & Marshall College is a hall that invites interactive conversation, since it is shaped like a horseshoe. It was the summer of 1994 in the middle of a rousing Center for Talented Youth* session, during which a full high school course is covered in three weeks of superb instruction with eager youth.

My assignment was to engage these young people one evening from 6:30 to 10:30 in exploring what we know of whales and the compelling research opportunities they offer.

I laid down ground rules. First, we would screen the fifty-five-minute documentary of my second Arctic expedition, *In Search of the Bowhead Whale*, by Bill Mason. Mason had made two award-winning series on whitewater canoeing and on wolves he had observed and lived with for five weeks.

The second hour would be given to questions about the bowhead whale, the beluga, and the Inuit with whom we worked in the Alaskan Arctic. The last two hours would be open to any questions about whales.

I had brought with me a copy of *Mind in the Waters: A Book to Celebrate the Consciousness of Whales and Dolphins*, to give to the student who asked the best question, but did not mention this beforehand.

I no sooner replied to one question than a forest of hands shot up.

It was already ten after ten when I pointed to a lad in the third tier on the right who was pumping his hand for recognition. He said, breathlessly, "What question are you waiting for you haven't gotten yet?"

I said, "Oh no—what is your question?"

"That is my question."

The question I had never gotten was, "How can a student in high school, college, and beyond prepare herself to crack the whale code?"

Yes, yes, how?

Then, for twenty minutes I sketched a scenario of courses and scientists with whom one could study at a series of institutions to create a multi-disciplined approach to a range of species, beginning with the beluga, "the canary of the sea," and including and extending our understanding of the mighty sperm whale, who seems to make only clicks.

At 10:30, six of these youth, in cahoots, crowded around and said, "You have to spend the night here. We have breakfast tomorrow from 7:00 to 9:00, and we have many more questions about whales and dolphins."

That was a breakfast peppered by questions and observations. I took down their names and addresses and sent each of them a copy of *Mind in the Waters* for the huge gift of the intensity of their exploratory spirit.

In giving hundreds of lectures on whales, which I enjoyed and often relished, I do not recall ever having so much fun.

*Today Johns Hopkins has more than thirty sites in America and abroad where bright kids come in the summer to study topics of fascination to them. Laughter is in the air as they discover others who are equally intellectually curious.

What is Important
in Life and Art?

What is important in life and art? You know,
when I was very young, I thought it didn't matter
what happened to me when I died, so long as
my work was immortal. As I age, I think, well,
perhaps if I had to trade dying right now and
being immortal with just living on, I would
choose living on.

— Elaine May, "Who's Afraid of Nichols & May?"
by Sam Kashner, *Vanity Fair*, January 2012

CAN YOUR QUESTIONS WAIT THAT LONG?

Lester Brown and Scott at the Cosmos Club, Washington, DC, 1994.

Since 1976, we have spent many hours with Lester Brown, founder and president of the Worldwatch Institute and then the Earth Policy Institute, and author now of fifty-four books translated into forty-one languages. Those translations comprise a total of 647 volumes! Not only is he known for describing the daunting issues facing humanity, but in each instance he also offers plausible solutions to stave off the calamitous risks we create for the planet and ourselves.

Therefore, we will here simply zoom in on a couple of priceless hours in 1994 on the occasion of Lester's sixtieth birthday.

Three months in advance, Reah Janise Kaufmann, his loyal, able, resourceful colleague, called to ask if Hella and I would be the decoys to lure Lester to the Cosmos Club for a surprise birthday party. Sure.

I telephoned Les and said that his latest paper prompted some questions. He asked, "What are they?" I said I wanted to review them in person.

"Are you coming to Washington next week?"

"No, but we will in three months."

"Can your questions wait that long?" he asked earnestly.

Fast forward. On the appointed day, we met Les at the Cosmos Club at five and went downstairs. I'd typed out a bunch of questions. Lester, Hella, and I were drinking cider as I recall. It was too early for a beer.

One or two individuals cruised by. Les said, "Isn't that so-and-so?"

"Let's stick to the questions."

And, again, familiar faces sailed by.

Then at 6:07, as instructed by RJ, I asked Les if we could see the library on the second floor.

"You want to see the library?"

"Yes, you have often spoken of it."

On the first floor we walked past photos of members of the club who were Nobel Prize winners, Pulitzer Prize winners, and recipients of the Presidential Medal of Freedom, then went up the stairs to the second floor. Just as Les was about to turn left, I said, "Let's see what's going on in here."

We pushed through the cracked doors. Two hundred and fifty people were inside, including his brother and sister, son and daughter, and relatives from Germany, who all greeted him with a whoop and a shout.

Les was stunned beyond reckoning. His life was so well ordered and organized that this event caught him off guard.

When a few remarks and toasts were offered an hour later—including reminiscences by Bill Dietel, former president of the Rockefeller Brothers

Fund, about how Worldwatch came to be founded and funded—Les was still somewhat shaken. When he finally spoke he said, "I should have known something was up when Reah Janise wore her red Chinese dress to the office today."

Knowing that Les did not like surprises, when it came time for his seventy-fifth birthday, he was consulted. Judy Gradwohl, chair of the Earth Policy Institute board, suggested a videotaped conversation at the Smithsonian with Marc Pachter, recently retired director of the National Portrait Gallery.

That was pulled off with aplomb and grace in 2010 (a year late since another version of Lester's book *Plan B 4.0: Mobilizing to Save Civilization* was being put out). Marc had done his homework, and he stayed for a while with Lester's youth, when he was a big-time tomato farmer* in South Jersey, probing the roots of his lifelong devotion to the health of the planet and its inhabitants.

*1.5 million pounds a year

A RHETORICAL QUESTION

Remarks for Lester Brown's Eightieth birthday
Omni Shoreham Hotel
Washington, DC

April 11, 2014

The scent of that Jersey tomato plant, Marion, lingers!

Of seven-plus billion of us on Earth, who saw the Earth as a patient and kept rigorously continuing to examine the vital signs and interlinkages?

Who?

Who cares day and night about the issues that determine whether this dear blue-green orb will persist with adequate food and water and topsoil to carry our "civilization"?

Who? Who has worked unflaggingly for five decades on the knot of issues we confront and offered off-the-shelf solutions?

Who? Who wrote the now-classic *Building a Sustainable Society* in 1981 that defined the tasks ahead and never took his hands off the oars of analysis, writing, explication, and exhortation?

Who? Who never ceased to tackle the population issue at the root of much of the mayhem while the leading environmental groups let that slip off their radar and off their roster? *The 29th Day.* Yes, and who wrote the book *Full House: Reassessing the Earth's Population Carrying Capacity* in advance of the United Nations International Conference on Population and Development in Cairo in 1994?

Who was among the first to write about "failed states"? Who? Who wrote early on about the millions of "environmental refugees"?

Who gives back his honoraria in the tens of thousands, millions now, to first Worldwatch and now Earth Policy Institute?

Who? Noting an anomaly in the grain harvests, who was the analyst and scholar to ask, in 1995, *Who Will Feed China?* It was a farmer from New Jersey, the Garden State, who grew 1.5 million pounds of tomatoes every year as a teen with brother Carl.

Never a doomsday scenario, ever a hope-filled action plan.

Who has been the exemplar and incubator of young talent like Erik Eckholm, Denis Hayes, Alan Durning, Sandra Postel? Yes, who?

Fifty-four books into as many as forty-one languages, plus Esperanto.

I want to acknowledge the board of Earth Policy Institute, well led by Judy Gradwohl, Reah Janise (his right arm), Janet Larson, and a dedicated team. I also acknowledge loyal competent translators the planet over, led by physicians Hamid Taravati and Farzaneh Bahar in Iran, where they have made twenty years of books available to leaders in Iran across discipline and workplace. This is a country we boycott and that suffers under our sanctions.

In fact, were you to construct a quiz on the issues and their solutions from our author's lexicon, Iranian leaders would stand pretty tall. Run a five-mile tape from a stake on Dupont Circle in a circle, and you may be astonished by the ecological illiteracy. Let's praise, too, the hundreds of professors who use these books—*World on the Edge, Plan B*, and their progeny—as part of their core curricula.

In fact, evoking loyalty is one of the cardinal traits of this author and speaker.

All of you here today have played essential roles and are part of the story, part of the celebration of a life well lived on behalf of Mother Earth and its dominant species' fervent hopes for the future.

Whenever I called Les, I would ask, "How are you?" In classic understatement, he always replied, NOT SO BAD. When one reflects on his lifework, it would not be overstating it to say, "Not so bad."

Let's hear it for Lester Brown. Lester Russell Brown, eighty years old, fifteen days ago.

BAR CODE WIZARD

*C. Harry Knowles and Frank von Hippel, a leader in efforts to reduce
and eliminate nuclear weapons, at our 55th anniversary in 2013.*

On March 12, 2014, Harry Knowles mailed us a book, *Genius
in America: The Story of C. Harry Knowles, Inventor*, inscribed: "Scott
& Hella—without whom much of this would not be! Thanks is not
enough. Harry."

The biography of 332 pages, plus fifty pages of notes, bibliography,
and index, was meticulously researched and written by Mary Ellen
Hendrix over a fifteen-year period, beginning with an in-depth profile
for *Auburn Magazine*.

What is striking about this biography is the unbridled honesty,
revealing not only a difficult relationship with Harry's mother and
the agony of his first marriage, but also the heady years at Bell Labs
(1953–1958), the Motorola years in Phoenix (1958–1962), those at
Westinghouse (1962–1968), the founding of Metrologic in Blackwood,

New Jersey, and the amassing of over 400 patents on transistors, lasers, and handheld scanning devices. Deep relationships with his father, his brother, and many colleagues along the trajectory of this inventor's life also burnish the story of working on bar code devices that were in time being sold in 100 countries when Harry and Janet Knowles had some 1,500 employees.

In early May 1999, Harry and Janet Knowles came to our home with David Brandt, an attorney and college classmate of mine, to explore the possibility of creating a foundation to advance the teaching of science and mathematics in high schools nationwide. That led to my conducting a national search for an executive director for what would become the Janet H. Knowles and C. Harry Knowles Science Teaching Foundation based in Moorestown, New Jersey.

I brought in seventeen candidates, each a little stronger in my view ("Don't snap at the first fly!"), for the Knowleses to interview. The last, Angelo Collins, had an impressive record of working in the zone of the Knowleses' primary interest and directly with Lee Shulman, president of the Carnegie Foundation for the Advancement of Teaching for four years. She was hired, and the first KSTF Fellows were chosen in 2002. Today 275 individuals are in or have completed the five-year fellowship program.

In the book, I am quoted as saying, when Harry was inducted into the New Jersey Business Hall of Fame in 2006, "Harry has phenomenal ability as an entrepreneur, is creative, wonderfully articulate, incisive, and witty. I continue with KSTF because I like Harry and respect what he's doing, but also because I believe in the mission. A lot of philanthropy is a soup kitchen. Good foundations can effect systemic change. Harry gets that. Harry's greatest legacy will be the foundation."

I must note here that Janet Knowles was a critical player throughout the years of growth and many challenges at Metrologic, from going bankrupt to the sale of the company, as is faithfully recorded in the book. She is also a frugal and attentive manager as I have seen in a fifteen-year association through the board of the Knowles Foundation.

Harry produced last summer a photo album from our fifty-fifth wedding anniversary celebrated at Prospect with 112 family and friends, which was deeply touching.

At the May 16, 2014, board meeting, Nicole Gillespie, the second executive director, presented a vision paper for where the foundation is going, building on the strong early years, which was discussed at length by the board and applauded.

On January 16, 2015, the founders' audacious written goal was circulated among the board, beginning:

"The overarching goal of the Knowles Science Teaching Foundation is greater understanding of science and mathematics across the United States through improved teaching and learning.

"Science and mathematics are crucial to our nation. As a field of knowledge and inquiry, 'hard' science and mathematics are both elegant and fundamental—and absolutely vital to innovation, economic growth, and informed public policy."

At eighty-five-plus, Harry Knowles is still a vital, passionate thinker driving a foundation that is assuming its place among those championing by example teacher-leaders in science and mathematics classroom learning.

DNA BAR CODING

the biologists have finally
begun to catch up with Harry
note the proceedings of the
National Academy of Sciences—don't tarry

the tropical skipper butterfly
Astraptes fulgerator, first
described in '75, 1775,
known for an occasional speed burst

is now thought to be
TEN species in Costa Rica
because the test gene—
a stretch of 645 bits

reveals variations
reaching back, say, four million years
reflected in feeding on different plants
& a different BAR CODING as caterpillars

Harry and Janet have created
a philanthropic foundation terrific
to spot and nurture great teachers
in science and mathematic

three cohorts of physics teachers
have been named, now math's in the wings
the genetic bar coding suggests
biology may be one of the new things

for your vision and erudition
love, joy, and inventiveness
we salute Harry and Janet
Bar Coding Emperor and Empress!

October 21, 2004, at a Metrologic dinner

WOULD YOU LIKE TO SEE MY BEDROOM?

Our fascination with the Storm King Art Center began in 1988 upon our first visit, which prompted a five-page celebratory poem that Peter Stern, the president, said he loved to read to VIP visitors. Storm King has 100 major works of art elegantly situated on land sculpted to show them off. Some six major stories about it appear every year in the *New York Times*. We, therefore, had a notion of what outdoor sculpture in a spectacular, albeit lovingly manipulated, natural setting could look like. We were not enamored at first by what J. Seward Johnson, Jr., was doing with his Grounds for Sculpture in Hamilton Township, New Jersey, less than a mile from Trenton.

Works were being acquired rapidly for what is now forty-two acres, and they seemed less enduring than those of Storm King, which is situated on 500 acres of rolling terrain. Also, Seward's own works were under fire for being too cute, too kitschy, too popular, and too everywhere.

Upon returning from Chautauqua in 2004, we saw Grounds for Sculpture with fresh eyes. We underwent a conversion. Seward's dream landscape—built on a former fairgrounds site, long a brown field—seemed to have materialized quite magically. This was a courageous thing, since the land was abused and forgotten. His own reputation as an artist was blessed by a major show at the Corcoran in 2003 in Washington. I fired off a love letter dated July 9, 2005, in gratitude for his wit, whimsy, and creativity in creating a major destination in our area.

He replied with a letter inviting me for a private tour. It took place in early October, beginning on the periphery where small maquettes were being made into large works for places far and wide, from China to Italy to cities across America that bought collections of his work.

For three hours, eleven to two o'clock, we were together. I do not remember ever being more amused or laughing more at his nonstop wit and aphorisms. For example, he ran around and into his three-dimensional version of Henri Rousseau's work *The Dream*, surrounded by bamboo, and grinned. Folks still gasp in amazement at the smiling insertion of himself in the three-dimensional *Luncheon of the Boating Party* by the lake. His adroit commentary and ineffable spirit warrant a full-time Boswell.

We eventually wound up at Rat's Restaurant for lunch. He uncorked, or had uncorked, a bottle of red and a bottle of white, his own artistic label, and the conversation clattered on.

His cell phone kept ringing, ever more urgently. As the hour of two o'clock approached, he asked if I wanted to see his studio. I said I thought we had seen it at the outset. No, he said, it's upstairs. Sure. We ascend the circular stair at Rat's. He touches a series of numbers on a panel, and the door swung open. Various items were there for corporate purchase. Then, he said, "Would you like to see my bedroom?"

Seward Johnson's three-dimensional version of van Gogh's painting of his bedroom, unveiled at the Corcoran Gallery of Art opening in Washington in 2003.

Well, okay.

"Stand here," he said, and he walked down a narrow hall and flipped a switch.

"All right, please come."

I walked down a little hall and on the right was a room, a full-size rendering of van Gogh's painting of his room in Arles. I ran my finger along an uneven edge of a window. He said, "That's what a blind woman did when this was first shown at the Corcoran."

I joined the board of Grounds for Sculpture in September 2009.

In December 2013, Seward published a book, *Grounds for Sculpture: A Living Legacy, Intuitive Encounters with Art in Nature* on the history and intention behind his sculpture park. He sent us a copy with a note: "I think it turned out very well, and I hope you enjoy it. Seward." His handwriting has a Gothic reach and a heavy tilt to the right, which some graphologists say denotes warmth. It should be noted that he loves to lead a sing-along of the great songs of yore.

In May 2014, a huge retrospective of Seward's work was created by bringing many pieces out there in the world to the grounds, orchestrated by Tom Moran, chief curator, including a monumental Marilyn with her skirt billowing, a gargantuan Abraham Lincoln with a common man at his side, and scores of others.

On September 16, 2014, Hella and I were invited to Grounds for Sculpture for the first visit of leaders from the Storm King Art Center, including John Stern, president, and David Collens, director and curator. Under Gary Garrido Schneider's leadership, Grounds for Sculpture openly shared how-to ideas for parking, crowd management, making disabled folks welcome, and the running of the acclaimed Rat's Restaurant. In Storm King's current eight-month season, a record number of 107,000 visitors came, and Grounds for Sculpture is projecting over 200,000 this calendar year, which will include a blockbuster exhibition of the manifold works of architect Michael Graves.

THE BAREFOOT SALESMAN

Most folks know the bruising play *Death of a Salesman* by Arthur Miller, wherein Willy Loman, exhausted and despairing, comes to know the depths of despair a salesman may know. This offering, by contrast, is about a happy, enormously successful salesman in Jodhpur, India.

like the Bolero, or an insistent drum,
the excitement grew ...
yet nothing like
Arthur Miller's *Death of a Salesman*

we walked up a nondescript
flight of stairs
then another to the right and sat about

the barefoot salesman in jeans
diamonds in his ears
said we landed at the biggest
wholesale rug place in India

"we are unorganized,"
said he, Chitranjan,
—oh yeah—
mountains of rugs
piled high all around

have you heard of
Richard Gere?
he bought 108 rugs
Bill Murray many, too
he likes Bill Murray* best—
spent seven days with him
in New York—a great guy
Madonna came by, too

some 8,000 desert families
make tapestries, one may
take 18 months, another
two years even three

would you like "chai" tea?
or a pepsi cola? good
no obligation

the tapestries or bedspreads
or what-have-yous kept
coming, being unfurled
billowing over us.

gently flipped
billowing again
shimmering in the light
colors and designs just right

the colors "clicked" every time
not an ugly piece

was shown, Jain desert people
know their craft

you'll only have regrets
when you get home
if you let this chance
pass ...

have you heard of Armani?
Donna Karan? DKNY?
so and so, the Italian designer,
Hermani?

well, their mark-ups in
New York or London
are huge once they get
their labels on ...

we held our breath
for the prices—
you want them in rupees
or dollars? no one said rupees

six were $100 or less
one $35!

for two hours Chitranjan
held us spellbound
unfurling, presenting,
lofting, lifting, lovingly opening

all these treasures
praising them
modeling the wraps
some nine paisleys in nine
color combinations
all at the ready
not missing a beat

one after another
was claimed, folded,
packed away in a see-through
envelope, inserted in a plastic bag

dozens moved
two "ancient" items
from 150 to 300 years old
refurbished, came on the block

one sold to Amy for six or seven hundred
then he pulled out a fabric
topping any anywhere, said he,
for softness from the underbelly of baby vicuña
in Kashmir
    (thought they were in Peru)
$269 for the softest shawl
on Earth and nibblers
bit, everyone was happy
having seen an utterly persuasive
phenom pitch his
gorgeous wares from

the desert people before
the massive mark-up
stitching in of labels
shipping to Fifth Avenue
or Savile Row,

we salute this razzle-dazzler
coming as a counter weight to Prakash
tour de force this morning
on his home territory
about the people and their astonishing
adaptations to desert life,
making oases of life in the sand

oh Jodhpur, what
other miracles do you have
as we move about by rattling rickshaw,
jeeps, shanks mare?

January 10, 2008
Maharani Art Exporters, Cycle Market Road near clock tower

*When he can, Bill Murray often participates in the annual Poet's Walk across the Brooklyn Bridge. After he read this poem at the high point over the East River, I asked him, "Is it true that Chitranjan visited you?" Bill's eyes widened, and he smiled. He said he got this call on his cell phone, saying that Chitranjan and his family were camped on the edge of his place—was it okay? Bill said, "I'm on my way home." The family stayed a week, and Murray was happy to show them around New York. In spring 2012, Poets House was celebrating twenty-five years, and some prominent poets, including Billy Collins, came. Murray spoke, too. "Tonight we will explore the mystery of poetry, and the mystery of why I am here."

Scott and Hella at Taj Mahal, 2008.

Ad Astra *by sculptor Mark di Suvero, 2005.*

Following a horrible accident, sculptor Mark di Suvero began using an arc welder and crane to create iconic, huge, red, sometimes-whimsical artworks. On this day on Roosevelt Island, in cooperation with the Storm King Art Center, a robust installation of his lifework was recognized by Mayor Bloomberg with an award.

YES, THAT'S HIM

in the orange shirt
moving briskly through the crowd
Yes, he's the one who made
the big red artworks,
part of the eleven carefully placed here
on Governors Island
Yes, he's the one
who rode unwobbly on a bike
'round the island

Yes, he's the one
who created the sculpture "Will"
'cause he's overcome a lot
since that horrific accident
in 1960 when, as a cabinetmaker
he was crushed in an elevator
under one ton of pressure
for an hour,
He knows about "overcoming,"
He understands what it took
for Ghandi to shake India
loose from the Brits' grip
yeah oh yeah that resides
in every molecule of "Mahatma"
also among the four at isle's
other end.

But the book of beguiling photos
of works daintily placed
here and there
abroad and here
is the DREAMBOOK, Berkeley,
aught eight
containing the poetry
that's part of this guy's DNA
in the original Farsi
for Rumi as well as Coleman's
tuned translation,
in the original German
for Goethe's *Faust*
"What you can do, or dream you can,
begin it,

Boldness has genius, power and
magic in it."

in the original Chinese
for Lao-tzu
"The surest test if a man be sane
Is if he accepts his life whole as it is ..."

He, too, loves the water
He, too, was born in thirty-three
He has a brother, older, Victor,
in Santa Fe who founded the Pennywhistle
Press, especially to help folks get published,
who has written good poetry himself,

YES, YES, YES,
Marco Polo "Mark" di Suvero is what
realized promise is.

Last month when he received
the arts medal from the President
he said, softly, just to him,
"Cut the military budget in half."

YES, YES, YES, that's him,
and we love 'im.

July 15, 2011

YOU ... WHAT?

*New Jersey's own Bruce Springsteen,
cover,* NJN Guide, *June 2007.*

In the August 2005 issue of New Jersey Network's *The Guide,* an image of Bruce Springsteen holding his guitar graces the cover because a documentary of his work was being broadcast.

Elizabeth "Tiz" Christopherson, president and CEO of New Jersey Network, asked me to invite "The Boss" to be the honoree at the NJN Gala in May 2006. Tiz and I had worked closely when she chaired the New Jersey Council on the Arts and later became president of NJN. After I retired from the Dodge Foundation, I served on the NJN board.

I did not know much about the "Born to Run" rock star and his band, so I spent a couple of days in the library, immersing myself in the nature and extent of his celebrity—over 200 songs, an annotated volume of his compositions and edits and re-edits, scores of books about him, annual scholarly retreats to explore and examine his creative imagination, and compelling performances where all the fans knew all the words to all his songs.

Finally, I fired off a letter inviting him to be the centerpiece of the next NJN Gala. The letter was conveyed by a member of the board of Two Rivers Theater Company in Red Bank, thanks to the kindness of Robert Rechnitz, its founder and producer.

A few weeks passed, and I had heard nothing.

Scott and Hella with Elizabeth Good Christopherson at NJN Gala.

I dropped by to see William Lockwood, the long-standing director of programming at McCarter Theatre in Princeton (and creator and producer of Mostly Mozart in New York and pioneer programmer for the New Jersey Performing Arts Center in Newark) to get advice on the courtship of Mr. Springsteen.

Bill Lockwood laughed, a knowing laugh based upon years of

courting complicated and expensive performers worldwide—luring them into a sparkling spot in a seasonal series of pearls.

He laughed and cried, "You ... what? What do you want him to do? Sit there and be honored?"

Well ... Bill explained that Bruce had a manager up in Connecticut who was the impenetrable palace guard. He scheduled his performances and managed all the details—and this was just plain beyond the bounds of what The Boss did.

I left discouraged, utterly naïve regarding the difficulty of scaling this mountain, which outstripped the challenges of recruiting folks to speak at Chautauqua in my three years there.

Then, a handwritten note arrived in an envelope dated January 13, 2006.

"Dear Scott, Thanks for the great letter. The Gala sounds like a wonderful evening but outside of the occasional musical award, I'm not sure the 'honoree' game is for me. If I've had any possible impact on the state, it was a result of doin' what comes 'naturally.' Thanks for thinking of me though.

"x Bruce Springsteen."

IT IS EASIER TO WRITE A BOOK
THAN TO GOVERN

Philip Pettit, now a professor of philosophy at Princeton, received word that a candidate for prime minister of Spain wanted to meet with him. José Luis Rodríguez Zapatero said that his platform for the job was based entirely upon Pettit's book, *Republicanism: A Theory of Freedom and Government* (1997) and that he was eager to speak with him.

Pettit was busy, and it was not a good time. Zapatero was elected prime minister of Spain in April 2004. (He continued as the leader of Spain until December 2011.) In a nonce, Professor Pettit was shuttling back and forth to Spain, meeting with the PM, giving talks in the most revered places in the country, and being interviewed by lead journalists.

A gorgeous, detailed book of this unlikely scenario has been published, *A Political Philosophy in Public Life*, written by José Luis Martí and Pettit and published by the Princeton University Press (2009), and it is a page-turner. Pettit holds that the lessons learned when thinking about problems in one area of philosophy often constitute ready-made solutions for problems faced in completely different areas.

When the PM chose to run for re-election, he asked Professor Pettit to do a detailed evaluation of his first four years and to make his report public. Reluctantly, Pettit undertook the task, noting, "It is easier to write a book than to govern."

On March 25, 2009, when I introduced Philip Pettit to the Old Guard of Princeton, a group of lifelong learners who gather weekly for a lecture, I asked the members where they were on August 7, 1974. They did not know. It was not a day like the bombing of Pearl Harbor, the assassination of JFK, or 9/11. I said that was the day when Philippe Petit (different spelling!) danced on a wire he had fastened at dawn between the Twin Towers of the World Trade Center.

I made clear that the only connection between our speaker and the *Man on Wire*,* a Frenchman, was their name. However, two or three days after that feat, our young Dr. Pettit, who was teaching at the University College Dublin, was approached by one of the young women students in his class who pleaded,

"Dr. Pettit, please don't ever do that again!"

The next week at the Old Guard meeting, the scribe for the prior week made the two Pettits one person, and ten members rushed up to set him straight without embarrassment.

*Name of film of this feat

Postscript

In April 2013, Philippe Petit published a book, *Why Knot? How to Tie More Than Sixty Ingenious, Useful, Beautiful, Lifesaving, and Secure Knots!*, that was reviewed with élan by James Barron in the *Times*.

Lucretius

What human beings can and should do is conquer their fears, accept the fact that they themselves and all the things they encounter are transitory, and embrace the beauty and pleasure of the world.

— Lucretius (99 BC–55 BC)
as summarized by Stephen Greenblatt,
"The Almost-Lost Poem That Changed The World,"
the *New York Times*, October 2, 2011

THE BACK STORY

Reunion photo of classmates Ralph Nader, Scott McVay, and Kenly Webster.

It was in February of 1980 that I called Ralph Nader to invite him to speak at our twenty-fifth reunion.

Ralph said, "No thanks."

He was upset that Princeton had not accepted his PIRG (public interest research group) idea the way Rutgers had.

I said the Rutgers's plan was flawed in that students were automatically billed upon entering as freshmen and that they needed to make a written request to stop the $3 charge. He saw this waivable fee as paying for students' civic education and practice. It seemed unethical to me.

We agreed to disagree on that one, and I persisted in asking Ralph to please consider coming back at least for Friday evening, since I planned to assemble about 200 alumni and others in the Nassau Presbyterian Church between nine o'clock and midnight.

Ralph asked, "Aren't they drinking beer at that time?"

I said, "Perhaps, but they would park it at the door."

After hesitating and further discussion, Ralph kindly agreed to come.

When he arrived at the reunion some three months later, our class had all eaten. It was about 7:40. Our reunion chairman, Lee Neuwirth, introduced Ralph to his wife, Sydney, son Peter, and daughter Bebe.

Ralph was wearing a dark suit with a narrow black tie. Our daughter Catherine, a student in engineering who had completed her sophomore year, led Ralph to the supply area since he lacked a reunion jacket.

He tried one on, and it was too small. His arms stuck out. He needed something more commodious.

Catherine helped him to get a good fit. Then, back at the sign-in table, she made him a reunion button and asked him to sign the book.

She said that would be $100. Ralph reached into his wallet and pulled out a check, somewhat worn from having been there for some time, and wrote out a check for that amount.

I asked Ralph if he had eaten. He said he had actually not eaten all day. I pointed to a little stand with hamburgers and hot dogs. He said that would be fine.

After that, we sauntered over to the Nassau Presbyterian Church where a couple of hundred people were waiting eagerly.

Ralph held the audience in thrall for three hours. It was a great day and a turning point in Ralph's relationship with Princeton and his Class of 1955, even though he had received the Woodrow Wilson Award on Alumni Day eleven years earlier, the highest distinction the university can bestow on an alumnus of the undergraduate college.

I remember picking Ralph up at the Newark airport in 1972 and driving him to Princeton for that occasion. En route he was reading and clipping and sorting news items from five newspapers.

Three years after our twenty-fifth reunion, another event in February

1983 sealed Ralph's now-close relationship with the class when he received our Class Award and spoke at a dinner at Prospect. He was, as usual, witty, often incandescent, as he recalled his life as a student. He remembered when he was on campus over spring break and most students were away, the trees were sprayed. He noticed a number of dead birds under the trees. He asked members of the biology and chemistry departments and administration about the connection between the spraying and the dead birds. The reply was none. That was the early 1950s.

As we were filing out at midnight, our classmate Stan Rubin of Tigertown Five fame, who had played at Grace Kelly's wedding in Monaco after our graduation, said to Ralph, "This was *the best* evening of my life."

Ralph smiled and said, "That's too bad."

Twenty-five years ago, during a driving rainfall, Ralph walked into the second-floor room of the Red Cross building in Washington with his sister Claire and gave a galvanizing talk that led quickly to Princeton Project 55—a not-for-profit established by our class to mobilize alumni and students in regards to civic leadership. That day he asked me, "How far can we go?"

I said, "It was all teed up."

When Ralph finished his remarks that noon, three classmates spoke with fervor in support of his idea of people in their fifties and sixties giving back, specifically working to place Princeton undergraduates in not-for-profit organizations across America. Ralph asked me what I thought.

"I am taken by the idea and your persuasiveness," I replied.

TWELVE WORDS THAT ALTERED DESTINY

Princeton president Harold Shapiro listened to our plans for Princeton Project 55 and blessed them. The classmates at the historic 1989 meeting, left to right, are Alan Willemsen, Steve Boyd, Kenly Webster, Ralph Nader, Tom Boyatt, and Scott McVay. Shapiro is far left and staff Bob Durkee and Joe Bolster are to the right.

"What are YOU going to do with the rest of your life?"

Those twelve words, a penetrating question, were the turning point in the history of the Class of 1955 at Princeton University. They were spoken by Ralph Nader on April 15, 1989, on the second floor of the Red Cross building in Washington, DC, to 150 classmates and their wives.

Ralph asked further, "Are you simply going to try to lower your golf score or go fishing?" These were thoughts swimming in the heads of more than a few.

The remarks of Ralph that day galvanized the class to see what we could do, individually and collectively, to give back to a society in which many of us had thrived beyond our wildest hopes after graduation. Ralph pointed out that our phone calls were still being returned and that we could become a phalanx for giving back that would redefine our later years. We could even broaden the mission of the university through community outreach and service on a footing with education, scholarship, and science.

Years later, at our fiftieth reunion, President Shirley Tilghman would pronounce the Class of 1955 among the three greatest Princeton classes in the twentieth century. It may well be true. (My guess is that the other two are the Class of 1909 with Judge Harold Medina and the Class of 1922 with Adlai Stevenson; the Class of 1942 with George Shultz is another contender).

Back to that pivotal day. After Ralph's remarks, which were sadly not recorded, even though they were seared into the souls of everyone present, educator Win Adkins leapt to his feet, seconding enthusiastically Ralph's charge to us, noting that his son had worked with Ralph and his various organizations for nearly ten years, an experience that changed his life.

John West, a California physician, said that if Ralph called a meeting, he could clear his calendar with two days notice and be there.

Charlie Bray stood up. With the grace and clout of a seasoned diplomat, he said, "Ralph, we must become five million strong within five years, giving back." Charlie captured the sense many of us shared.

Ralph turned to me and said, "Scott, what you think?"

"I feel like I am at a Baptist revival."

Soon about thirty of us gathered at Kenly Webster's law firm to plan the next steps. A board of fifteen was chosen. With the gathering enthusiasm, we had the pick of the litter, and yet, oddly, only five of the first fifteen members of the board of Princeton Project 55 understood the nature of systemic change. Having been in philanthropy for several years at that point, I was aware that systemic change was what we should strive for, not Band-Aids or palliatives or soup kitchens. Instead we should teach a man to fish so he could think beyond the next meal.

After we were underway, I arranged for a meeting with President Harold Shapiro for a handful of us, and he encouraged us in every way.

The triumph and signature of Princeton Project 55 is the fellowship program, conceived, sparked, guided, and nourished by John Fish. The idea was to place carefully selected Princeton undergraduates in intern positions with not-for-profits in eight geographic locations and graduating seniors in such nonprofits for longer duration, often altering their life trajectories. John's life in Chicago has been a celebration of the city where he has connected countless students from liberal arts colleges with not-for-profits that seek to address issues of equity, education, health, access, justice, and opportunity.

It was a pleasure for Hella and me to interview Princeton students in the early years to see who might be a candidate for an internship with a major environmental group, many of whom hire only graduate students with advanced degrees. Once some good matches clicked, these groups became eager to work with successive students.

Ralph also deserves kudos for providing strategic leadership and inspiration, including generic funding by board members, in getting Princeton Project 55 solidly launched—and for focusing on tuberculosis, a long-term plague of humanity, with Gordon Douglas, an MD who had headed Merck's research division.

Building in the next generation, and encouraging dozens of other universities to pursue similar strategies, has led to an evolution of the name to AlumniCorps. Most of the spots on the board now are occupied by more recent Princeton alumni who have been among more than 1,600 interns and fellows to date. Some fifty new fellows are carefully screened and added every year.

Postscript

This write-up is taken mostly from my entry in the book, *Shared Effort, Shared Values: Princeton Project 55—The Founders*, wherein thirty-eight classmates and wives recorded their recollections in an eighty-one-page book in 2008.

Author of many books, Ralph Nader ran for president of the United States in 1992 as a write-in candidate, in 1996 with Winona LaDuke for the Green Party, and again in 2000, when he garnered 2,882,955 votes. Those votes are often cited as the reason that Al Gore lost the election. That is not so—Gore won the election even with Nader's impressive showing.

AN ENIGMA FOR MORE THAN 750 YEARS

"If you haven't read the *Divine Comedy*—you know who you are—now is the time, because Robert and Jean Hollander have just completed a beautiful translation of the astonishing fourteenth-century poem. ... It is more idiomatic than any other English version I know. At the same time, it is lofty, the more so for being plain. Jean Hollander, a poet, was in charge of the verse; Robert Hollander, her husband, oversaw its accuracy. The notes are by Robert, who is a Dante scholar and a professor emeritus at Princeton, where he taught the *Divine Comedy* for forty-two years.

"Dante's poem is fiendishly difficult to translate into verse, partly because of its lovely, garlanded rhyme scheme, terza rima—or aba, bcb, cdc. To reproduce the *Comedy* in English terza rima, it has been calculated, that approximately forty-five hundred triple rhymes are needed. In Italian, where almost every word ends in a vowel, you can come up with such a number. In English, it is next to impossible, as can be seen in the frequency of ridiculous forced rhymes in terza-rima translations. Some translators have compromised on aba, cdc—in other words, rhyming in twos, not threes—but that's not easy, either, if you're trying to be faithful to Dante's text.

"Jean Hollander made a bigger compromise. She has used blank verse, primarily: unrhymed iambic pentameter. Relieved of the task of rhyming, she is able to stay closer to Dante's wording. Nevertheless, her translation is a poem, and it sounds like one."

—Article by Joan Acocella, the *New Yorker*,
September 3, 2007, "Cloud Nine: A new translation of the *Paradiso*"

Among the original 804 members of the Class of 1955 at Princeton University who spent four years on campus, only two returned as members of the faculty: Robert Hollander, the Dante scholar, and Frederick Almgren, a mathematician with a focus on geometric measure theory and the calculus of variation, the surfaces of least area such as soap bubble clusters. Both joined the faculty in 1962 and rose through the ranks to full professor in the early 1970s. Both were superb teachers and they were recipients of the Class of 1955 Award in 1988.

Over dinner on May 28, 2011, Bob Hollander mentioned that his long study of *The Decameron* by Giovanni Boccaccio (1313–1375) had yielded a fresh interpretation. That very evening he sent me a seventy-two-page manuscript that was later published by *Studi sul Boccaccio*, the major and only Italian journal devoted solely to study of that author.

In that conversation Bob said that the serious stroke he suffered in 2004, followed by a coma and the slow recovery of speech, seems to have opened for him this new interpretation, which he believes gets close to the author's ultimate intent in writing the masterwork.

Hollander's revolutionary interpretation centers on Boccaccio's pivot in being an ironic manager of the tales of the last day. He wants us to understand something quite different from what he seems to say. Boccaccio's view of human strivings is characterized by the sense that everybody is a self-seeking animal—the utter selfishness of every protagonist shines through again and again—yet the announced topic for these last ten tales is magnanimity. Perhaps the most crushing example occurs in the third tale of that day when the man who has striven to be considered the most magnanimous in the kingdom learns that there is one more magnanimous. His response? He realizes that he can never outdo his neighbor in magnanimity and, as a result, sets out to kill him.

As I read into this dazzling, meticulously argued analysis, I became so taken by what my friend and classmate had written that I felt frankly undeserving of this access. I felt that I had to return to the original work and chose the translation by G. H. McWilliam, first published in 1972, second edition in 1995 (Penguin Classics).

What a sleigh ride it has been to read these rollicking, sometimes ribald one hundred tales, each carrying a message or a moral turn as in Aesop's fables.

My conclusion is that Bob Hollander, a diligent and ever-congenial friend, has crafted another priceless scholarly work that deepens our regard for both immortal Italian writers, Boccaccio and Dante.

Postscript

Hollander's commentary of just under 900 pages on *The Divine Comedy* has been translated into Italian by Simone Marchesi (Florence: Olschki, 2011) and is being used, to Bob's delight, in Italian schools.

WE WILL DO EACH OTHER'S EULOGIES

I suggested that the Princeton University Class of 1955 Award for service beyond the usual nine to five be inaugurated in the late 1970s and that the annual recipient be the speaker at our midwinter dinner on Alumni Day every February.

For years, I chaired the selection committee and the likes of Ralph Nader, Bill Ruckelshaus, and others were honored and recognized in turn. These were rapturous evenings as each told his story.

In the late 1990s, at an event at Prospect House for Isles, the lead not-for-profit in Trenton, I cornered Harold Shapiro, Princeton's president, to inquire about the recent appointment of Peter Lewis, president and CEO of Progressive Insurance in Cleveland, to the university's board of trustees.

I felt I was anything but a prude. However, when I was checking out Peter as a possible recipient for the Class Award, I called Princeton alumni in Cleveland not in our class to get their read. The response in three or four instances was that Peter was going great guns at Progressive, he was the lead philanthropist in Cleveland, and he had amassed a superb collection of contemporary art, which his former wife has handled since 1981.

But his private life was flaunted in the newspapers. He seemed to have a woman for every occasion, and he did not operate with the hypocrisy typical of some others. He seemed to parade his lifestyle.

Harold Shapiro responded with a smile, saying that Princeton's board was large, numbering forty, and that it operated mainly by committees. Actually, he said, it might be healthy to have an eccentric or two just to keep things lively.

I reconvened the committee and proposed not only Peter Lewis for the Class Award, but also his best friend, Paul Sigler, MD, an accomplished researcher at Yale, who had served on Progressive's board since 1984.

In calling Peter, he said he would be sailing in the South Pacific at the time of the dinner but would be willing to fly back for it.

He was in the process of hanging up when I said the committee felt the award—in no ways diminished—should be given at the same time to Sigler if he was comfortable with the idea.

Peter said, "Yes, we talked just last night for three hours. We'll do each other's eulogies."

I remember calling Paul at his laboratory on a Saturday afternoon just after a distinguished visitor had left. He was cheerful, enthusiastic about the idea, and said he planned to bring down to Princeton nine members of his family. Tragically, Paul Sigler died a few weeks later walking to his laboratory.

Peter did Paul's eulogy at the dinner with Paul's family present.

Peter's gifts to Princeton exceed $220 million, more than any other donor or alumnus: a contemporary gallery at the back of the art museum; cumulative gifts to annual giving; the new Lewis Science Library designed by Frank Gehry (completed in 2009, $60 million); and the Lewis Center for the Arts ($101 million pledged in 2006).

Peter died on November 23, 2013, in Coconut Grove, Florida, of an apparent heart attack. Shirley Tilghman, former president of Princeton, said, "I think he was one of the last great patrons of universities who was prepared to say, 'What is your highest priority, and how can I help you achieve it?'" When asked how involved he was in establishing the Lewis-Sigler Institute for Integrative Genomics, she said, "The amount he knew about genomics could fit into a thimble with room for lots of other things. He was really driven by his desire to be as helpful as he could."

President Tilghman said further, "He believed he received a really world-class education at Princeton, and it held him in good stead the rest of his life. He was also grateful to the university for embracing him at a time when he was getting a lot of criticism in the press about his support for legalized marijuana, and his lifestyle that he never pretended was anything other than what it was. He was, let's say, a free spirit." (*Town Topics*, November 27, 2013)

TO WHAT EXTENT DO THE ARTS AFFECT HUMAN AFFAIRS?

Lisa Gay Hamilton and South African playwright Athol Fugard play lead roles as Veronica and Buks in Valley Song, *Fugard's powerful drama addressing generational issues and his first post-apartheid play at McCarter Theatre in Princeton.*

I'll have grounds
More relative than this—the play's the thing
Wherein to catch the conscience of the King.

— *Hamlet*, Act 2, scene 2

This is a departure from other vignettes. It is a rumination in nine parts.

Stephen Wadsworth, director of opera and theater, impresario, translator, in speaking to the Old Guard of Princeton on February 19, 2014, said the play *The Marriage of Figaro* by Pierre Beaumarchais, a comedy in five acts mocking royalty, was not performed until the king lifted his ban of six years in 1784. A mere five years after the first performance, Wadsworth points out, the Women's March on Versailles took place, which led to democracy in France (and the United States!). The apparently causal relationship between these two events prompts one to ask about the influence of the arts on what happens in the world.

In 1996, a conference for 400 artists and arts leaders in New Jersey was held, opened by then–US Poet Laureate Robert Hass, who from memory walked us through the literary lights in the Garden State over four centuries, quoting readily from dozens of them. The conference was closed by the South African playwright Athol Fugard, who asked me, a half hour before he spoke, "What should I talk about?" I suggested he speak about the impact of the arts in South Africa on the ending of Apartheid. Fugard said, improbably, he had not thought about it, even though his work was part of the impetus for reform—plays such at *Blood Knot, Sizwe Bansi Is Dead*, and many others—but then went on to give what he felt was his best talk ever on that very topic.

Consider, too, Pablo Picasso's monumental painting *Guernica* in 1937, protesting the unbearable dictatorship in Spain and the bombing of a Basque country village of the same name during the country's civil war. It brought the war to the world's attention.

George Bernard Shaw created an astonishing canon of more than sixty plays addressing a staggering set of issues. Shaw saw the play as a crucible for confronting topics of public concern and as a vehicle for promoting reform in public attitudes and policy. Remember only

Mrs. Warren's Profession (1893, about prostitution), *Arms and the Man* (1894, which made the ultimate case against munitions and war), *Man and Superman* (1903, about the new woman), *Pygmalion* (1913, about literacy as a function of exposure), and *Saint Joan* (1923, a dramatization of Joan of Arc's life, which ends with Joan despairing that mankind will never accept its saints: "How long, O Lord, how long?"). Initially a music critic, Shaw's brilliance as a playwright (and polemicist) may well be second only to Shakespeare in the English language. In retrospect, it seems prophetic that I chose as my college thesis topic in an exploration of "The Consciousness of George Bernard Shaw."

Where would Martin Luther King Jr.'s crusade and marches for civil rights have gone without the compelling altered Gospel song, "We Shall Overcome"?

While serving as painter to the court of Spain and doing endless portraits of odd members of the royal family, Goya quietly made a series of eighty-two prints (1810–1820) known as *The Disasters of War*. This was the artist's ringing response to the brutality of both Napoleon's assaults in 1808 and the restoration of the Bourbon monarchy in 1814. Failing health and being almost deaf did not deter Goya from depicting his anguish at horrific behavior. Goya called the series *Fatal Consequences of Spain's bloody war with Bonaparte, and other emphatic caprices.* The work was not published until 1863, thirty-five years after his death, but it reverberates as a searing indictment of our inhumanity in hundreds of instances down the long dark corridors of history.

In photography, what iconic image gave us a jolting fresh perception? One candidate might be Dorothea Lange's 1936 image of a woman, a migrant worker with her children huddled around her. That brought the plight of the poor and forgotten migrant farm workers to public attention and aid was actually provided. Another might well be that arresting image of the Earth, the entire blue-white sphere, taken on December 7,

1972, by the crew of Apollo 17. It showed us our planet whole without national boundaries and, in a way, spurred the environmental movement triggered by Rachel Carson's eloquence on DDT's lethal impact on bird life.

Editorial cartooning is a trenchant critical art. In our local morning paper, the choice of a cartoon is often right on the mark, and a regular contributor these days is *Jimmy Margulies*, whose works appear in many New Jersey papers. But in the pantheon of all-time greats, Herbert Lawrence Block (1909–2001) is a towering exemplar in his lifelong fight against abuses by the powerful. Garnering three Pulitzer Prizes (1942, 1954, and 1979), Herblock did almost daily cartoons for seventy-nine years, fifty-five of them at the *Washington Post*. He coined the term "McCarthyism" in a devastating cartoon of March 29, 1950. In 2014, an HBO documentary called *Herblock: The Black and the White* sought to capture his courageous, telling probes with pen and ink. We sound the trumpet for such fearlessness, wit, insight, and truth-seeking.

In the realm of song and protest music, one person appears on stage with a five-string banjo, Pete Seeger. He and his folk songs, where everyone is encouraged to join in, form a courageous, persisting musical force by re-envisioning the issues of our day, from the Vietnam War and all wars ("Where have all the flowers gone?") to civil rights and environmental causes. Pete's sloop, *The Clearwater*, was a potent reminder of the urgent need to clean up the PCBs spewed by GE into the Mohawk River, and, hence, the Hudson River. Building on the legacies of Woody Guthrie ("This Land is Your Land") and Lead Belly, Seeger even had a hand in turning the gospel song, "We Will Overcome" into "We Shall Overcome," making the goal of full equality seemingly more attainable.

WHAT TRAITS AT FIFTY WILL PREDICT JOY AND HEALTH AT EIGHTY?

At our fiftieth reunion of the Exeter Class of 1951, a fascinating classmate was George E. Valliant, who then divided his time between Australia and Vermont, where he gardened. He was an undergrad at Harvard and went on to become a psychiatrist at Harvard Medical School. He spent his research career charting adult development and the recovery process of schizophrenia, heroin addiction, alcoholism, and personality disorder. George spent thirty years as director of the Study of Adult Development at Harvard, charting the lives of 724 men and women for over sixty years.

In 2003, when I was at Chautauqua, George sent me the galleys for his book *Aging Well*, which noted seven items that before the age of fifty can predict joy and health at eighty. They are: your education, a good marriage, having stopped smoking, no alcohol abuse, exercise (moderate), normal weight, and learning to play and create after retirement. In one of my Saturday columns for *The Chautauquan Daily*, I summed up the points briefly and then noted the values added for folks who came every summer to Chautauqua, such as engagement in a variety of cultural, spiritual, recreational, and educational activities; inter-generational opportunities; porch conversations; and so on. I wrote George to see if I got it right. He replied, "Yes," and I could imagine his friendly grin.

Looking afresh at *Aging Well*, it still holds enduring interest well after my eightieth birthday. At the outset, George cites differing views of old age in Robert Browning ("Grow old with me! / The best is yet to be") and Shakespeare ("Bare ruin'd choirs, where late the sweet birds sang").

Among my countless favorite lines in the book are: "In personality traits, the (Lewis) Terman women showed significantly more humor, common sense, perseverance, leadership, and even popularity than their classmates." (p. 22)

"An ordinary wine tastes very different if poured from a bottle with a Château Lafitte label than from a screw-top jug labeled Thunderbird." (p. 34)

"A certain amount of good luck is involved in growing old without accident, disease, or social catastrophe." (p. 73)

"Viewed from the perspective of a fifty-year study, the maturation of great human beings becomes as miraculous as the birth of a child." (p. 131)

"Being needed is a luxury that the young allow the middle-aged, but it is a luxury that wise grandparents learn to relinquish." (p. 144)

"Great poets can continue to create not only after forty but after eighty-five!" (p. 182)

"Healthy aging, then, is being both contented and vigorous as well as being not sad or sick or dead." (p. 187)

The cover article in the *Atlantic*, June 2009, "What Makes Us Happy," by Joshua Wolf Shenk, who gained access to Vaillant's files for the long-term landmark Harvard study, rounds out this sketch. George's interview is online and worth a read, and among many nuggets is the thought, "Enjoy where you are now ... Happiness is love. Full stop."

What is more marvelous in the long arc of a life than requited love?

Toshiko bell residing in stand of black locust designed by Robert Brander before gate and fence created by David Robinson. The bell is rung to welcome visitors.

EPILOGUE

ONE LOVE.

ah, the slit drum,

an adroit
manifestation of man,
another way to serenade a woman,

greeting us in Freetown,
Sierra Leone,

the erect old man*
saying he's ninety-three
in red ever-tapping slippers
like the Pope
& red brush-studded cap
an old baobab
comes forward

slapping the slit drum
slapping the slit drum
thumping the slit drum,

my gawd, do we feel welcome.

*Known as "one man gang,"
his name is Yalaba Sesay.

Poetry and the highest reaches of scientific imagination are very much akin; each seeks to crack the kernel of the particular in order to liberate the universal.

— Stanley Kunitz

This happy narrative is winding down and out. Every time I write my date of birth, June 1, 1933, that day seems to stand at a small distant point receding at the speed of light. Everything, every gesture, touch, taste, smile, laugh, splash of sunshine, every wild turkey, leaping squealing frog, darting fish, skipping tripping red fox, white squirrel, and great blue heron seems precious, incredibly precious.

At the outset, I sought to capture the essence of diverse encounters along life's way in anecdotes or longer-form stories of individuals, often stories with a point or an Aesop's fable épée.

Nearly everyone found herein I admire, some enormously, like John Gardner, Bob Goheen, or Shirley Tilghman. A small subset of vignettes reveal a toe or two of clay, foibles, or vanities.

Among the threads of the book is a regard for persons whose obsessions led them to the pinnacle of their fields: Ted Parker with birds, Merlin Tuttle with bats, George Archibald with cranes, E. O. Wilson with ants, and—in interspecies communication—Aimee Morgana with an African gray parrot named N'Kisi.

Throughout my adult life, I sought to find ways to redress injustices, a big one being the wholesale slaughter of whales. Others included slowing the chemical contamination of all life on Earth, encouraging Theo Colborn's work with endocrine disruptors, and reducing the disfigurement and mutilation of the planet.

I sought to tackle issues strategically in heading two foundations— Robert Sterling Clark and Geraldine R. Dodge—and in active service on the boards of two other foundations—W. Alton Jones, and the Knowles Science Teaching Foundation.

Looking backward now, I see a coherence in these stories that suggests an awe before the mystery and workings of the natural world initially provoked by a fascination with the leviathan of literature and dwelling yet in the seas of this blue-green water planet.

This began, I guess, with a desire to have a dog in Denver. My New York–bred Mother said, "Okay, but keep him in our garage out back." Dog after dog disappeared. Hmm. When we had kids, we had cats, notably Petrosian; a German Shepherd named CRI; dachshunds Curio and Timoly; gerbils; et al. But it was whales who tore open the natural world for me and it is Hella who sees daily miracles in nature at our home or in our travels.

Four years ago, I began setting down encounters, some one shot, others spanning decades. Of interest to me was the crackle of each one. Being of a curious, questioning nature with broad interests, I have savored the meetings and tried to capture their resonance in these yarns. Readers pressed for more about the family, details of my early years, and the organic tissue of the overall narrative landing in the ninth decade.

In a closing thought in Marcela Serrano's revelatory book, *Ten Women*, she recalls, "Edward Said, that admirable Palestinian writer, talked about the 'late style.' The term is generally used for artists. It's the final stage, when the creator lets go of the reins and starts to do what he wants, with no consideration of or coherence with his previous work. By releasing the moorings, extremely valuable work is often created."

I don't know about that. I only know that at this stage of life it is fun to put down selected recollections in the hope they might be of interest to others.

— Scott McVay
January 2015

VILLANELLE

For Scott McVay

Hard to sustain our humanity and vision.
The world seems to have other plans for us.
After each fraught choice comes another decision.

When in trouble, most save their own skin,
abandon the cause, make an excuse.
So hard to sustain our humanity and vision.

The whales were in danger, poetry needed a champion,
Scott didn't sit by in cool ambivalence
After each fraught choice he made another decision.

Daniel Moynihan once said he trusted tall men,
they had a long history of being conspicuous.
Still, it's hard to sustain humanity and vision.

Tall Scott is, but broad is a better designation
Under him, the Dodge was brilliantly various.
After each fraught choice came another decision.

If one's character, finally, is always in question,
Then Scott's his own answer, his own exegesis.
Hard to sustain one's humanity and vision
After each fraught choice: another decision.

— Stephen Dunn
May 11, 1998
Dunn has published fifteen collections of poetry and
received the Pulitzer Prize for Poetry in 2001.

ACKNOWLEDGEMENTS

I thought I would write one hundred vignettes in the spirit of Boccaccio.

Some twenty-five or thirty persons encountered here have read and signed off on their brief sketches, often with enthusiasm.

As I shared early drafts, friends encouraged me to connect the stories of my life and family in a narrative arc. So *Surprise Encounters* was shaped by folks whom I admire who gave generously of their time and guidance.

First and foremost, I acknowledge Hella, wife and caring counselor, for encouraging this joyful undertaking and offering ideas regarding these recollected stories, which we often experienced together.

Susan Danoff, champion storyteller in the Garden State; Ron Rapoport, a sports writer all his life whom we met on an African safari; Areta Parle, a rigorous, professional editor; David Rothenberg, who wrote *Thousand Mile Song*, which nudged writing the larger story; Jim Haba, poet, professor of literature, and a colleague, all read the manuscript and offered telling suggestions.

Joy Stocke, editor-in-chief and publisher of Wild River Books, expressed an interest in publishing the book after reading it. She asked Raquel Pidal in Boston to read the manuscript closely and make suggestions. They were penetrating, precise, and contributory. She, too, pushed for more about the family and asked for context regarding the players in the book. After a major reordering and revising, Joy read the text afresh with purple pen in hand, sharpening, tightening.

She is a terrific coach and cheerleader. Her approach is grounded in an education in journalism at the University of Wisconsin in Madison with a literary flair. That led her to create, with co-founder Kim Nagy, the imaginative *Wild River Review*. She loves and resonates with poetry and has said to me, "Don't forget—whatever our suggestions, this is *your* book."

Kim Nagy, from the get-go, has been a diligent, imaginative, encouraging player in getting the book out. She handles publicity, marketing, and distribution of Wild River Books and has been wonderful to work with. She is also a superb interviewer and writer. Our gratitude to her is unending.

The cover of this book, *Guide* (4' 8" by 5' 9"), is a work by master teacher and artist Diane Churchill. She created *Guide* in 1988 as part of a "Gorilla Series" for an exhibition at the William Carlos Williams Center in Rutherford, New Jersey.

Churchill drew a huge gorilla face staring ahead and dominating the large canvas. Below her—Churchill thinks of this creation as female—dance small indistinguishable beasts like little demons in a ritual dance. The *Guide* appears wise and calm. On her forehead is painted a triangle, which Churchill links to the seat of consciousness. Profound as she hopes her gorillas' messages are, she also intended the painting to be humorous. The *Guide*, for example, she sees as a kind of contemporary comment on the *Mona Lisa* with its enigmatic smile and simian face. Hella and I have the daily joy of beholding it in our home. We share it gladly here as a hint of the contents of the book.

As fellow design wonks ourselves, we applaud the layout that Tim Ogline has created. We like the font, the airiness of the text—and the touch of genius in using the "little demons" at the base of Diane's *Guide* as connective icons through the book. The images have small frames around them that will resonate with an older audience. We like, too, the subtle interweaving of the name of the book with section titles at the top of each page.

PERMISSIONS

The majority of the photographs in the book are by Hella McVay. Many others are from Dodge Foundation annual reports during the period of McVay's leadership. The remainder are owned by the McVays. Individual permissions for other images are listed below:

Page 246: Pont Neuf wrapped by Christo (1985), by Airair, used under Creative Commons license.

Page 342: Dalai Lama at Newark Museum (1990), image © Newark Museum, used with permission of Newark Museum.

Page 100: George Nakashima tree drawing used with permission of Mira Nakashima.

Page 360: Photograph of David Hunter McAlpin used with permission of David H. McAlpin Jr.

Scott McVay

ABOUT THE AUTHOR

Scott McVay graduated from Princeton University in English literature and served for three years as a special agent of the US Army's Counter Intelligence Corps in Berlin. Returning to Princeton, he became the University's first recording secretary and later assistant to President Robert F. Goheen, who brought about the admission of women to Princeton in 1969.

McVay's avocational interest in whales and dolphins led him to work for John C. Lilly, MD, and to serve on the US delegation to the International Whaling Commission. With Roger Payne, he discovered and described the six-octave song of the humpback whale, which became an anthem for whale conservation.

He has served as founding executive director of the Robert Sterling Clark Foundation and the Geraldine R. Dodge Foundation, and as the sixteenth president of the Chautauqua Institution. He has served on two dozen not-for-profit boards including the World Wildlife Fund, the Smithsonian Institution, the W. Alton Jones Foundation, and currently serves on the boards of the Knowles Science Teaching Foundation, the Endocrine Disruption Exchange, and Grounds for Sculpture.

McVay's honors include the Albert Schweitzer Award from the Animal Welfare Institute, the Joseph Wood Krutch medal from the Humane Society of the United States, the Princeton University Class of 1955 award, the Lyndon Baines Johnson award by the White House Commission on Presidential Scholars, the New Jersey Council of the Humanities Citizen of the Year 1998, and an honorary doctorate from Middlebury College for initiating a nationwide program to spark and sustain Chinese language instruction in high schools.

He lives in Princeton, New Jersey, with his wife Hella. They have two daughters and three grandchildren.

SELECT PUBLICATIONS

Periodicals

"The Last of the Great Whales." *Scientific American*, August 1966, 13–21.

"How Hears the Dolphin?" *Princeton Alumni Weekly*, cover article, October 10, 1967, 6–9, 17–18.

"Initiation of a Whale Campaign in Japan," paper, New York Zoological Society, August 1970, 45 pages.

"Can Leviathan Long Endure So Wide a Chase?" *Natural History*, January 1971, 36–40, 68–72.

"Does the Whale's Magnitude Diminish?—Will He Perish?" *Bulletin of the Atomic Scientists*, February 1971, 38–41.

"Whales: A Skirmish Won, But What About the War?" *National Parks*, cover article, February 1971, 14–19, photos of Ayakaya Whaling Station by Hella McVay.

"Songs of the Humpback Whales," cover article with Roger Payne, *Science*, August 13, 1971, 587–597.

"Saving the Whales: Any Hint of Hope?", *Audubon*, November 1971.

"The Great Porpoise Massacre," *New York Times*, March 19, 1972.

"Leviathan's Last Song?", *Passages*, April 1972, 10–14.

"The Jaws of the Whale," *New York Times*, September 3, 1972.

"Another View of Whales: Let's Take a Good Long Look," *Newsday*, October 1972, illustration by Larry Foster.

"Stalking the Arctic Whale," *American Scientist*, cover article, January–February 1973, 24–37.

"The Plants and Animals of Détente," *Washington Post*, April 2, 1973.

"Alaska's Trumpets of Spring: Bowhead Spouts Along Arctic Coast," *Mainstream* (Animal Protection Institute of America), Fall 1974.

"Bowhead Whale—Migration and Behavior," *World Wildlife Fund Yearbook*, 1973–74.

"Robert Sterling Clark Foundation: Building Bridges Across Moats," *Foundation News*, January/February 1976.

"Gifted Children—A Neglected Minority?", *Foundation News*, ca. 1978.

"Triptych to the Ice Whale" and "A Sign, Look for a Sign," *Project Interspeak*, 1979, 71–76.

"A Regard for Life: Getting Through to the Casual Visitor," *The Philadelphia Zoo Review*, March 1987.

"Symphony Beneath the Sea," comment, *Natural History*, June 1991.

"Doing Ecology," editorial, *Orion*, Autumn 1991.

"Imagine the Joyful Reunion," *Progressive Welfare Society*, Autumn 1997.

"How to Deal with Critics," *Foundation News & Commentary*, May/June 1998.

"Where Is Walt Whitman? Weren't We Supposed to Look Under Our Boot Soles?", *US 1*, July 22, 2009.

Books and Chapters in Books

"Reflections on the Management of Whaling," chapter in *The Whale Problem: A Status Report*, William E. Schevill, ed. (Cambridge: Harvard University Press, 1974, 369–382).

"One Strand in the Rope of Concern," chapter in *Mind in the Waters: A Book to Celebrate the Consciousness of Whales and Dolphins*, Joan McIntyre, ed. (New York: Charles Scribner's Sons, 1974, pgs. 72, 92, 208–9, 225–229).

Introduction in *New Jersey at the Crossroads of Migration*, Peter Dunne (New Jersey Audubon Society, 1989).

"How to Heal the Sickness? Cherish Women, Children, and Animals," chapter in *Child Abuse, Domestic Violence, and Animal Abuse*, Frank R. Ascione and Phil Arkow, eds. (West Lafayette: Purdue University Press, 1999).

"A Siamese Connexion with a Plurality of Other Mortals," prelude in *The Biophilia Hypothesis*, Stephen R. Kellert and Edward O. Wilson, eds. (Washington, DC: Island Press, 1993, pgs 3–19).

"What Are You Going to Do with the Rest of Your Life?" in *Shared Effort, Shared Values: Princeton Project 55—The Founders*, Project 55 members (Princeton 2007).

"The Philanthropic Tipping Point: The Intimate, Albeit Frail, Connection between Survival and the Work of the Independent Sector," in *Just Money: A Critique of Contemporary American Philanthropy*, H. Peter Karoff, ed. (Boston: The Philanthropic Initiative Editions, 2004, 73–100).

"Philanthropists as Explorers," in *A Passion for Giving: Tools and Inspiration for Creating a Charitable Foundation*, Peter J. Klein and Angelica Berrie, eds. (Hoboken: Wiley, 2012, 233–242).

Whales Sing and Other Exuberances, poetry collection, 2012.

Miscellaneous

Hearings Before the Subcommittee on International Organizations and Movements of the Committee on Foreign Affairs, H. J. Res. 706 Instructing the Secretary of State to Call for an International Moratorium of Ten Years on the Killing of all Species of Whales, H. Con. Res. 375, Requesting the Secretary of State to Call for an International Moratorium of Ten Years on the Killing of all Species of Whales, July 26, 1971, 10–15.

In Search of the Bowhead Whale, directed by Bill Mason. National Film Board of Canada, 1974, documentary film, 50 min.

"Bowhead Migration Along Arctic Coast: A Spectacular Manifestation of Spring," Boston's Museum of Science, In Celebration of the Living Whale, April 11–13, 1975.

Book of poetry, Whales Sing and Other Exuberances, *2012. Cover gouache by Tom George.*

CPSIA information can be obtained at www.ICGtesting.com
Printed in the USA
BVOW08*1717151215

428916BV00001B/1/P

9 781941 948026